The Essential American

The Essential American

A PATRIOT'S RESOURCE

---

25 DOCUMENTS AND SPEECHES EVERY AMERICAN SHOULD OWN

FOREWORD BY

NEWT GINGRICH

EDITED BY

JACKIE GINGRICH CUSHMAN

Since 1947
REGNERY
PUBLISHING, INC.
An Eagle Publishing Company • Washington, DC

Library of Congress Cataloging-in-Publication Data

   The essential American / edited by Jackie Cushman ; foreword by Newt Gingrich.
        p. cm.
    Includes bibliographical references.
    ISBN 978-1-59698-643-5
    1. United States--Politics and government--Sources. 2. United States--History--Sources. 3. Speeches, addresses, etc., American. 4. Political oratory--United States. I. Cushman, Jackie Gingrich.
      E183.E83 2010
      973--dc22

2010040286

Published in the United States by
Regnery Publishing, Inc.
One Massachusetts Avenue, NW
Washington, DC 20001
www.regnery.com

Manufactured in the United States of America
10 9 8 7 6 5 4 3 2 1

Books are available in quantity for promotional or premium use. Write to Director of Special Sales, Regnery Publishing, Inc., One Massachusetts Avenue NW, Washington, DC 20001, for information on discounts and terms or call (202) 216-0600.

Distributed to the trade by:
Perseus Distribution
387 Park Avenue South
New York, NY 10016

To my husband Jimmy Cushman, Junior,
and our children Maggie and Robert

Contents

FOREWORD

THE BEST WAY TO LEARN ABOUT AMERICA IS TO STUDY THE WORDS OF those leaders who wrestled with the great issues and the great decisions that came to define us as a country and a people.

In the history of the United States, certain speeches and documents are so appropriate, so fitting, and so worthy of study that they become instantaneous fixtures in the American canon. We remember exactly where we were on the day we heard them, we listen to or read them over and over again, and we teach our children and our grandchildren why they are important.

However, sometimes a groundbreaking address goes unnoticed by contemporaries.

When Ronald Reagan passed away in 2004, the *Washington Post* recalled his 1987 address at the Brandenburg Gate as "one of the most famous speeches of his presidency." In the shadow of the Berlin Wall, which divided Communist East Berlin from democratic West Berlin, Reagan had issued a now-famous challenge to Soviet Premier Mikhail Gorbachev, daring him to "tear down this wall." But, the *Post* only saw fit to run a single news story about the Friday speech in the following day's newspaper, and much of the rest of the press followed suit. The story had disappeared by the following Monday.

The *Post's* op-ed page had a few more things to say. Staff columnist Frank Getlein penned a column entitled "Keep Germany Divided; The Dirty Little Secret Is That It Means a Europe at Peace." His colleague Richard Cohen opined that Reagan's message was out of vogue, noting "in the streets of East Berlin, rock fans shout the name of Gorbachev. It's a foreboding sound of the future to which the Reagan administration has turned a tin ear."

It wasn't until the Berlin Wall crumbled twenty-nine months later that the Brandenburg Gate speech received due credit as one of the most important addresses of the late 20th century. We finally recognized Reagan's appeal to "tear down this wall" as a watershed moment in which he called on the world to remember that the Cold War was just as much a moral and spiritual struggle as a geopolitical one. But at the time, the press passed it off as just another speech.

In November 1863, one of the darkest periods of the Civil War, President Abraham Lincoln approached the dais at the military cemetery dedication at the Gettysburg battlefield. Despite being commander-in-chief, Lincoln was not the top-billed speaker; that honor went to former Massachusetts governor and Harvard president Edward Everett, who had prepared a two-hour address.

Lincoln's invitation was an afterthought, and his brief remarks were just one of many events on the agenda for the day—hardly the setting for a ground-breaking speech.

However, what followed was a profoundly simple yet unforgettable articulation of the American spirit, rivaled only by the Declaration of Independence for encapsulating the principles by which we live.

Though the Gettysburg Address is today read by every American schoolchild and regarded universally as perhaps the best two minutes of oratory in our nation's history, even it was hardly celebrated in its time. The *Chicago Times* knocked the speech, noting that "the cheek of every American must tingle with shame as he reads the silly, flat and dishwatery utterances of the man who has to be pointed out to intelligent foreigners as the President of the United States."

The speeches that have the most enduring appeal are not always the ones that were the most eagerly hyped or anticipated in their time. Nor were all of them considered immediate classics. Subsequent events catapulted many of these speeches into immortality many months, years, or even generations after their delivery. Leaders regarded as erratic or quixotic in their time have been deemed prescient with the benefit of hindsight.

Regardless of context or immediate reception, the twenty-five historic American speeches Jackie has assembled in this volume share three common themes.

First, our greatest leaders understand that there is something exceptional in the origins of our nation and character of the American people. Their most powerful speeches recognize this fact. Even in moments of extreme somberness or vulnerability, like that which prevailed during Franklin Roosevelt's address to the nation following the Pearl Harbor attacks, or while confronting the nation's flaws, such as occured when the Reverend Martin Luther King, Jr. confronted the legacy of racism on the steps of the Lincoln Memorial, the fundamental decency and character of Americans is affirmed as a guidepost for hope.

FDR knew better than to wallow in self-pity or succumb to righteous anger when he spoke to the nation following the Japanese attack on Pearl Harbor in December 1941. The most effective way to lead in America's soberest hour was to appeal to the innate resilience and vigor of the American people:

> I believe I interpret the will of the Congress and of the people when I assert that we will not only defend ourselves to the uttermost but will make very certain that this form of treachery shall never endanger us again.
>
> Hostilities exist. There is no blinking at the fact that our people, our territory and our interests are in grave danger.
>
> With confidence in our armed forces—with the unbounded determination of our people—we will gain the inevitable triumph—so help us God.

Even as Dr. King courageously denounced the scourges of racism and seg-regation, he invoked the hopes and language of the Founding Fathers and called upon Americans of 1963 to live up to the words of these exceptional men:

> When the architects of our republic wrote the magnificent words of the Constitution and the Declaration of Independence, they were signing a promissory note to which every American was to fall heir. This note was a promise that all men, yes, black men as well as white men, would be guaranteed the "unalienable Rights" of "Life, Liberty and the pursuit of Happiness." It is obvious today that America has defaulted on this promissory note, insofar as her citizens of color are concerned. Instead of honoring this sacred obligation, America has given the Negro people a bad check, a check which has come back marked "insufficient funds." But we refuse to believe that the bank of justice is bankrupt.

In perhaps the darkest moment in American history since Pearl Harbor, Presi-dent George W. Bush glowingly recapitulated what he had seen in the days following September 11—tough, unwavering Americans who had graciously risen to support one another and were eagerly prepared to defend their security.

> In the normal course of events, presidents come to this chamber to report on the state of the union. Tonight, no such report is needed; it has already been delivered by the American people.... My fellow citizens, for the last nine days, the entire world has seen for itself the state of union, and it is strong.

The second common theme of these works is that each does not merely lec-ture, but challenges the audience, the American public, to rise and engage as citizens. Our most enduring icons, such as John F. Kennedy and Theodore Roosevelt, understood that American democracy requires an active and engaged citizenry, and used their speeches to compel and inspire.

President Kennedy perhaps expressed this most famously during his 1961 inauguration speech, when he declared, "Ask not what your country can do for you—ask what you can do for your country."

Theodore Roosevelt believed that a physically and mentally vigorous populace was essential to a rapidly growing and expanding America at the dawn of the twentieth century, and he used his visibility to inspire Americans about these beliefs. In his famed "Strenuous Life" address in 1899, Roosevelt extolled the virtues of intellectual and bodily exertion, and called on his audience to strive both on behalf of themselves as individuals and for their nation:

> Above all, let us shrink from no strife, moral or physical, within or without the nation, provided we are certain that the strife is justified, for it is only through strife, through hard and dangerous endeavor, that we shall ultimately win the goal of true national greatness.

Third, each speech and document uses language to clarify, not obfuscate. The best speeches do not equivocate. They are intellectually honest and morally explicit. The audience is left understanding exactly what the speaker believes and how he or she plans to act upon these stated beliefs. Oftentimes, these speeches can be identified by a sentence or even just a few words.

Addressing the Virginia Convention in March 1775, Patrick Henry made it clear that his individual rights were not negotiable. Confronting those who were hesitant to go to war against the king to preserve such rights, Henry famously bellowed: "Is life so dear, or peace so sweet, as to be purchased at the price of chains and slavery? Forbid it, Almighty God! I know not what course others may take; but as for me, give me liberty or give me death!" His passion swayed a wavering legislature to adopt a resolution for preparation of a militia.

Thomas Jefferson understood that he was presiding over a divided nation following the bitter and controversial 1800 election. He knew he had to make it painstakingly clear to both his supporters and foes what a Jefferson Administration would believe and how it would behave. His March 1801 inaugural address leaves little room for doubt:

It is proper you should understand what I deem the essential principles of our Government, and consequently those which ought to shape its Administration. I will compress them within the narrowest compass they will bear, stating the general principle, but not all its limitations. Equal and exact justice to all men, of whatever state or persuasion, religious or political; peace, commerce, and honest friendship with all nations, entangling alliances with none; the support of the State governments in all their rights, as the most competent administrations for our domestic concerns and the surest bulwarks against antirepublican tendencies; the preservation of the General Government in its whole constitutional vigor, as the sheet anchor of our peace at home and safety abroad . . .

Ronald Reagan came to power at a time when it was fashionable for American political elites to vacillate about the nature of the Soviet threat and the evils of Soviet communism. Reagan was not one for clouded morals. When asked about how he envisioned a satisfactory end to the Cold War, he famously replied, "We win, they lose."

Jackie has put together a collection of writings and speeches that I believe to be the most seminal and influential in our history. I hope that you will find hope, inspiration, and clarity in these great patriots' words, which have been drawn from the earliest days of our Revolution to the recent battles against Communism and Islamist terrorism. Although the eras, dispositions, ideologies, and motivations of these leaders may sometimes be divergent, their belief in the power of words to engage and compel our exceptional nation binds them all together.

You and your family will find this book an essential companion in learning about America and the American people.

—Newt Gingrich
September 2010

INTRODUCTION

FOR A NATION FOUNDED A LITTLE OVER TWO CENTURIES AGO, AMERICA'S history is replete with remarkable individuals. For those in search of the core moments that shaped America's story, this book contains the twenty-five most essential speeches and documents created, written, shared, and preserved by and for citizens of the United States.

Some of the selections were immediately clear: the Declaration of Independence, the Constitution, President George Washington's Farewell Address, and the Emancipation Proclamation. It would be impossible to understand our nation without reading, reviewing, and thinking about how these were created, the times in which they were written, how they changed the course of American history, and their continuing influence today.

Other selections were less obvious and raised difficult questions. For example, how long ago must a speech have been delivered for it to be considered a key part of America's history? Though recent in historical terms, President

George W. Bush's address to the nation from the well of the United States House of Representatives after the terrorist attacks of September 11, 2001 was an easy choice, as the courageous response to the worst violation of American sovereignty since our founding.

Each of the twenty-five selections in this volume reflect our American heritage, providing insight into how our national character was forged. Most were born from challenging times in our nation's history; those times of trouble when character is developed and witnessed most clearly.

In facing our current troubles, we must remember that a higher power gathers us for a common purpose. Reliance on that power is one of our best traditions, as He has gotten us through many times of trial. To recall, reread, reconsider, and repeat the stories that have resulted from that reliance provides us with the strength and inspiration to continue to fight for liberty and freedom.

Individual character is passed down from parents to children through stories, experiences, and practice. Every family has different stories—the life narratives that describe what they have lived through, where they came from, and how they acted and reacted to events in their lives. These accounts provide the next generation with a foundation and understanding of their family values. This allows children to create their underlying belief system, which helps determine how they will respond to events in their lives.

In my family, it's my mother's story of completing college in three years, taking extra classes and studying during the summer so that her sister could go to college, too. We're a family that values education.

It's my father's story of running for Congress and losing twice, but running a third time—and winning. We're a family that values persistence.

It's my husband's grandfather's story of helping start the Atlanta Botanical Garden. We value civic involvement.

It's the story of how my husband drove our family through the Teton Pass from Wyoming to Idaho in a 38-foot RV. We're a family that enjoys adventure.

As a nation, we build character in a similar manner. It's how we talk about shared experiences, how we remember them, and what we emphasize that builds national character. If we want to continue to be an extraordinary nation, we have to remember what we have done that is extraordinary. Today, it is evident that Americans are passionate about rediscovering our national character by remembering our country's greatest stories.

What are America's stories?

Our Pilgrim forefathers fled religious persecution—we believe in freedom of religion. They held the first Thanksgiving and gave thanks to their Creator—we have a tradition of belief in God. We also value hard work because without hard work the Pilgrims would have perished.

Revolutionary leader Patrick Henry understood it was inevitable that we would fight the British for our freedom, even as others hoped for a peaceful resolution. His speech in support of a colonists' militia ended with the now-famous line, "Give me liberty or give me death." America values liberty.

President Abraham Lincoln fought to keep the union together, then fought to end slavery. We value unity and equality.

Theodore Roosevelt—an asthmatic, sickly child—pushed himself physically to become a rough rider and a champion of the strenuous life. We value overcoming personal obstacles.

General Dwight D. Eisenhower led more than 73,000 American troops as they stormed the beaches of Normandy on D-Day and helped free Europe from Nazi rule. We value freedom.

The Reverend Martin Luther King, Jr. championed equal rights. He described in his speech at the Lincoln Memorial his dream that "my four little children will one day live in a nation where they will not be judged by the color of their skin but by the content of their character." As a nation, we value personal character.

President John F. Kennedy challenged the nation to put a man on the moon. We met that challenge. America values exploration and achievement.

Ronald Reagan challenged Mikhail Gorbachev, who was then General Secretary of the Communist Party of the Soviet Union, to "tear down this wall," based on the President's belief that freedom—free speech, free elections, and free markets—would win over a totalitarian regime. We value political and economic freedom.

As a nation, we have a choice: wander forward without direction or a sense of our American identity, or recount the moments and fundamental values that define us so that they may guide us into future generations of American exceptionalism.

America *is* exceptional not because of who we are as individuals, but because of the model of self-government our Founding Fathers created that we continue today. We recognize that each of us was created by God and given certain unalienable rights: life, liberty, and the pursuit of happiness. We then loan these rights to the government, which we replace if it fails to heed the will of the people.

These essential American documents and speeches remind us of this all-important principle and of our forefathers' ongoing fight to defend it.

I hope you find this book inspiring, informative, and, most importantly, useful. Useful in leading to a better understanding of our nation's historic moments, useful in helping you identify the ideas and individuals that have deeply influenced America's development, and useful in helping you engage in determining America's future.

Together we can uphold America's foundation and once again make her strong.

May God bless you and God bless America.

I

"Give me liberty, or give me death!"

Patrick Henry's Address at the Second Virginia Convention (1775)

PATRICK HENRY HAS RECEIVED LESS ATTENTION THAN MANY OF THE other Founding Fathers. The commentaries regarding his personality are often at odds with each other, with one claiming he was illiterate and next that he was schooled in Latin; or a different one claiming that he was lazy, with another asserting that he was industrious. Even the speech that coined "Give me liberty or give me death" is not well-documented. There is not an authoritative version of the speech; rather there are reflections, recollections, and remembrances.

What we do know is that the spirit of Patrick Henry is with us today. It is a spirit we recognize and emulate. It's the desire for liberty and freedom above security and safety. Henry, a Virginian, first encountered Thomas Jefferson in 1759. At that time, Henry had been unsuccessful, first as a farmer and then as a merchant, and was filling in on occasion for his father-in-law, a tavern owner.

Jefferson was struck by Henry's manner—"His passion was music, dancing, and pleasantry, and it attached every one to him."

According to Patrick Henry Fontaine, Henry's grandson, it was Patrick Henry's uncle who taught him to live according to the catechism from the Book of Common Prayer, "to be true and just in all my dealings. To bear no malice nor hatred in my heart ... to do my duty in that state of life unto which it shall please God to call me." We would be well-served to live by these words today.

In 1760, Henry traveled to Williamsburg to seek admittance to the bar. George Wythe, John Randolph, Peyton Randolph, and Edmund Pendleton examined his qualifications. As is normal with Henry's life, several versions exist on who did and did not vote for his acceptance, but in any event, by the time he left for home, he had been approved to practice law. All five men would become important Revolutionary leaders.

In 1763, Henry gained fame for his oratorical skills in arguing for the power of colonial legislatures over the Crown in a dispute known as the Parson's Cause. Virginia's clergy was paid in tobacco, but following a surge in its price, the legislature capped the rate of compensation. King George subsequently vetoed this legislation. Consequently, Anglican minister Reverend James Maury—essentially assuming a proxy for the power of the Crown—filed a suit seeking back-compensation. Though Henry lost, he displayed such oratorical skill that the award to Maury was one penny and Henry became well-known locally and highly sought-after as a speaker.

At this time, the colonists were beginning to chafe under British rule. The king's government had begun to require the colonists to pay taxes to London in the 1760s but had not granted the Americans due representation. In 1765, Parliament passed the Stamp Act, requiring a government "stamp" or tax on colonial transactions. Prior to its passage, the colonists had protested this act. Once it passed into law, the British expected that the colonists would quiet down and follow the law, paying the tax for the stamps to the Crown. London assumed this tax was reasonable, as it was created to pay for the costs of maintaining a standing army in America following the French and Indian War.

When the Virginia House of Burgesses met in May of 1765, one of the new members, Patrick Henry, offered resolutions that questioned the right of

Britain to tax the colonists. As Henry spoke zealously in support of these res-olutions saying, "Caesar had his Brutus, Charles the First his Cromwell; and George the Third," a listener supposedly shouted, "Treason!" Henry continued, "and George the Third may profit by their example. If this be treason make the most of it."

From that point on, Henry was known as a leader and a passionate orator on the side of the colonists and freedom.

The Virginia House of Burgesses ended up accepting parts of Henry's pro-posed resolutions. Though they were not as strong or defiant as Henry might have wanted, they represented a protestation of the Stamp Act by the govern-ing body in Virginia, the largest colony.

While tension mounted throughout the colonies, Henry continued to serve in the House of Burgesses and was a Virginia delegate to the First Continen-tal Congress in 1774, which declared to the citizenry, "We think ourselves bound in duty to observe to you that schemes agitated against the colonies have been so conducted as to render it prudent that you should extend your views to mournful events, and be in all respects prepared for every emergency."

One of the attendees, John Dickinson, wrote to an American in Britain, "The most peaceful provinces are now animated; and a civil war is unavoidable, unless there be a quick change of British measures."

But there was no quick change.

The following February, Massachusetts convoked the Provincial Congress. Led by Joseph Warren and John Hancock, the congress began to prepare for a possible war. In response, Parliament declared Massachusetts to be in a "state of rebellion." Maryland, Rhode Island, Connecticut, Pennsylvania, and Delaware followed Massachusetts' lead.

The next month, the delegates from Virginia, the largest of the colonies, met in Richmond. Normally they would have met in Williamsburg, the capital, but because British troops were present in Williamsburg, they moved their loca-tion, and convened in St. John's Church. These men were American patriots dedicated to resisting the British tax. Other colonial legislatures had also met and considered a possible war, but at this point, all assemblies outside of Rich-mond were hoping for peace.

Henry proposed a resolution to raise a militia as "the only security of a free government." He continued, "This colony is immediately put into a posture of defense."

A great debate followed. While other conventions had adopted similar language, they all referred to a possible war, leaving the door open to peace, if Britain made certain concessions.

Henry's resolutions were different—they treated war as inevitable. If adopted, they posed an irrevocable step whose ramifications inspired fear among many.

The revolutionary cause faced long odds at this moment in 1775. The colonies had no standing army, were only loosely associated, and were contemplating challenging the world's largest navy and one of its largest armies.

Approving Henry's resolutions would close the door to peace and practically invite war against Britain. Patrick Henry, sure of his convictions, stood up to address the group and began his speech—his argument—addressing the president of the convention, as was custom. No transcript exists, and first- and second-hand accounts differ in their descriptions. What we do know is that Henry's talk transfixed the group. He spoke with conviction and his final words still ring in our ears, "but as for me, give me liberty or give me death."

Henry became the first governor of the Commonwealth of Virginia, and was a vocal opponent to the Constitution in the late 1780s. He believed it would encroach on individual rights and give too much power to the national government.

Historic political figures "are able to perceive the gathering of historical forces in a way in which their contemporaries are unable to do," thereby sensing the big picture, Claire Berlinski writes in *There Is No Alternative: Why Margaret Thatcher Matters*. They are prescient, able to determine what might happen due to historical forces. According to Berlinski, "Those who matter are able to master these historical forces ... they are able to shift the forces into a different outcome."

Henry had the ability to see the gathering of political forces and determine that war was inevitable before his contemporaries could. Additionally, he was able to propose a resolution to the Virginia convention and provide the only real American option to liberty—death.

His speech set the stage for the birth of a nation.

—JGC

Note: the following description is taken from William Wirt's biography of Patrick Henry.

🐚　🐚　🐚

These proceedings were not adapted to the taste of Mr. Henry; on the contrary, they were "gall and wormwood" to him. The house required to be wrought up to a bolder tone. He rose, therefore, and moved the following manly resolutions:

"Resolved, That a well regulated militia, composed of gentlemen and yeomen, is the natural strength and only security of a free government; that such a militia in this colony, would forever render it unnecessary for the mother country to keep among us for the purpose of our defence, any standing army of mercenary soldiers, always subversive of the quiet, and dangerous to the liberties of the people, and would obviate the pretext of taxing us for their support.

"That the establishment of such a militia is, *at this time*, peculiarly necessary, by the state of our laws, for the protection and defence of the country, some of which are already expired, and others will shortly be so; and that the known remissness of government in calling us together in legislative capacity, renders it too insecure, in this time of danger and distress, to rely that opportunity will be given of renewing them, in general assembly, *or making any provision to secure our inestimable rights and liberties, from those further violations with which they are threatened.*

"Resolved, therefore, That this colony be immediately put into a state of defence, and that [there] be a committee to prepare a plan for embodying, arming, and disciplining such a number of men, as may be sufficient for that purpose."

The alarm which such a proposition must have given to those who had contemplated no resistance of a character more serious than petition, non-importation, and passive fortitude, and who still hung with suppliant tenderness on the skirts of Britain, will be readily conceived by the reflecting reader.

The shock was painful. It was almost general. The resolutions were opposed as not only rash in policy, but as harsh and well nigh impious in point of feeling. Some of the warmest patriots of the convention opposed them. Richard Bland, Benjamin Harrison, and Edmund Pendleton, who had so lately drunk of the fountain of patriotism in the continental congress, and Robert C. Nicholas, one of the best as well as ablest men and patriots in the state, resisted them with all their influence and abilities.

They urged the late gracious reception of the congressional petition by the throne. They insisted that national comity, and much more filial respect, demanded the exercise of a more dignified patience. That the sympathies of the parent country were now on our side. That the friends of American liberty in parliament, were still with us, and had, as yet, had no cause to blush for our indiscretion. That the manufacturing interests of Great Britain, already smart-ing under the effects of our non-importation, co-operated powerfully towards our relief. That the sovereign himself had relented, and showed that he looked upon our sufferings with an eye of pity. "Was this a moment," they asked, "to disgust our friends, to extinguish all the conspiring sympathies which were working in our favour; to turn their friendship into hatred, their pity into revenge? And what was there, they asked, in the situation of the colony, to tempt us to this? Were we a great military people? Were we ready for war? Where were our stores—where were our arms—where our soldiers—where our generals—where our money, the sinews of war? They were no where to be found. In truth, we were poor—we were naked—we were defenceless. And yet we talk of assuming the front of war! Of assuming it too, against a nation, one of the most formidable in the world! A nation ready and armed at all points! Her navies riding triumphant in every sea; her armies never marching but to certain victory! What was to be the issue of the struggle we were called upon to court? What could be the issue, in the comparative circumstances of the two countries, but to yield up this country an easy prey to Great Britain, and to con-vert the illegitimate right which the British parliament now claimed, into a firm and indubitable right, by conquest? The measure might be brave; but it was the bravery of madmen. It had no pretension to the character of prudence; and as little to the grace of genuine courage. It would be time enough to resort to measures of despair, when every well founded hope had entirely vanished."

To this strong view of the subject, supported as it was, by the stubborn fact of the well known helpless condition of the colony, the opponents of those resolutions superadded every topic of persuasion, which belonged to the cause.

"The strength and lustre which we derived from our connexion with Great Britain—the domestic comforts which we had drawn from the same source, and whose value we were now able to estimate by their loss—that ray of reconciliation which was dawning upon us from the east, and which promised so fair and happy a day:—with this they contrasted the clouds and storms which the measure now proposed, was so well calculated to raise—and in which, we should not have even the poor consolation of being pitied by the world, since we should have so needlessly and rashly, drawn them upon ourselves."

These arguments and topics of persuasion, were so well justified by the appearance of things, and were moreover so entirely in unison with that love of ease and quiet which is natural to man, and that disposition to hope for happier times, even under the most forbidding circumstances, that an ordinary man, in Mr. Henry's situation, would have been glad to compound with the displeasure of the house, by being permitted to withdraw his resolutions in silence.

Not so, Mr. Henry. His was a spirit fitted to raise the whirlwind, as well as to ride in it. His was that comprehensive view, that unerring prescience, that perfect command over the actions of men, which qualified him not merely to guide, but almost to create the destinies of nations.

He rose at this time with a majesty unusual to him in an exordium, and with all that self-possession by which he was so invariably distinguished. "No man," he said, "thought more highly than he did, of the patriotism, as well as abilities, of the very worthy gentlemen who had just addressed the house. But different men often saw the same subject in different lights; and therefore, he hoped it would not be thought disrespectful to those gentlemen, if, entertaining as he did, opinions of a character very opposite to theirs, should speak forth his sentiments freely, and without reserve. This," he said, "was no time for ceremony. The question before the house was one of awful moment to this country. For his own part, he considered it as nothing less than a question of freedom or slavery. And in proportion to the magnitude of the subject, ought to be the freedom of the debate. It was only in this way that they could hope to arrive at truth, and fulfil the great responsibility which they held to God and their country. Should he keep back his opinions, at such a time, through fear of giving offence, he should consider himself as guilty of treason towards his country, and of an act of disloyalty toward the majesty of Heaven, which he revered above all earthly kings."

"Mr. President, said he, "it is natural to man to indulge in the illusions of hope. We are apt to shut our eyes against a painful truth—and listen to the song of that syren, till she transforms us into beasts. Is it," he asked, "the part of wise men, engaged in a great and arduous struggle for liberty? Were we disposed to be of the number of those, who having eyes, see not, and having ears, hear not, the things which so nearly concern their temporal salvation? For his part, whatever anguish of spirit it might cost, he was willing to know the whole truth to know the worst, and to provide for it."

"He had," he said, "but one lamp by which his feet were guided: and that was the lamp of experience. He knew of no way of judging of the future, but by the past. And judging by the past, he wished to know what there had been in the conduct of the British ministry for the last ten years, to justify those hopes with which gentlemen had been pleased to solace themselves and the house? Is it that insidious smile with which our petition has been lately received? Trust it not, sir; it will prove a snare to your feet. Suffer not yourselves to be betrayed with a kiss. Ask yourselves how this gracious reception of our petition, comports with those warlike preparations which cover our waters and darken our land? Are fleets and armies necessary to a work of love and reconciliation? Have we shown ourselves so unwilling to be reconciled, that force must be called in to win back our love? Let us not deceive ourselves, sir. These are the implements of war and subjugation—the last arguments to which kings resort. I ask gentlemen, sir, what means this martial array, if its purpose be not to force us to submission? Can gentlemen assign any other possible motive for it? Has Great Britain any enemy in this quarter of the world, to call for all this accumulation of navies and armies? No, sir: she has none. They are meant for us: they can be meant for no other. They are sent over to bind and rivet upon us those chains, which the British ministry have been so long forging. And what have we to oppose to them? Shall we try argument? Sir, we have been trying that for the last ten years. Have we any thing new to offer upon the subject? Nothing. We have held the subject up in every light of which it is capable; but it has been all in vain. Shall we resort to entreaty and humble supplication? What terms shall we find, which have not been already exhausted? Let us not, I beseech you, sir, deceive ourselves longer. Sir, we have done every thing that could be done, to avert the storm which is now coming on. We have petitioned—we have remonstrated—we have supplicated—we have prostrated ourselves before the throne, and have implored its interposition to arrest the tyrannical hands of the ministry and parliament. Our petitions have been slighted; our remonstrances have produced additional violence and insult; our supplications have been disregarded; and we have been spurned, with contempt, from the foot of the throne. In vain, after these things, may we indulge the fond hope of peace and reconciliation. There is no longer any room for hope. If we wish to be free—if we mean to preserve inviolate those inestimable privileges for which we have been so long contending—if we mean not basely to abandon the noble struggle in which we have been so long engaged, and which we have pledged ourselves never to abandon, until the glorious object of our contest shall be obtained—we must fight!—I repeat it, sir; we must fight!! An appeal to arms and to the God of Hosts, is all that is left us!"

"They tell us, sir," continued Mr. Henry, "that we are weak—unable to cope with so formidable an adversary. But when shall we be stronger? Will it be the next week, or the next year? Will it be when we are totally disarmed; and when a British guard shall be stationed in every house? Shall we gather strength by irresolution and inaction? Shall we acquire the means of effectual resistance, by lying supinely on our back, and hugging the delusive phantom of hope, until our enemies shall have bound us, hand and foot? Sir, we are not weak, if we make a proper use of those means which the God of nature hath placed in our power. Three millions of people, armed in the holy cause of liberty, and in such a country as that which we possess, are invincible by any force which our enemy can send against us. Besides, sir, we shall not fight our battles alone. There is a just God who presides over the destinies of nations; and who will raise up friends to fight our battles for us. The battle, sir, is not to the strong alone; it is to the vigilant, the active, the brave. Besides, sir, we have no election. If we were base enough to desire it, it is now too late to retire from the contest. There is no retreat, but in submission and slavery! Our chains are forged. Their clanking may be heard on the plains of Boston! The war is inevitable—and let it come!! I repeat it, sir; let it come!!!

"It is in vain, sir, to extenuate the matter. Gentlemen may cry, peace, peace— but there is no peace. The war is actually begun! The next gale that sweeps from the north, will bring to our ears the clash of resounding arms! Our brethren are already in the field! Why stand we here idle? What is it that gentlemen wish? What would they have? Is life so dear; or peace so sweet, as to be purchased at the price of chains, and slavery? Forbid it, Almighty God!—I know not what course others may take; but as for me," cried he, with both his arms extended aloft, his brows knit, every feature marked with the resolute purpose of his soul, and his voice swelled to its boldest note of exclamation—"give me liberty, or give me death!"

He took his seat. No murmur of applause was heard. The effect was too deep. After the trance of a moment, several members started from their seats. The cry, "to arms," seemed to quiver on every lip, and gleam from every eye! Richard H. Lee arose and supported Mr. Henry, with his usual spirit and elegance. But his melody was lost amidst the agitations of that ocean, which the master spirit of the storm had lifted up on high. That supernatural voice still sounded in their ears, and shivered along their arteries. They heard, in every pause, the cry of liberty or death. They became impatient of speech—their souls were on fire for action.

The resolutions were adopted; and Patrick Henry, Richard H. Lee, Robert C. Nicholas, Benjamin Harrison, Lemuel Riddick, George Washington, Adam Stevens, Andrew Lewis, William Christian, Edmund Pendleton, Thomas Jefferson, and Isaac Zane, esquires, were appointed a committee to prepare the plan called for by the last resolution.

II

"I am your ever faithful friend"

LETTER FROM
ABIGAIL ADAMS
(1776)

Male landowners dominated the Revolutionary period. They were the ones who were able to serve in the state legislatures and in the Constitutional Conventions. However, women assisted in the revolutionary cause. The letters between John and Abigail Adams provide us with an example of the impact women had on the events taking place, despite being legally shut out of the process.

Abigail Adams was born to Elizabeth Quincy Smith and the Reverend William Smith in 1744. She was the second of three daughters in a highly regarded family. Her maternal grandfather, Colonel John Quincy, was a leader of Braintree, Massachusetts, a town south of Boston. Her husband John was born and raised in Braintree.

Unlike many women of her time, Abigail was well educated and loved literature. John Adams, a lawyer, found Abigail's intellect and wit stimulating.

They began spending time together after a friend of John's married Abigail's sister. Family stories noted that the Smith family did not initially approve of Abigail's proposed marriage, but finally relented.

Abigail Adams lived in a time when men and women were seen as inhabiting separate spheres; men belonged at the forefront of public life while women's province was children and the home. Abigail and John's correspondence during the American Revolutionary War provides an intimate glimpse of a marriage unusual in its partnership of minds as well as hearts.

John's detailed inquiries about the state of home affairs underscores how important he considered Abigail's role in raising and educating their children, the future citizens and inheritors of the nation he was helping create. Abigail certainly understood that, while John was helping create a new nation, he could do so only because of the firm foundation she was creating at home.

"Every day we sit, the more we are convinced that the designs against us are hostile and sanguinary, and that nothing but fortitude, vigor, and perseverance can save us," wrote John to his wife on June 17, 1775. "But America is a great, unwieldy body. Its progress must be slow. It is like a large fleet sailing under convoy. The fleetest sailors must wait for the dullest and slowest. Like a coach and six, the swiftest horses must be slackened, and the slowest quickened, that all may keep an even pace."

Abigail provided community and family news to John, but also asked questions regarding the progress and understanding of those working on founding a nation. Theirs was a two-way conversation between partners, friends, and confidants.

"Does every member feel for us?" Abigail asked her husband five days later, referring to the delegates from outside Massachusetts who were not experiencing the British occupation. "Can they realize what we suffer? And can they believe with what patience and fortitude we endure the conflict?"

Even during the darkest days of the Continental Army's struggle against the King's army, Abigail remained optimistic about a peaceful future, and often posed questions to John about the formation of an American government. Her questions must have been valuable to John as he worked with the other founders to create the foundation for our emerging government.

"If a form of government is to be established here, what one will be assumed?" Abigail asked in a letter dated November 27, 1775. "Will it be left to our Assemblies to choose one? And will not many men have many minds? And shall we not run into dissensions among ourselves?"

John shared with Abigail many of the materials he was reading while at war, and kept her engaged in the politics of the revolution by sending her newspaper clippings and influential political tracts. On February 18, 1776, John sent her a copy of Thomas Paine's "Common Sense," a political pamphlet published anonymously in January 1776, which provided an argument for American independence from the British.

Her response: "I am charmed with the sentiments of 'Common Sense,' and wonder how an honest heart, one who wishes the welfare of his country and the happiness of posterity, can hesitate one moment at adopting them."

On March 31, 1776, in anticipation of American independence, Abigail wrote to John asking him to "remember the ladies and be more generous and favorable to them than your ancestors. Do not put such unlimited power into the hands of the husbands. Remember, all men would be tyrants if they could. If particular care and attention is not paid to the ladies, we are determined to foment a rebellion, and will not hold ourselves bound by any laws in which we have no voice or representation."

John frequently asked Abigail's opinion of political developments as the new nation came together and provided updates on their progress along with his private doubts and fears. His letters indicate that he valued her thoughts and ideas.

On April 14, 1776, he provided detailed responses to her questions:

> You ask where the fleet is? The inclosed [sic] papers will inform you. You ask what sort of defense Virginia can make? I believe they will make an able defense. Their militia and minute-men have been some time employed in training themselves, and they have nine battalions of regulars, as they call them, maintained among them, under good officers, at the Continental expense. They have set up a number of manufactories of fire-arms, which are busily employed. They are

tolerably supplied with powder, and are successful and assiduous in making saltpetre.

The right of women to vote moved backward after the Revolutionary War. In 1777, women lost the right to vote in New York. By 1807, women had lost the right to vote in all states. It was not until more than 100 years later, in 1920, that the 19th Amendment was ratified, giving women throughout the nation the right to vote. While women in the Revolutionary era were not normally in the forefront, nor did they have power at the ballot box, Abigail Adams proves that women were yet instrumental to the Revolutionary War in the early days of the Republic.

—JGC

∾ ∾ ∾

Braintree, March 31, 1776

I wish you would ever write me a Letter half as long as I write you; and tell me if you may where your Fleet are gone? What sort of Defence Virginia can make against our common Enemy? Whether it is so situated as to make an able Defence? Are not the Gentery Lords and the common people vassals, are they not like the uncivilized Natives Brittain represents us to be? I hope their Riffel Men who have shewen themselves very savage and even Blood thirsty; are not a specimen of the Generality of the people.

I am willing to allow the Colony great merrit for having produced a Washington but they have been shamefully duped by a Dunmore.

I have sometimes been ready to think that the passion for Liberty cannot be Eaquelly Strong in the Breasts of those who have been accustomed to deprive their fellow Creatures of theirs. Of this I am certain that it is not founded upon that generous and christian principal of doing to others as we would that others should do unto us.

Do not you want to see Boston; I am fearfull of the small pox, or I should have been in before this time. I got Mr. Crane to go to our House and see what state it was in. I find it has been occupied by one of the Doctors of a Regiment, very dirty, but no other damage has been done to it. The few things which were left in it are all gone. Cranch [Crane?] has the key which he never deliverd up. I have wrote to him for it and am determined to get it cleand as soon as possible and shut it up. I look upon it a new acquisition of property, a property which one month ago I did not value at a single Shilling, and could with pleasure have seen it in flames.

The Town in General is left in a better state than we expected, more owing to a percipitate flight than any Regard to the inhabitants, tho some individuals discoverd a sense of honour and justice and have left the rent of the Houses in which they were, for the owners and the furniture unhurt, or if damaged sufficent to make it good.

Others have committed abominable Ravages. The Mansion House of your President [John Hancock] is safe and the furniture unhurt whilst both the House and Furniture of the Solisiter General [Samuel Quincy] have fallen a prey to their own merciless party. Surely the very Fiends feel a Reverential awe for Virtue and patriotism, whilst they Detest the paricide and traitor.

I feel very differently at the approach of spring to what I did a month ago. We knew not then whether we could plant or sow with safety, whether when we had toild we could reap the fruits of our own industery, whether we could rest in our own Cottages, or whether we should not be driven from the sea coasts to seek shelter in the wilderness, but now we feel as if we might sit under our own vine and eat the good of the land.

I feel a gaieti de Coar to which before I was a stranger. I think the Sun looks brighter, the Birds sing more melodiously, and Nature puts on a more chearfull countanance. We feel a temporary peace, and the poor fugitives are returning to their deserted habitations.

Tho we felicitate ourselves, we sympathize with those who are trembling least the Lot of Boston should be theirs. But they cannot be in similar circumstances unless pusilanimity and cowardise should take possession of them. They have time and warning given them to see the Evil and shun it.—I long to hear that you have declared an independency—and by the way in the new

Code of Laws which I suppose it will be necessary for you to make I desire you would Remember the Ladies, and be more generous and favourable to them than your ancestors. Do not put such unlimited power into the hands of the Husbands. Remember all Men would be tyrants if they could. If perticuliar care and attention is not paid to the Laidies we are determined to foment a Rebelion, and will not hold ourselves bound by any Laws in which we have no voice, or Representation.

That your Sex are Naturally Tyrannical is a Truth so thoroughly established as to admit of no dispute, but such of you as wish to be happy willingly give up the harsh title of Master for the more tender and endearing one of Friend. Why then, not put it out of the power of the vicious and the Lawless to use us with cruelty and indignity with impunity. Men of Sense in all Ages abhor those customs which treat us only as the vassals of your Sex. Regard us then as Beings placed by providence under your protection and in immitation of the Supreem Being make use of that power only for our happiness.

April 5

Not having an opportunity of sending this I shall add a few lines more; tho not with a heart so gay. I have been attending the sick chamber of our Neighbour Trot whose affliction I most sensibly feel but cannot discribe, striped of two lovely children in one week. Gorge the Eldest died on wednesday and Billy the youngest on fryday, with the Canker fever, a terible disorder so much like the thr[o]at distemper, that it differs but little from it. Betsy Cranch has been very bad, but upon the recovery. Becky Peck they do not expect will live out the day. Many grown person[s] are now sick with it, in this [street?] 5. It rages much in other Towns. The Mumps too are very frequent. Isaac is now confined with it. Our own little flock are yet well. My Heart trembles with anxiety for them. God preserve them.

I want to hear much oftener from you than I do. March 8 was the last date of any that I have yet had.—You inquire of whether I am making Salt peter. I have not yet attempted it, but after Soap making believe I shall make the experiment. I find as much as I can do to manufacture cloathing for my family which would else be Naked. I know of but one person in this part of the Town who has made any, that is Mr. Tertias Bass as he is calld who has got very near an hundred weight which has been found to be very good. I have heard of some others in the other parishes. Mr. Reed of Weymouth has been applied to, to go to Andover to the mills which are now at work, and has gone. I have lately seen a small Manuscrip de[s]cribing the proportions for the various sorts of pow-der, fit for cannon, small arms and pistols. If it would be of any Service your way I will get it transcribed and send it to you.—Every one of your Friend[s] send their Regards, and all the little ones. Your Brothers youngest child lies bad with convulsion fitts. Adieu. I need not say how much I am Your ever faithfull Friend.

III

"All men are created equal"

DECLARATION OF INDEPENDENCE
(1776)

A S A NATION, WE CELEBRATE OUR INDEPENDENCE ON JULY 4TH, THE DAY the Declaration of Independence was signed. However, the decision to assert our independence from Great Britain was the culmination of years of grievances—in 1775, these finally became intolerable.

The King's government had begun to require the colonists to pay taxes to London in the 1760s, but had not granted the Americans due representation in Parliament. The colonists began to protest, and tensions grew. Five colonists died in 1770 at the Boston Massacre, which occurred when British soldiers fired into a crowd of Bostonians who were heckling them.

In 1773, the colonists protested a new tea tax by dumping dozens of boxes of tea into Boston Harbor, an event that became known as the Boston Tea Party.

However, open hostilities did not break out until April 19, 1775 with the Battles of Lexington and Concord, the opening battles of the American Revolution. On June 7, 1776, the Second Continental Congress voted for a resolution, stating "these United Colonies are, and of right ought to be, free and independent States."

A committee of five delegates, including John Adams, a delegate from Massachusetts, and Thomas Jefferson, a Virginia delegate, were chosen to draft a declaration of independence. Jefferson was picked from the group to write the first draft. He finished a draft within three weeks and, after a few revisions, Congress adopted it on July 4, 1776.

It says, in part:

> We hold these truths to be self-evident, that all men are created equal, that they are endowed by their Creator with certain unalienable rights, that among these are life, liberty and the pursuit of happiness.—That to secure these rights, governments are instituted among 'men, deriving their just powers from the consent of the governed ...

This document is incredibly important because it acknowledges that fundamental human rights are granted solely by God, not men; it is the people who then grant legitimacy to government for the protection of their rights. In this model, the Creator is the ultimate authority. Next are the people as the beneficiaries of the Creator's generosity. Consequently, a government holds only as much power as the people are willing to yield.

There is great importance in these "self-evident" truths. First, all men are *created* equal. That means that we all have equal value at birth. It does not say that all men, regardless of whether they work, shall end up equal. We are created equal and given equal rights by our Creator. We are a nation of believers in God. This provides us with optimism, a belief in the future, and solace and strength in times of crisis.

Our rights are "life, liberty, and the pursuit of happiness." We are not guaranteed health care, education, houses, or even happiness. Our founders acknowledge that life and liberty came from God and that he gave us the ability to pursue happiness, not a guarantee that it would be achieved.

The end of the American Revolution came six years after it began, when British General Charles Cornwallis formally surrendered at Yorktown on October 19, 1781.

However, our new country still had a lot of work to do. Our freedom from colonial rule was won, but we had yet to learn how to govern ourselves, or how to practice the high ideals we had asserted in the Declaration of Independence. As a young nation, we argued over the structure of government, how much government we should have, and how we would determine its limits.

The thirteen colonies' initial attempt to create a government was reflected in our first constitution, the Articles of Confederation, drafted in 1777 and fully ratified in 1781. The Articles of Confederation gave very little power to a federal government. So little that, as a nation at war, we had challenges raising troops and paying them. In 1787, the Constitution was written and the Articles of Confederation were repealed as the new Constitution was ratified state-by-state.

On April 30, 1789, we inaugurated George Washington as our first president. This was a move toward order and stability: our freedom had been declared and won, and our government was being created peacefully according to guidelines set out in the Constitution.

Our model was designed for the people, not the government, to hold power. Our Declaration reduced the status of government from master of the people (as under English rule) to servant of the people. In the years since our government came together, we have learned that the government must continually be held accountable and continually reminded that it derives its powers from the consent of the governed (the people).

Today, our unalienable right of liberty—the power to make individual choices—is coming under attack from our own government. Congress is passing legislation that the people do not agree to, ranging from mandated health care to intrusive bailouts.

While we might be pessimistic about the current path our country is taking, we should remind ourselves that our country has the ability to build on our past and create a bright future. We, the people, still retain the power to elect a government that listens and responds to us.

—JGC

✿   ✿   ✿

IN CONGRESS, July 4, 1776.

The unanimous Declaration of the thirteen united States of America,

When in the Course of human events, it becomes necessary for one people to dissolve the political bands which have connected them with another, and to assume among the powers of the earth, the separate and equal station to which the Laws of Nature and of Nature's God entitle them, a decent respect to the opinions of mankind requires that they should declare the causes which impel them to the separation.

We hold these truths to be self-evident, that all men are created equal, that they are endowed by their Creator with certain unalienable Rights, that among these are Life, Liberty and the pursuit of Happiness.—That to secure these rights, Governments are instituted among Men, deriving their just powers from the consent of the governed,—That whenever any Form of Government becomes destructive of these ends, it is the Right of the People to alter or to abolish it, and to institute new Government, laying its foundation on such principles and organizing its powers in such form, as to them shall seem most likely to effect their Safety and Happiness. Prudence, indeed, will dictate that Governments long established should not be changed for light and transient causes; and accordingly all experience hath shewn, that mankind are more disposed to suffer, while evils are sufferable, than to right themselves by abolishing the forms to which they are accustomed. But when a long train of abuses and usurpations, pursuing invariably the same Object evinces a design to reduce them under absolute Despotism, it is their right, it is their duty, to throw off such Government, and to provide new Guards for their future security.—Such has been the patient sufferance of these Colonies; and such is now the necessity which constrains them to alter their former Systems of Government. The history of the present King of Great Britain is a history of repeated injuries and usurpations, all having in direct object the establishment of an absolute Tyranny over these States. To prove this, let Facts be submitted to a candid world.

He has refused his Assent to Laws, the most wholesome and necessary for the public good.

He has forbidden his Governors to pass Laws of immediate and pressing importance, unless suspended in their operation till his Assent should be obtained; and when so suspended, he has utterly neglected to attend to them.

He has refused to pass other Laws for the accommodation of large districts of people, unless those people would relinquish the right of Representation in the Legislature, a right inestimable to them and formidable to tyrants only.

He has called together legislative bodies at places unusual, uncomfortable, and distant from the depository of their public Records, for the sole purpose of fatiguing them into compliance with his measures.

He has dissolved Representative Houses repeatedly, for opposing with manly firmness his invasions on the rights of the people.

He has refused for a long time, after such dissolutions, to cause others to be elected; whereby the Legislative powers, incapable of Annihilation, have returned to the People at large for their exercise; the State remaining in the mean time exposed to all the dangers of invasion from without, and convulsions within.

He has endeavoured to prevent the population of these States; for that purpose obstructing the Laws for Naturalization of Foreigners; refusing to pass others to encourage their migrations hither, and raising the conditions of new Appropriations of Lands.

He has obstructed the Administration of Justice, by refusing his Assent to Laws for establishing Judiciary powers.

He has made Judges dependent on his Will alone, for the tenure of their offices, and the amount and payment of their salaries.

He has erected a multitude of New Offices, and sent hither swarms of Officers to harrass our people, and eat out their substance.

He has kept among us, in times of peace, Standing Armies without the Consent of our legislatures.

He has affected to render the Military independent of and superior to the Civil power.

He has combined with others to subject us to a jurisdiction foreign to our constitution, and unacknowledged by our laws; giving his Assent to their Acts of pretended Legislation:

For Quartering large bodies of armed troops among us:

For protecting them, by a mock Trial, from punishment for any Murders which they should commit on the Inhabitants of these States:

For cutting off our Trade with all parts of the world:

For imposing Taxes on us without our Consent: For depriving us in many cases, of the benefits of Trial by Jury:

For transporting us beyond Seas to be tried for pretended offences.

For abolishing the free System of English Laws in a neighbouring Province, establishing therein an Arbitrary government, and enlarging its Boundaries so as to render it at once an example and fit instrument for introducing the same absolute rule into these Colonies:

For taking away our Charters, abolishing our most valuable Laws, and altering fundamentally the Forms of our Governments:

For suspending our own Legislatures, and declaring themselves invested with power to legislate for us in all cases whatsoever.

He has abdicated Government here, by declaring us out of his Protection and waging War against us.

He has plundered our seas, ravaged our Coasts, burnt our towns, and destroyed the lives of our people.

He is at this time transporting large Armies of foreign Mercenaries to compleat the works of death, desolation and tyranny, already begun with circumstances of Cruelty & perfidy scarcely paralleled in the most barbarous ages, and totally unworthy the Head of a civilized nation.

He has constrained our fellow Citizens taken Captive on the high Seas to bear Arms against their Country, to become the executioners of their friends and Brethren, or to fall themselves by their Hands.

He has excited domestic insurrections amongst us, and has endeavoured to bring on the inhabitants of our frontiers, the merciless Indian Savages, whose known rule of warfare, is an undistinguished destruction of all ages, sexes and conditions.

In every stage of these Oppressions We have Petitioned for Redress in the most humble terms: Our repeated Petitions have been answered only by repeated injury. A Prince whose character is thus marked by every act which may define a Tyrant, is unfit to be the ruler of a free people.

Nor have We been wanting in attentions to our Brittish brethren. We have warned them from time to time of attempts by their legislature to extend an unwarrantable jurisdiction over us. We have reminded them of the circumstances of our emigration and settlement here. We have appealed to their native justice and magnanimity, and we have conjured them by the ties of our common kindred to disavow these usurpations, which, would inevitably interrupt our connections and correspondence. They too have been deaf to the voice of justice and of consanguinity. We must, therefore, acquiesce in the necessity, which denounces our Separation, and hold them, as we hold the rest of mankind, Enemies in War, in Peace Friends.

We, therefore, the Representatives of the united States of America, in General Congress, Assembled, appealing to the Supreme Judge of the world for the rectitude of our intentions, do, in the Name, and by Authority of the good People of these Colonies, solemnly publish and declare, That these United Colonies are, and of Right ought to be Free and Independent States; that they are Absolved from all Allegiance to the British Crown, and that all political connection between them and the State of Great Britain, is and ought to be totally dissolved; and that as Free and Independent States, they have full Power to levy War, conclude Peace, contract Alliances, establish Commerce, and to do all other Acts and Things which Independent States may of right do. And for the support of this Declaration, with a firm reliance on the protection of divine Providence, we mutually pledge to each other our Lives, our Fortunes and our sacred Honor.

The 56 signatures on the Declaration appear in the positions indicated:

COLUMN 1

Georgia:
Button Gwinnett
Lyman Hall
George Walton

COLUMN 2

North Carolina:
William Hooper
Joseph Hewes
John Penn

South Carolina:
Edward Rutledge
Thomas Heyward, Jr.
Thomas Lynch, Jr.
Arthur Middleton

COLUMN 3

Massachusetts:
John Hancock

Maryland:
Samuel Chase
William Paca
Thomas Stone
Charles Carroll of Car-
rollton

Virginia:
George Wythe
Richard Henry Lee
Thomas Jefferson
Benjamin Harrison
Thomas Nelson, Jr.
Francis Lightfoot Lee
Carter Braxton

COLUMN 4

Pennsylvania:
Robert Morris
Benjamin Rush
Benjamin Franklin
John Morton
George Clymer
James Smith
George Taylor
James Wilson
George Ross

Delaware:
Caesar Rodney
George Read
Thomas McKean

COLUMN 5

New York:
William Floyd
Philip Livingston
Francis Lewis
Lewis Morris

New Jersey:
Richard Stockton
John Witherspoon
Francis Hopkinson
John Hart
Abraham Clark

COLUMN 6

New Hampshire:
Josiah Bartlett
William Whipple

Massachusetts:
Samuel Adams
John Adams
Robert Treat Paine
Elbridge Gerry

Rhode Island:
Stephen Hopkins
William Ellery

Connecticut:
Roger Sherman
Samuel Huntington
William Williams
Oliver Wolcott

New Hampshire:
Matthew Thornton

IV

"The United States of America"

ARTICLES OF CONFEDERATION
(1777)

AFTER WE DECLARED OUR INDEPENDENCE ON JULY 4, 1776, AMERICANS had to determine how our country would be run. The Second Continental Congress formed a committee to "prepare and digest the form of confederation." There was one representative from each state (as the colonies were now known). John Dickinson, a well-known lawyer from Pennsylvania, was the principal writer.

Their task was complex. How should the states conduct their business? They knew what they did not want—a government that would take control and dictate what Americans had to do, like a monarchy—but the question of what they *did* want was much harder to answer.

The states were hesitant to apportion too many of their rights to a national government—they covered a large geographic area and had different economic interests—but acknowledged one was necessary for "their common defence, the security of their liberties, and their mutual and general welfare." Since the nation was at war, the articles had to address military and foreign policy concerns.

The Articles of Confederation represented our first attempt to define how our country would be run. Once drafted, they were returned to the Congress for debate. As they were debated, the congressmen (yes, they were all men) increased the rights of the states and decreased the power of the national government.

The lawmakers' emphasis on states' rights over those of the federal government caused much frustration among many of the men who would ultimately preside over the first American government. For example, Washington and Hamilton were both critics of the Articles from the outset. Additionally there were no provisions for national taxation, and handling of national debt, which we had to address because we had borrowed extensively during the Revolutionary War.

The Articles of Confederation was the first document to debut our new country's name: "The United States of America." We were united as a single country but also recognized in our very name the importance of each state. The national government was given the ability to conduct diplomacy and make war, though the provision of funds and troops was up to each individual state.

The relationship between the states was identified as "perpetual." In other words, this was not intended to be a temporary situation, but one that would last forever. The states were described as being in "a firm league of friendship with each other," and all powers not specifically given to the United States were to be retained by each state respectively.

Each state could determine how to pick its delegates to the Congress. And each state reserved the power "to recall its delegates, or any of them, at any time within the year, and to send others in their stead for the remainder of the year." The Articles included term limits; representatives could serve no more than three years out of every six.

The national government did not have the ability to tax states or people, but could only request that states contribute for the common good. As for a national military, it relied on the states to provide "a well-regulated and disciplined militia." Perhaps most surprisingly to modern audiences, the Articles envisioned no executive or president of the United States.

One of the more interesting aspects of the Articles was an offer to Canada to join the United States. It noted that, if Canada were to join the United States, Canadians would be "entitled to all the advantages of this union." Canada declined.

Congress passed the Articles on November 15, 1777, but all thirteen states had to ratify it for it to be adopted as our government structure.

Ratification was a slow process. Virginia ratified it on December 16, 1777. Maryland delayed ratification until March 1, 1781. Once Virginia conceded to transfer large tracts of unsettled western land to the national government, Maryland ratified the Articles.

The states' reluctance to embrace a centralized power—even if they were part of it this time—made sense for an infant country that had just announced its independence on grounds that Britain's centralized power was tyrannical. They certainly did not want to cast off one yoke only to exchange it for another.

As Joseph Ellis wrote in *Founding Brothers*, "The national government established during the war under the Articles of Confederation accurately embodies the cardinal conviction of revolutionary-era republicanism. Namely, that no central authority empowered to coerce or discipline the citizenry was permissible, since it merely duplicated the monarchial and aristocratic principles that the American Revolution had been fought to escape."

While this first step in creating a government provided a framework for ongoing governance, it soon became evident to many that the powers of the national government were not strong enough to create a lasting union. The next step was a rewrite of the Articles that turned into the United States Constitution. But without the Articles as the forerunner, the Constitution would not have been the great document that has successfully governed our nation for more than 200 years.

—JGC

➣ ➣ ➣

To all to whom these Presents shall come,

We, the undersigned, Delegates of the States affixed to our Names, send greeting:

Whereas the Delegates of the United States of America in Congress assembled, did on the fifteenth day of November, in the year of our Lord one thousand seven hundred and seventy seven, and in the second year of the Independence of America, agree to certain articles of Confederation and perpetual Union between the states of New Hampshire, Massachusetts-bay, Rhode Island and Providence Plantations, Connecticut, New York, New Jersey, Pennsylvania, Delaware, Maryland, Virginia, North Carolina, South Carolina, and Georgia, in the words following, viz.

Articles of Confederation and perpetual union,

between the States of New Hampshire, Massachusetts-bay, Rhode Island and Providence Plantations, Connecticut, New York, New Jersey, Pennsylvania, Delaware, Maryland, Virginia, North Carolina, South Carolina, and Georgia.

Article I. The stile of this confederacy shall be, "The United States of America."

Article II. Each State retains its sovereignty, freedom, and independence, and every power, jurisdiction, and right, which is not by this confederation, expressly delegated to the United States, in Congress assembled.

Article III. The said States hereby severally enter into a firm league of friendship with each other, for their common defence, the security of their liberties, and their mutual and general welfare, binding them-selves to assist each other against all force offered to, or attacks made upon them, or any of them, on account of religion, sovereignty, trade, or any other pretence whatever.

Article IV. The better to secure and perpetuate mutual friendship and intercourse among the people of the different States in this union, the free inhabitants of each of these States, paupers, vagabonds, and fugitives from justice excepted, shall be entitled to all privileges and immunities of free citizens in the several States; and the people of each State shall have free ingress and regress to and from any other State, and shall enjoy therein all the privileges of trade and commerce, subject to the same duties, impo-sitions, and restrictions, as the inhabitants thereof respectively; provided that such restrictions shall not extend so far as to prevent the removal of property imported into any State, to any other State, of which the owner is an inhabitant; provided also, that no imposition, duties, or restriction, shall be laid by any State on the property of the United States, or either of them.

If any person guilty of, or charged with, treason, felony, or other high misdemeanor in any State, shall flee from justice, and be found in any of the united States, he shall, upon demand of the governor or executive power of the State from which he fled, be delivered up, and re-moved to the State having jurisdiction of his offence.

Full faith and credit shall be given, in each of these States, to the records, acts, and judicial proceedings of the courts and magistrates of every other State.

Article V. For the more convenient management of the general interests of the united States, delegates shall be annually appointed in such manner as the legislature of each State shall direct, to meet in Congress on the first Monday in November, in every year, with a power reserved to each State to recall its delegates, or any of them, at any time within the year, and to send others in their stead, for the remainder of the year.

No State shall be represented in Congress by less than two, nor by more than Seven Members; and no person shall be capable of being delegate for more than three years, in any term of Six years; nor shall any person, being a delegate, be capable of holding any office under the united States, for which he, or another for his benefit, receives any salary, fees, or emolument of any kind.

Each State shall maintain its own delegates in a meeting of the States, and while they act as members of the committee of the States.

In determining questions in the united States in Congress assembled, each State shall have one vote.

Freedom of speech and debate in Congress shall not be impeached or questioned in any Court or place out of Congress; and the members of Congress shall be protected in their persons from arrests and imprisonments during the time of their going to and from, and attendance on, Congress, except for treason, felony or breach of the peace.

Article VI. No State, without the consent of the united States, in congress assembled, shall send any embassy to, or receive any embassy from, or enter into any conference, agreement, alliance, or treaty, with any King, prince or State; nor shall any person holding any office of profit or trust under the united States, or any of them, accept of any present, emolument, office, or title of any kind whatever, from any king, prince, or foreign State; nor shall the united States, in congress assembled, or any of them, grant any title of nobility.

No two or more States shall enter into any treaty, confederation, or alliance whatever, between them, without the consent of the united States, in Congress assembled, specifying accurately the purposes for which the same is to be entered into, and how long it shall continue.

No State shall lay any imposts or duties, which may inter-fere with any stipulations in treaties, entered into by the united States, in congress assembled, with any king, prince, or State, in pursuance of any treaties already proposed by congress to the courts of France and Spain.

No vessels of war shall be kept up in time of peace, by any State, except such number only as shall be deemed necessary by the united States, in congress assembled, for the defence of such State, or its trade; nor shall any body of forces be kept up, by any State, in time of peace, except such number only as, in the judgment of the united States, in congress assembled, shall be deemed requisite to garrison the forts necessary for the defence of such State; but every State shall always keep up a well-regulated and disciplined militia, sufficiently armed and accounted, and shall provide and constantly have ready for use, in public stores, a due number of field-pieces and tents, and a proper quantity of arms, ammunition, and camp equipage.

No State shall engage in any war without the consent of the united States, in congress assembled, unless such State be actually invaded by enemies, or shall have received certain advice of a resolution being formed by some nation of Indians to invade such State, and the danger is so immi-nent as not to admit of a delay till the united States, in congress assembled, can be consulted; nor shall any State grant commissions to any ships or vessels of war, nor letters of marque or reprisal, except it be after a declaration of war by the united States, in congress assembled, and then only against the kingdom or State, and the subjects thereof, against which war has been so declared, and under such regulations as shall be established by the united States, in congress assembled, unless such State be infested by pirates, in which case vessels of war may be fitted out for that occasion, and kept so long as the danger shall continue, or until the united States, in congress assembled, shall determine otherwise.

Article VII. When land forces are raised by any State, for the common defence, all officers of or under the rank of colonel, shall be appointed by the legislature of each State respectively by whom such forces shall be raised, or in such manner as such State shall direct, and all vacancies shall be filled up by the State which first made appointment.

Article VIII. All charges of war, and all other expenses that shall be incurred for the common defence or general welfare, and allowed by the united States, in congress assembled, shall be defrayed out of a common treasury, which shall be supplied by the several States, in proportion to the value of all land within each State, granted to, or surveyed for, any person, as such land and the buildings and improvements thereon shall be estimated, according to such mode as the united States, in congress assembled, shall, from time to time, direct and appoint. The taxes for paying that proportion shall be laid and levied by the authority and direction of the legislatures of the several States, within the time agreed upon by the united States, in congress assembled.

Article IX. The united States, in congress assembled, shall have the sole and exclusive right and power of determining on peace and war, except in the cases mentioned in the sixth Article, of sending and receiving ambassadors; entering into treaties and alliances, provided that no treaty of commerce shall be made, whereby the legislative power of the respective States shall be restrained from imposing such imposts and duties on foreigners, as their own people are subjected to, or from prohibiting the exportation or importation of any species of goods or commodities whatsoever; of establishing rules for de-ciding, in all cases, what captures on land or water shall be legal, and in what manner prizes taken by land or naval forces in the service of the united Sates, shall be divided or appropriated; of granting letters of marque and reprisal in times of peace; appointing courts for the trial of piracies and felonies committed on the high seas; and establishing courts; for receiving and determine-ing finally appeals in all cases of captures; provided that no member of congress shall be appointed a judge of any of the said courts.

The united States, in congress assembled, shall also be the last resort on appeal, in all disputes and differences now subsisting, or that hereafter may arise between two or more States concerning boundary, jurisdiction, or any other cause whatever; which authority shall always be exercised in the manner following. Whenever the legislative or executive authority, or lawful agent of any State in controversy with another, shall present a petition to congress, stating the matter in question, and praying for a hearing, notice thereof shall be given, by order of congress, to the legislative or executive authority of the other State in con- troversy, and a day assigned for the appearance of the parties by their lawful agents, who shall then be directed to appoint, by joint consent, commissioners or judges to constitute a court for hearing and determining the matter in question: but if they cannot agree, congress shall name three persons out of each of the united States, and from the list of such persons each party shall alternately strike out one, the petitioners beginning, until the number shall be reduced to thirteen; and from that number not less than seven, nor more than nine names, as congress shall direct, shall, in the presence of congress, be drawn out by lot, and the persons whose names shall be so drawn, or any five of them, shall be commissioners or judges, to hear and finally determine the controversy, so always as a major part of the judges, who shall hear the cause, shall agree in the determi-nation: and if either party shall neglect to attend at the day appointed, without showing reasons which congress shall judge sufficient, or being present, shall refuse to strike, the congress shall proceed to nominate three persons out of each State, and the secretary of congress shall strike in behalf of such party absent or refusing; and the judgment and sentence of the court, to be appointed in the manner before prescribed, shall be final and conclusive; and if any of the parties shall refuse to submit to the authority of such court, or to appear or defend their claim or cause, the court shall nevertheless proceed to pronounce sentence, or judgment, which shall in like manner be final and decisive; the judgment or sentence and other proceedings being in either case transmitted to congress, and lodged among the acts of congress, for the security of the parties con-cerned: provided that every commissioner, before he sits in judgment, shall take an oath to be administered by one of the judges of the Supreme or Superior court of the State where the cause shall be tried, "well and truly to hear and determine the matter in question, according to the best of his judgment, without favour, affection, or hope of reward: "Provided, also, that no State shall be deprived of territory for the benefit of the united States.

All controversies concerning the private right of soil claimed under different grants of two or more States, whose jurisdictions as they may respect such lands, and the States which passed such grants are adjusted, the said grants or either of them being at the same time claimed to have originated ante-cedent to such settlement of jurisdiction, shall, on the petition of either party to the congress of the united States, be finally determined, as near as may be, in the same manner as is before prescribed for deciding disputes respecting territorial jurisdiction between different States.

The united States, in congress assembled, shall also have the sole and exclusive right and power of regulating the alloy and value of coin struck by their own authority, or by that of the respective States fixing the standard of weights and measures throughout the united States; regulating the trade and managing all affairs with the Indians, not members of any of the States; provided that the legislative right of any State, within its own limits, be not in-fringed or violated; establishing and regulating post-offices from one State to another, throughout all the United States, and exacting such postage on the papers passing through the same, as may be requisite to defray the expenses of the said office; appointing all officers of the land forces in the service of the united States, excepting regimental officers; appointing all the officers of the naval forces, and commissioning all officers whatever in the service of the united States; making rules for the government and regulation of the said land and naval forces, and directing their operations.

The united States, in congress assembled, shall have authority to appoint a committee, to sit in the recess of congress, to be denominated, "A Committee of the States," and to consist of one delegate from each State; and to appoint such other committees and civil officers as may be necessary for managing the general affairs of the united States under their direction; to appoint one of their number to preside; provided that no person be allowed to serve in the office of president more than one year in any term of three years; to ascertain the necessary sums of money to be raised for the service of the united States, and to appropriate and apply the same for defraying the public expenses; to borrow money or emit bills on the credit of the united States, transmitting every half year to the respective States an account of the sums of money so borrowed or emitted; to build and equip a navy; to agree upon the number of land forces, and to make requisitions from each State for its quota, in proportion to the number of white inhabitants in such State, which requi-sition shall be binding; and thereupon the Legislature of each State shall appoint the regimental officers, raise the men, and clothe, arm, and equip them, in a soldier-like manner, at the expense of the united States; and the officers and men so clothed, armed, and equipped, shall march to the place appointed, and within the time agreed on by the united States, in congress assembled; but if the united States, in congress assembled, shall, on consideration of circumstances, judge proper that any State should not raise men, or should raise a smaller number than its quota, and that any other State should raise a greater number of men than the quota thereof, such extra number shall be raised, officered, clothed, armed, and equipped in the same manner as the quota of such State, unless the Legislature of such State shall judge that such extra number cannot be safely spared out of the same, in which case they shall raise, officer, clothe, arm, and equip, as many of such extra number as they judge can be safely spared. And the officers and men so clothed, armed, and equipped, shall march to the place appointed, and within the time agreed on by the united States in congress assembled.

The united States, in congress assembled, shall never engage in a war, nor grant letters of marque and reprisal in time of peace, nor enter into any treaties or alliances, nor coin money, nor regulate the value thereof nor ascertain the sums and expenses necessary for the defence and welfare of the united States, or any of them, nor emit bills, nor borrow money on the credit of the united States, nor appropriate money, nor agree upon the number of vessels of war to be built or purchased, or the number of land or sea forces to be raised, nor appoint a commander in chief of the army or navy, unless nine States assent to the same, nor shall a question on any other point, except for adjourning from day to day, be determined, unless by the votes of a majority of the united States in congress assembled.

The congress of the united States shall have power to adjourn to any time within the year, and to any place within the united States, so that no period of adjournment be for a longer duration than the space of six months, and shall publish the journal of their proceedings monthly, except such parts thereof relating to treaties, alliances, or military operations, as in their judgment require secrecy; and the yeas and nays of the delegates of each State, on any question, shall be entered on the journal, when it is desired by any delegate; and the delegates of a State, or any of them, at his or their request, shall be furnished with a transcript of the said journal, except such parts as are above excepted, to lay before the legislatures of the several States.

Article X. The committee of the States, or any nine of them, shall be authorized to execute, in the recess of congress, such of the powers of congress as the united States, in congress assembled, by the consent of nine States, shall, from time to time, think expedient to vest them with; provided that no power be delegated to the said committee, for the exercise of which, by the articles of con-federation, the voice of nine States, in the congress of the united States assembled, is requisite.

Article XI. Canada acceding to this confederation, and joining in the measures of the united

States, shall be admitted into, and entitled to all the advantages of this union: but no other colony shall be admitted into the same, unless such admission be agreed to by nine States.

Article XII. All bills of credit emitted, monies borrowed, and debts contracted by or under the authority of congress, before the assembling of the united States, in pursuance of the present confederation, shall be deemed and considered as a charge against the united States, for payment and satisfaction whereof the said United States and the public faith are hereby solemnly pledged.

Article XIII. Every State shall abide by the determinations of the united States, in congress assembled, on all questions which by this confederation are submitted to them. And the articles of this confederation shall be inviolably observed by every State, and the Union shall be perpetual; nor shall any alteration at any time hereafter be made in any of them, unless such alteration be agreed to in a congress of the united States, and be afterwards confirmed by the legislatures of every State.

And Whereas it hath pleased the Great Governor of the World to incline the hearts of the legislatures we respectively represent in congress, to approve of, and to authorize us to ratify the said articles of confederation and perpetual union, Know Ye, that we, the undersigned delegates, by virtue of the power and authority to us given for that purpose, do, by these presents, in the name and in behalf of our respective constituents, fully and entirely ratify and confirm each and every of the said articles of confederation and perpetual union, and all and singular the matters and things therein contained. And we do further solemnly plight and engage the faith of our respective constituents, that they shall abide by the determinations of the united States, in congress assembled, on all questions which by the said confederation are submitted to them; and that the articles thereof shall be inviolably observed by the States we respectively represent, and that the Union shall be perpetual. In witness whereof, we have hereunto set our hands, in Congress.

Done at Philadelphia, in the State of Pennsylvania, the ninth day of July, in the year of our Lord one thousand seven hundred and seventy eight, and in the third year of the Independence of America.

On the part and behalf of the State of New Hampshire.—Josiah Bartlett, John Wentworth, Jun. (August 8, 1778.)

On the part and behalf of the State of Massachusetts Bay.—John Hancock, Samuel Adams, Elbridge Gerry, Francis Dana, James Lovell, Samuel Holten.

On the part and behalf of the State of Rhode Island and Providence Plantations.—William Ellery, Henry Marchant, John Collins.

On the part and behalf of the State of Connecticut.—Roger Sherman, Samuel Huntington, Oliver Wolcott, Titus Hosmer, Andrew Adams.

On the part and behalf of the State of New York.—James Duane, Francis Lewis, William Duer, Gouv. Morris.

On the part and behalf of the State of New Jersey.—Jno. Witherspoon, Nath. Scudder, (November 26, 1778.)

On the part and in behalf of the State of Pennsylvania.—Robert Morris, Daniel Roberdeau, Jona. Bayard Smith, William Clingan, Joseph Reed, (July 22, 1778.)

On the part and behalf of the State of Delaware.—Thomas M'Kean, (February 12, 1779,) John Dickinson, (May 5, 1779,) Nicholas Van Dyke.

On the part and behalf of the State of Maryland.—John Hanson, (March 1, 1781,) Daniel Carroll, (March 1, 1781)

On the part and behalf of the State of Virginia.—Richard Henry Lee, John Banister, Thomas Adams, Jno. Harvie, Francis Lightfoot Lee.

On the part and behalf of the State of North Carolina.—John Penn, (July 21, 1778,) Corns. Harnett, Jno. Williams.

On the part and behalf of the State of South Carolina.—Henry Laurens, William Henry Drayton, Jno. Mathews, Richard Hutson, Thos. Heyward, Jun.

On the part and behalf of the State of Georgia.—Jno. Walton, (July 24, 1778,) Edwd. Telfair, Edward Langworthy.

V

"For the government of the Territory"

NORTHWEST ORDINANCE
(1787)

CONGRESS AGREED TO THE ARTICLES OF CONFEDERATION ON NOVEMber 15, 1777. All thirteen colonies had to ratify them. Maryland held out for Virginia to give up part of its vast unsettled territory. When Virginia did, Maryland ratified the Articles on March 1, 1781. This was just before the end of the American Revolution, when British General Charles Cornwallis formally surrendered at Yorktown on October 19, 1781, and two years before the formal terms of peace were agreed to with Great Britain in 1783.

The debates and discussion around the Articles of Confederation provide a window into the concerns of the states at the time. Where would the power reside? Would the big state or small states wield more power? How would slavery be dealt with? While these questions were temporarily answered for the thirteen states, the same questions resurfaced in thinking through how the territories would become states.

The fledgling U.S. government had been granted territory around the Great Lakes following the 1783 Peace of Paris with Britain. Today, this area covers the states of Ohio, Indiana, Illinois, Michigan, Wisconsin, and Minnesota. However, in the early 1780s, there were no provisions governing how this vast area would be administered. Furthermore, many of the existing thirteen states had laid claims to territory in this region.

The members of the Congress of the Confederation, the legislature created by the Articles of Confederation, knew that they had to address the issues of geographic growth. Congressmen Thomas Jefferson, Jeremiah Chase, and David Howell submitted a report on March 1, 1784 with recommendations for "division and government of the western edges of United states [sic] territory." In addition to creating a process for this territorial area to become new states, the recommendation called for the abolition of slavery in the new states with the clause, "after the year 1800 of the Christian era, there shall be neither slavery nor involuntary servitude in any of the said States." Congress debated the issues, but the recommendation to limit slavery foundered.

This report eventually became the Land Ordinance of 1784, which noted that any new state should be included "on an equal footing with the said original States." The next year, the Land Ordinance of 1785 established guidelines for selling land in the territorial area to private owners.

A few years later, the Northwest Ordinance passed on July 13, 1787. It was one of the most important acts passed by Congress under the Articles of Confederation. It laid out the process through which a territory could move into statehood. It guaranteed that any new states would enter into the union on an equal footing with the old, and it protected civil liberties in the new territories. This ordinance was also the first national legislation that set limits on the expansion of slavery.

Written by Nathan Dane and Rufus King, delegates to the Continental Congress from Massachusetts, the Northwest Ordinance decreed that the territory should become "not less than three nor more than five States." It also listed rights including freedom of religion, "benefits of the writ of *habeas corpus*, and of the trial by jury; of a proportionate representation of the people in the legislature; and of judicial proceedings according to the course of the common law."

While it guaranteed freedom of religious worship, it also noted that religion and morality as well as education were the backbone of a republican government. "Religion, morality, and knowledge, being necessary to good government and the happiness of mankind, schools and the means of education shall forever be encouraged."

It is interesting to note that the writers believed that education should include teachings about religion and morality. America has more recently focused on education as a separate subject—without the religious or moral underpinning—and seen the character of our citizens decline.

The ordinance said the new states should have "equal footing with the original States in all respects whatever, and shall be at liberty to form a permanent constitution and State government: Provided, the constitution and government so to be formed, shall be republican, and in conformity to the principles contained in these articles."

Without this important document, the United States would have remained only thirteen states and would not have been able to grow in size and power into the nation we cherish today.

—JGC

〰 〰 〰

Section 1.

Be it ordained by the United States in Congress assembled, That the said territory, for the purposes of temporary government, be one district, subject, however, to be divided into two districts, as future circumstances may, in the opinion of Congress, make it expedient.

Sec. 2.

Be it ordained by the authority aforesaid, That the estates, both of resident and nonresident proprietors in the said territory, dying intestate, shall descent to, and be distributed among their children, and the descendants of a deceased child, in equal parts; the descendants of a deceased child or grandchild to take the share of their deceased parent in equal parts among them:

And where there shall be no children or descendants, then in equal parts to the next of kin in equal degree; and among collaterals, the children of a deceased brother or sister of the intestate shall have, in equal parts among them, their deceased parents' share; and there shall in no case be a distinction between kindred of the whole and half blood; saving, in all cases, to the widow of the intestate her third part of the real estate for life, and one third part of the personal estate; and this law relative to descents and dower, shall remain in full force until altered by the legislature of the district. And until the governor and judges shall adopt laws as hereinafter mentioned, estates in the said territory may be devised or bequeathed by wills in writing, signed and sealed by him or her in whom the estate may be (being of full age), and attested by three witnesses; and real estates may be conveyed by lease and release, or bargain and sale, signed, sealed and delivered by the person being of full age, in whom the estate may be, and attested by two witnesses, provided such wills be duly proved, and such conveyances be acknowledged, or the execution thereof duly proved, and be recorded within one year after proper magistrates, courts, and registers shall be appointed for that purpose; and personal property may be transferred by delivery; saving, however to the French and Canadian inhabitants, and other settlers of the Kaskaskies, St. Vincents and the neighboring villages who have heretofore professed themselves citizens of Virginia, their laws and customs now in force among them, relative to the descent and conveyance, of property.

Sec. 3.

Be it ordained by the authority aforesaid, That there shall be appointed from time to time by Congress, a governor, whose commission shall continue in force for the term of three years, unless sooner revoked by Congress; he shall reside in the district, and have a freehold estate therein in 1,000 acres of land, while in the exercise of his office.

Sec. 4.

There shall be appointed from time to time by Congress, a secretary, whose commission shall continue in force for four years unless sooner revoked; he shall reside in the district, and have a freehold estate therein in 500 acres of land, while in the exercise of his office. It shall be his duty to keep and preserve the acts and laws passed by the legislature, and the public records of the district, and the proceedings of the governor in his executive department, and transmit authentic copies of such acts and proceedings, every six months, to the Secretary of Congress: There shall also be appointed a court to consist of three judges, any two of whom to form a court, who shall have a common law jurisdiction, and reside in the district, and have each therein a freehold estate in 500 acres of land while in the exercise of their offices; and their commissions shall continue in force during good behavior.

Sec. 5.

The governor and judges, or a majority of them, shall adopt and publish in the district such laws of the original States, criminal and civil, as may be necessary and best suited to the circumstances of the district, and report them to Congress from time to time: which laws shall be in force in the district until the organization of the General Assembly therein, unless disapproved of by Congress; but afterwards the Legislature shall have authority to alter them as they shall think fit.

Sec. 6.

The governor, for the time being, shall be commander in chief of the militia, appoint and commission all officers in the same below the rank of general officers; all general officers shall be appointed and commissioned by Congress.

Sec. 7.

Previous to the organization of the general assembly, the governor shall appoint such magistrates and other civil officers in each county or township, as he shall find necessary for the preservation of the peace and good order in the same: After the general assembly shall be organized, the powers and duties of the magistrates and other civil officers shall be regulated and defined by the said assembly; but all magistrates and other civil officers not herein otherwise directed, shall during the continuance of this temporary government, be appointed by the governor.

Sec. 8.

For the prevention of crimes and injuries, the laws to be adopted or made shall have force in all parts of the district, and for the execution of process, criminal and civil, the governor shall make proper divisions thereof; and he shall proceed from time to time as circumstances may require, to lay out the parts of the district in which the Indian titles shall have been extinguished, into counties and townships, subject, however, to such alterations as may thereafter be made by the legislature.

Sec. 9.

So soon as there shall be five thousand free male inhabitants of full age in the district, upon giving proof thereof to the governor, they shall receive authority, with time and place, to elect a representative from their counties or townships to represent them in the general assembly: Provided, That, for every five hundred free male inhabitants, there shall be one representative, and so on progressively with the number of free male inhabitants shall the right of representation increase, until the number of representatives shall amount to twenty five; after which, the number and proportion of representatives shall be regulated by the legislature: Provided, That no person be eligible or qualified to act as a representative unless he shall have been a citizen of one of the United States three years, and be a resident in the district, or unless he shall have resided in the district three years; and, in either case, shall likewise hold in his own right, in fee simple, two hundred acres of land within the same; Provided, also, That a freehold in fifty acres of land in the district, having been a citizen of one of the states, and being resident in the district, or the like freehold and two years residence in the district, shall be necessary to qualify a man as an elector of a representative.

Sec. 10.

The representatives thus elected, shall serve for the term of two years; and, in case of the death of a representative, or removal from office, the governor shall issue a writ to the county or township for which he was a member, to elect another in his stead, to serve for the residue of the term.

Sec. 11.

The general assembly or legislature shall consist of the governor, legislative council, and a house of representatives. The Legislative Council shall consist of five members, to continue in office five years, unless sooner removed by Congress; any three of whom to be a quorum: and the members of the Council shall be nominated and appointed in the following manner, to wit: As soon as representatives shall be elected, the Governor shall appoint a time and place for them to meet together; and, when met, they shall nominate ten persons, residents in the district, and each possessed of a freehold in five hundred acres of land, and return their names to Congress; five of whom Congress shall appoint and commission to serve as aforesaid; and, whenever a vacancy shall happen in the council, by death or removal from office, the house of representatives shall nominate two persons, qualified as aforesaid, for each vacancy, and return their names to Congress; one of whom congress shall appoint and commission for the residue of the term. And every five years, four months at least before the expiration of the time of service of the members of council, the said house shall nominate ten persons, qualified as aforesaid, and return their names to Congress; five of whom Congress shall appoint and commission to serve as members of the council five years, unless sooner removed. And the governor, legislative council, and house of representatives, shall have authority to make laws in all cases, for the good government of the district, not repugnant to the principles and articles in this ordinance established and declared. And all bills, having passed by a majority in the house, and by a majority in the council, shall be referred to the governor for his assent; but no bill, or legislative act whatever, shall be of any force without his assent. The governor shall have power to convene, prorogue, and dissolve the general assembly, when, in his opinion, it shall be expedient.

Sec. 12.

The governor, judges, legislative council, secretary, and such other officers as Congress shall appoint in the district, shall take an oath or affirmation of fidelity and of office; the governor before the president of congress, and all other officers before the Governor. As soon as a legislature shall be formed in the district, the council and house assembled in one room, shall have authority, by joint ballot, to elect a delegate to Congress, who shall have a seat in Congress, with a right of debating but not voting during this temporary government.

Sec. 13.

And, for extending the fundamental principles of civil and religious liberty, which form the basis whereon these republics, their laws and constitutions are erected; to fix and establish those principles as the basis of all laws, constitutions, and governments, which forever hereafter shall be formed in the said territory: to provide also for the establishment of States, and permanent government therein, and for their admission to a share in the federal councils on an equal footing with the original States, at as early periods as may be consistent with the general interest:

Sec. 14.

It is hereby ordained and declared by the authority aforesaid, That the following articles shall be considered as articles of compact between the original States and the people and States in the said territory and forever remain unalterable, unless by common consent, to wit:

Art. 1.

No person, demeaning himself in a peaceable and orderly manner, shall ever be molested on account of his mode of worship or religious sentiments, in the said territory.

Art. 2.

The inhabitants of the said territory shall always be entitled to the benefits of the writ of habeas corpus, and of the trial by jury; of a proportionate representation of the people in the legislature; and of judicial proceedings according to the course of the common law. All persons shall be bailable, unless for capital offenses, where the proof shall be evident or the presumption great. All fines shall be moderate; and no cruel or unusual punishments shall be inflicted. No man shall be deprived of his liberty or property, but by the judgment of his peers or the law of the land; and, should the public exigencies make it necessary, for the common preservation, to take any person's property, or to demand his particular services, full compensation shall be made for the same. And, in the just preservation of rights and property, it is understood and declared, that no law ought ever to be made, or have force in the said territory, that shall, in any manner whatever, interfere with or affect private contracts or engagements, bona fide, and without fraud, previously formed.

Art. 3.

Religion, morality, and knowledge, being necessary to good government and the happiness of mankind, schools and the means of education shall forever be encouraged. The utmost good faith shall always be observed towards the Indians; their lands and property shall never be taken from them without their consent; and, in their property, rights, and liberty, they shall never be invaded or disturbed, unless in just and lawful wars authorized by Congress; but laws founded in justice and humanity, shall from time to time be made for preventing wrongs being done to them, and for preserving peace and friendship with them.

Art. 4.

The said territory, and the States which may be formed therein, shall forever remain a part of this Confederacy of the United States of America, subject to the Articles of Confederation, and to such alterations therein as shall be constitutionally made; and to all the acts and ordinances of the United States in Congress assembled, conformable thereto. The inhabitants and settlers in the said territory shall be subject to pay a part of the federal debts contracted or to be contracted, and a proportional part of the expenses of government, to be apportioned on them by Congress according to the same common rule and measure by which apportionments thereof shall be made on the other States;

and the taxes for paying their proportion shall be laid and levied by the authority and direction of the legislatures of the district or districts, or new States, as in the original States, within the time agreed upon by the United States in Congress assembled. The legislatures of those districts or new States, shall never interfere with the primary disposal of the soil by the United States in Congress assembled, nor with any regulations Congress may find necessary for securing the title in such soil to the bona fide purchasers. No tax shall be imposed on lands the property of the United States; and, in no case, shall non-resident proprietors be taxed higher than residents. The navigable waters leading into the Mississippi and St. Lawrence, and the carrying places between the same, shall be common highways and forever free, as well to the inhabitants of the said territory as to the citizens of the United States, and those of any other States that may be admitted into the confederacy, without any tax, impost, or duty therefor.

Art. 5.

There shall be formed in the said territory, not less than three nor more than five States; and the boundaries of the States, as soon as Virginia shall alter her act of cession, and consent to the same, shall become fixed and established as follows, to wit: The western State in the said territory, shall be bounded by the Mississippi, the Ohio, and Wabash Rivers; a direct line drawn from the Wabash and Post Vincents, due North, to the territorial line between the United States and Canada; and, by the said territorial line, to the Lake of the Woods and Mississippi. The middle State shall be bounded by the said direct line, the Wabash from Post Vincents to the Ohio, by the Ohio, by a direct line, drawn due north from the mouth of the Great Miami, to the said territorial line, and by the said territorial line. The eastern State shall be bounded by the last mentioned direct line, the Ohio, Pennsylvania, and the said territorial line: Provided, however, and it is further understood and declared, that the boundaries of these three States shall be subject so far to be altered, that, if Congress shall hereafter find it expedient, they shall have authority to form one or two States in that part of the said territory which lies north of an east and west line drawn through the southerly bend or extreme of Lake Michigan. And, whenever any of the said States shall have sixty thousand free inhabitants therein, such State shall be admitted, by its delegates, into the Congress of the United States, on an equal footing with the original States in all respects whatever, and shall be at liberty to form a permanent constitution and State government: Provided, the constitution and government so to be formed, shall be republican, and in conformity to the principles contained in these articles; and, so far as it can be consistent with the general interest of the confederacy, such admission shall be allowed at an earlier period, and when there may be a less number of free inhabitants in the State than sixty thousand.

Art. 6.

There shall be neither slavery nor involuntary servitude in the said territory, otherwise than in the punishment of crimes whereof the party shall have been duly convicted: Provided, always, That any person escaping into the same, from whom labor or service is lawfully claimed in any one of the original States, such fugitive may be lawfully reclaimed and conveyed to the person claiming his or her labor or service as aforesaid.

Be it ordained by the authority aforesaid, That the resolutions of the 23rd of April, 1784, relative to the subject of this ordinance, be, and the same are hereby repealed and declared null and void.

Done by the United States, in Congress assembled, the 13th day of July, in the year of our Lord 1787, and of their soveriegnty and independence the twelfth.

VI

"We the People"

CONSTITUTION
OF THE UNITED STATES
(1787)

As the war wound down, it became evident that the Articles of Confederation needed to be strengthened. The United States could not pay the soldiers for their service in the American Revolutionary war, nor could the country repay foreign debts taken out during the war.

The states were concerned over debts as well. Rhode Island passed a law to forgive debts. Soon after, Daniel Shays led a rebellion in Massachusetts in the hopes that private citizens would be able to win debt relief from the government. Something had to be done. Independence was won—but there had to be internal control and structure for the union to last.

In 1786, James Madison, a Virginia State Legislator, called for a conference to discuss rules and regulations for intra-national trade. Delaware, New Jersey, New York, Pennsylvania, and Virginia sent delegates to participate at the Annapolis Convention, but more participation was needed.

The conference participants sent a report to the Continental Congress and requested a full conference of all thirteen states. On February 21, 1787, the Continental Congress announced, "it is expedient that on the second Monday in May next a Convention of delegates who shall have been appointed by the several States be held at Phlladelphia for the sole and express purpose of revising the Articles of Confederation."

Madison and the other Virginia delegates, including General George Washington, arrived early for the 1787 Constitutional Convention. While they waited, they drew up a draft structure for the government and presented it when the Convention met.

Called the Virginia Plan, it envisioned the federal government being divided among three branches—legislative, executive, and judicial. The two legislative bodies would be composed of representatives whose numbers would be based on the populations of the states. While this structure was welcomed by large states such as Virginia, the small states were very concerned. This would give the big states much more power than had been given by the Articles of Confederation, which gave each state one representative.

As an alternative, New Jersey's William Patterson submitted the New Jersey Plan. It, too, proposed three branches of government, but called for a single legislative body in which each state would have an equal number of votes.

But the big states were opposed and the convention was deadlocked—how were they to bridge the gap between the small states and the large states?

A compromise rescued the convention: bicameralism, under which the composition of one of two legislative bodies was to be determined by population, with the other giving each state equal representation.

Roger Sherman of Connecticut, the only member of the Continental Congress who had signed the Association of 1774, the Declaration of Independence, the Articles of Confederation, and the Constitution, proposed the solution, which came to be known as the Great Compromise.

The slavery question remained unaddressed. Some colonies had slaves, some did not. Forcing the issue one way or the other would have resulted in some states pulling away from the young nation to go out on their own. It was not simply a matter of allowing or disallowing slaves, but also the question of whether slaves should be counted in determining how many representatives each state got in Congress.

Another compromise was put forth—every five slaves would count as three people for purposes of determining representation, though they could not vote. It became known as the Three-Fifths Compromise.

As for who was sovereign in our new nation, it was not the president, the national legislature, or the state. It was "the people." While "the people" were not defined in the Constitution, we have come to interpret "the people" as the nation's citizens, who exert their power over the government by participating in elections of their representatives.

The convention, composed of fifty-five delegates, met in Philadelphia for four months, hashing out ideas and compromises while looking for solutions on how best to create a framework for government. Though Philadelphia was the largest city in the country in 1787, with a population of about 40,000, there were few places to eat and even fewer to stay. This meant that those on opposing sides often stayed in the same inns and ate in the same restaurants. Quite often, these settings allowed for differences to be aired and relationships to be built. Finally, on September 17, 1787, the Continental Congress signed the Constitution.

Soon after the Constitution was adopted, John Adams, who was serving in London at the time, wrote to Thomas Jefferson and asked, "What think you of a Declaration of Rights? Should not such a thing have preceded the model?"

Jefferson wrote to Adams that he was concerned that the office of president seemed to him to be "a bad edition of a Polish king."

The Federalists, who promoted the idea of a strong national government, were concerned that the masses would pull apart the nation. The anti-Federalists, who desired less national control and more states' rights, were concerned that a centralized government would concentrate too much power in the hands of a few—leading to tyranny and despotism.

Adams responded to Jefferson, "You are afraid of the one, I, the few.... I would have given more power to the president and less to the Senate."

While a Declaration of Rights was not included, Adams believed that, on the whole, the Constitution was well thought out, writing to John Jay, who had previously served as the president of the Continental Congress, "the great principles necessary to order, liberty, and safety are respected in it, and provision is made for corrections and amendments, as they may be found necessary."

Necessary they were. Others shared Adams' concern about the absence of a "Declaration of Rights." There was great concern that providing more power to the federal government would result in the loss of individual freedoms.

In Article Five, the Constitution provided a way to change the Constitution, but it wasn't easy.

> The Congress, whenever two thirds of both Houses shall deem it necessary, shall propose Amendments to this Constitution, or, on the Application of the Legislatures of two thirds of the several States, shall call a Convention for proposing Amendments, which, in either Case, shall be valid to all Intents and Purposes, as Part of this Constitution, when ratified by the Legislatures of three fourths of the several States, or by Conventions in three fourths thereof, as the one or the other Mode of Ratification may be proposed by the Congress; Provided that no Amendment which may be made prior to the Year One thousand eight hundred and eight shall in any Manner affect the first and fourth Clauses in the Ninth Section of the first Article; and that no State, without its Consent, shall be deprived of its equal Suffrage in the Senate.

The first state to ratify the Constitution was Delaware. Rhode Island, who did not send delegates to the convention as they saw it as an overthrow of the existing government, refused to call a ratifying convention. Massachusetts, concerned about individual rights, added language asking for the newly formed Congress to amend the Constitution.

The United States Constitution went into effect March 4, 1789.

When the new Congress met March 4, 1789, one of its first orders of business was to recommend a list of amendments to the Constitution. Of the twelve amendments recommended, ten were passed. These amendments became known as the Bill of Rights and include the right to freedom of speech, freedom of religion, the right to bear arms, and the right to trial by jury. Proposed amendments regarding congressional pay and apportionment were not passed.

Since that time, seventeen additional amendments have been approved. Additional amendments have included those that address civil rights, women's suffrage, congressional pay, and limits on presidential service.

Today it is important we remember that the Constitution balances a national government with individuals' liberties. It is a living document that can grow and change over time, although sometimes those changes are slow in coming. The last amendment, the Twenty-seventh, concerns congressional pay. It was first proposed on September 25, 1789. It was ratified on May 5, 1992.

—JGC

❧ ❧ ❧

Note: The following text is a transcription of the Constitution in its original form. Items that are italicized have since been amended or superseded.

We the People of the United States, in Order to form a more perfect Union, establish Justice, insure domestic Tranquility, provide for the common defence, promote the general Welfare, and secure the Blessings of Liberty to ourselves and our Posterity, do ordain and establish this Constitution for the United States of America.

Article. I.

Section. 1.

All legislative Powers herein granted shall be vested in a Congress of the United States, which shall consist of a Senate and House of Representatives.

Section. 2.

The House of Representatives shall be composed of Members chosen every second Year by the People of the several States, and the Electors in each State shall have the Qualifications requisite for Electors of the most numerous Branch of the State Legislature.

No Person shall be a Representative who shall not have attained to the Age of twenty five Years, and been seven Years a Citizen of the United States, and who shall not, when elected, be an Inhabitant of that State in which he shall be chosen.

Representatives and direct Taxes shall be apportioned among the several States which may be included within this Union, according to their respective Numbers, which shall be determined by adding to the whole Number of free Persons, including those bound to Service for a Term of Years, and excluding Indians not taxed, three fifths of all other Persons. The actual Enumeration shall be made within three Years after the first Meeting of the Congress of the United States, and within every subsequent Term of ten Years, in such Manner as they shall by Law direct. The Number of Representatives shall not exceed one for every thirty Thousand, but each State shall have at Least one Representative; and until such enumeration shall be made, the State of New Hampshire shall be entitled to chuse three, Massachusetts eight, Rhode-Island and Providence Plantations one, Connecticut five, New-York six, New Jersey four, Pennsylvania eight, Delaware one, Maryland six, Virginia ten, North Carolina five, South Carolina five, and Georgia three.

When vacancies happen in the Representation from any State, the Executive Authority thereof shall issue Writs of Election to fill such Vacancies.

The House of Representatives shall chuse their Speaker and other Officers; and shall have the sole Power of Impeachment.

Section. 3.

The Senate of the United States shall be composed of two Senators from each State, *chosen by the Legislature* thereof for six Years; and each Senator shall have one Vote.

Immediately after they shall be assembled in Consequence of the first Election, they shall be divided as equally as may be into three Classes. The Seats of the Senators of the first Class shall be vacated at the Expiration of the second Year, of the second Class at the Expiration of the fourth Year, and of the third Class at the Expiration of the sixth Year, so that one third may be chosen every second Year; *and if Vacancies happen by Resignation, or otherwise, during the Recess of the Legislature of any State, the Executive thereof may make temporary Appointments until the next Meeting of the Legislature, which shall then fill such Vacancies.*

No Person shall be a Senator who shall not have attained to the Age of thirty Years, and been nine Years a Citizen of the United States, and who shall not, when elected, be an Inhabitant of that State for which he shall be chosen.

The Vice President of the United States shall be President of the Senate, but shall have no Vote, unless they be equally divided.

The Senate shall chuse their other Officers, and also a President pro tempore, in the Absence of the Vice President, or when he shall exercise the Office of President of the United States.

The Senate shall have the sole Power to try all Impeachments. When sitting for that Purpose, they shall be on Oath or Affirmation. When the President of the United States is tried, the Chief Justice shall preside: And no Person shall be convicted without the Concurrence of two thirds of the Members present.

Judgment in Cases of Impeachment shall not extend further than to removal from Office, and disqualification to hold and enjoy any Office of honor, Trust or Profit under the United States: but the Party convicted shall nevertheless be liable and subject to Indictment, Trial, Judgment and Punishment, according to Law.

Section. 4.

The Times, Places and Manner of holding Elections for Senators and Representatives, shall be prescribed in each State by the Legislature thereof; but the Congress may at any time by Law make or alter such Regulations, except as to the Places of chusing Senators.

The Congress shall assemble at least once in every Year, and such Meeting shall *be on the first Monday in December,* unless they shall by Law appoint a different Day.

Section. 5.

Each House shall be the Judge of the Elections, Returns and Qualifications of its own Members, and a Majority of each shall constitute a Quorum to do Business; but a smaller Number may adjourn from day to day, and may be authorized to compel the Attendance of absent Members, in such Manner, and under such Penalties as each House may provide.

Each House may determine the Rules of its Proceedings, punish its Members for disorderly Behaviour, and, with the Concurrence of two thirds, expel a Member.

Each House shall keep a Journal of its Proceedings, and from time to time publish the same, excepting such Parts as may in their Judgment require Secrecy; and the Yeas and Nays of the Members of either House on any question shall, at the Desire of one fifth of those Present, be entered on the Journal.

Neither House, during the Session of Congress, shall, without the Consent of the other, adjourn for more than three days, nor to any other Place than that in which the two Houses shall be sitting.

Section. 6.

The Senators and Representatives shall receive a Compensation for their Services, to be ascertained by Law, and paid out of the Treasury of the United States. They shall in all Cases, except Treason, Felony and Breach of the Peace, be privileged from Arrest during their Attendance at the Session of their respective Houses, and in going to and returning from the same; and for any Speech or Debate in either House, they shall not be questioned in any other Place.

No Senator or Representative shall, during the Time for which he was elected, be appointed to any civil Office under the Authority of the United States, which shall have been created, or the Emoluments whereof shall have been encreased during such time; and no Person holding any Office under the United States, shall be a Member of either House during his Continuance in Office.

Section. 7.

All Bills for raising Revenue shall originate in the House of Representatives; but the Senate may propose or concur with Amendments as on other Bills.

Every Bill which shall have passed the House of Representatives and the Senate, shall, before it become a Law, be presented to the President of the United States: If he approve he shall sign it, but if not he shall return it, with his Objections to that House in which it shall have originated, who shall enter the Objections at large on their Journal, and proceed to reconsider it. If after such Reconsideration two thirds of that House shall agree to pass the Bill, it shall be sent, together with the Objections, to the other House, by which it shall likewise be reconsidered, and if approved by two thirds of that House, it shall become a Law. But in all such Cases the Votes of both Houses shall be determined by yeas and Nays, and the Names of the Persons voting for and against the Bill shall be entered on the Journal of each House respectively. If any Bill shall not be returned by the President within ten Days (Sundays excepted) after it shall have been presented to him, the Same shall be a Law, in like Manner as if he had signed it, unless the Congress by their Adjournment prevent its Return, in which Case it shall not be a Law.

Every Order, Resolution, or Vote to which the Concurrence of the Senate and House of Representatives may be necessary (except on a question of Adjournment) shall be presented to the President of the United States; and before the Same shall take Effect, shall be approved by him, or being disapproved by him, shall be repassed by two thirds of the Senate and House of Representatives, according to the Rules and Limitations prescribed in the Case of a Bill.

Section. 8.

The Congress shall have Power To lay and collect Taxes, Duties, Imposts and Excises, to pay the Debts and provide for the common Defence and general Welfare of the United States; but all Duties, Imposts and Excises shall be uniform throughout the United States;

To borrow Money on the credit of the United States;

To regulate Commerce with foreign Nations, and among the several States, and with the Indian Tribes;

To establish an uniform Rule of Naturalization, and uniform Laws on the subject of Bankruptcies throughout the United States;

To coin Money, regulate the Value thereof, and of foreign Coin, and fix the Standard of Weights and Measures;

To provide for the Punishment of counterfeiting the Securities and current Coin of the United States;

To establish Post Offices and post Roads;

To promote the Progress of Science and useful Arts, by securing for limited Times to Authors and Inventors the exclusive Right to their respective Writings and Discoveries;

To constitute Tribunals inferior to the supreme Court;

To define and punish Piracies and Felonies committed on the high Seas, and Offences against the Law of Nations;

To declare War, grant Letters of Marque and Reprisal, and make Rules concerning Captures on Land and Water;

To raise and support Armies, but no Appropriation of Money to that Use shall be for a longer Term than two Years;

To provide and maintain a Navy;

To make Rules for the Government and Regulation of the land and naval Forces;

To provide for calling forth the Militia to execute the Laws of the Union, suppress Insurrections and repel Invasions;

To provide for organizing, arming, and disciplining, the Militia, and for governing such Part of them as may be employed in the Service of the United States, reserving to the States respectively, the Appointment of the Officers, and the Authority of training the Militia according to the discipline prescribed by Congress;

To exercise exclusive Legislation in all Cases whatsoever, over such District (not exceeding ten Miles square) as may, by Cession of particular States, and the Acceptance of Congress, become the Seat of the Government of the United States, and to exercise like Authority over all Places purchased by the Consent of the Legislature of the State in which the Same shall be, for the Erection of Forts, Magazines, Arsenals, dock-Yards, and other needful Buildings;—And

To make all Laws which shall be necessary and proper for carrying into Execution the foregoing Powers, and all other Powers vested by this Constitution in the Government of the United States, or in any Department or Officer thereof.

Section. 9.

The Migration or Importation of such Persons as any of the States now existing shall think proper to admit, shall not be prohibited by the Congress prior to the Year one thousand eight hundred and eight, but a Tax or duty may be imposed on such Importation, not exceeding ten dollars for each Person.

The Privilege of the Writ of Habeas Corpus shall not be suspended, unless when in Cases of Rebellion or Invasion the public Safety may require it.

No Bill of Attainder or ex post facto Law shall be passed.

No Capitation, or other direct, Tax shall be laid, *unless in Proportion to the Census or enumeration herein before directed to be taken.*

No Tax or Duty shall be laid on Articles exported from any State.

No Preference shall be given by any Regulation of Commerce or Revenue to the Ports of one State over those of another; nor shall Vessels bound to, or from, one State, be obliged to enter, clear, or pay Duties in another.

No Money shall be drawn from the Treasury, but in Consequence of Appropriations made by Law; and a regular Statement and Account of the Receipts and Expenditures of all public Money shall be published from time to time.

No Title of Nobility shall be granted by the United States: And no Person holding any Office of Profit or Trust under them, shall, without the Consent of the Congress, accept of any present, Emolument, Office, or Title, of any kind whatever, from any King, Prince, or foreign State.

Section. 10.

No State shall enter into any Treaty, Alliance, or Confederation; grant Letters of Marque and Reprisal; coin Money; emit Bills of Credit; make any Thing but gold and silver Coin a Tender in Payment of Debts; pass any Bill of

Attainder, ex post facto Law, or Law impairing the Obligation of Contracts, or grant any Title of Nobility.

No State shall, without the Consent of the Congress, lay any Imposts or Duties on Imports or Exports, except what may be absolutely necessary for executing it's inspection Laws: and the net Produce of all Duties and Imposts, laid by any State on Imports or Exports, shall be for the Use of the Treasury of the United States; and all such Laws shall be subject to the Revision and Controul of the Congress.

No State shall, without the Consent of Congress, lay any Duty of Tonnage, keep Troops, or Ships of War in time of Peace, enter into any Agreement or Compact with another State, or with a foreign Power, or engage in War, unless actually invaded, or in such imminent Danger as will not admit of delay.

Article. II.

Section. 1.

The executive Power shall be vested in a President of the United States of America. He shall hold his Office during the Term of four Years, and, together with the Vice President, chosen for the same Term, be elected, as follows:

Each State shall appoint, in such Manner as the Legislature thereof may direct, a Number of Electors, equal to the whole Number of Senators and Representatives to which the State may be entitled in the Congress: but no Senator or Representative, or Person holding an Office of Trust or Profit under the United States, shall be appointed an Elector.

The Electors shall meet in their respective States, and vote by Ballot for two Persons, of whom one at least shall not be an Inhabitant of the same State with themselves. And they shall make a List of all the Persons voted for, and of the Number of Votes for each; which List they shall sign and certify, and transmit sealed to the Seat of the Government of the United States, directed to the President of the Senate. The President of the Senate shall, in the Presence of the Senate and House of Representatives, open all the Certificates, and the Votes shall then be counted. The Person having the greatest Number of Votes shall be the President, if such Number be a Majority of the whole Number of Electors

appointed; and if there be more than one who have such Majority, and have an equal
Number of Votes, then the House of Representatives shall immediately chuse by Ballot one
of them for President; and if no Person have a Majority, then from the five highest on the
List the said House shall in like Manner chuse the President. But in chusing the Presi-
dent, the Votes shall be taken by States, the Representation from each State having one
Vote; A quorum for this purpose shall consist of a Member or Members from two thirds
of the States, and a Majority of all the States shall be necessary to a Choice. In every Case,
after the Choice of the President, the Person having the greatest Number of Votes of the
Electors shall be the Vice President. But if there should remain two or more who have
equal Votes, the Senate shall chuse from them by Ballot the Vice President.

The Congress may determine the Time of chusing the Electors, and the Day
on which they shall give their Votes; which Day shall be the same throughout
the United States.

No Person except a natural born Citizen, or a Citizen of the United States,
at the time of the Adoption of this Constitution, shall be eligible to the Office
of President; neither shall any Person be eligible to that Office who shall not
have attained to the Age of thirty five Years, and been fourteen Years a Resident
within the United States.

In Case of the Removal of the President from Office, or of his Death, Resignation, or
Inability to discharge the Powers and Duties of the said Office, the Same shall devolve on
the Vice President, and the Congress may by Law provide for the Case of Removal, Death,
Resignation or Inability, both of the President and Vice President, declaring what Officer
shall then act as President, and such Officer shall act accordingly, until the Disability be
removed, or a President shall be elected.

The President shall, at stated Times, receive for his Services, a Compensation, which shall neither be increased nor diminished during the Period for
which he shall have been elected, and he shall not receive within that Period
any other Emolument from the United States, or any of them.

Before he enter on the Execution of his Office, he shall take the following
Oath or Affirmation:—"I do solemnly swear (or affirm) that I will faithfully
execute the Office of President of the United States, and will to the best of my
Ability, preserve, protect and defend the Constitution of the United States."

Section. 2.

The President shall be Commander in Chief of the Army and Navy of the United States, and of the Militia of the several States, when called into the actual Service of the United States; he may require the Opinion, in writing, of the principal Officer in each of the executive Departments, upon any Subject relating to the Duties of their respective Offices, and he shall have Power to grant Reprieves and Pardons for Offences against the United States, except in Cases of Impeachment.

He shall have Power, by and with the Advice and Consent of the Senate, to make Treaties, provided two thirds of the Senators present concur; and he shall nominate, and by and with the Advice and Consent of the Senate, shall appoint Ambassadors, other public Ministers and Consuls, Judges of the supreme Court, and all other Officers of the United States, whose Appointments are not herein otherwise provided for, and which shall be established by Law: but the Congress may by Law vest the Appointment of such inferior Officers, as they think proper, in the President alone, in the Courts of Law, or in the Heads of Departments.

The President shall have Power to fill up all Vacancies that may happen during the Recess of the Senate, by granting Commissions which shall expire at the End of their next Session.

Section. 3.

He shall from time to time give to the Congress Information of the State of the Union, and recommend to their Consideration such Measures as he shall judge necessary and expedient; he may, on extraordinary Occasions, convene both Houses, or either of them, and in Case of Disagreement between them, with Respect to the Time of Adjournment, he may adjourn them to such Time as he shall think proper; he shall receive Ambassadors and other public Ministers; he shall take Care that the Laws be faithfully executed, and shall Commission all the Officers of the United States.

Section. 4.

The President, Vice President and all civil Officers of the United States, shall be removed from Office on Impeachment for, and Conviction of, Treason, Bribery, or other high Crimes and Misdemeanors.

Article. III.

Section. 1.

The judicial Power of the United States shall be vested in one supreme Court, and in such inferior Courts as the Congress may from time to time ordain and establish. The Judges, both of the supreme and inferior Courts, shall hold their Offices during good Behaviour, and shall, at stated Times, receive for their Services a Compensation, which shall not be diminished during their Continuance in Office.

Section. 2.

The judicial Power shall extend to all Cases, in Law and Equity, arising under this Constitution, the Laws of the United States, and Treaties made, or which shall be made, under their Authority;—to all Cases affecting Ambassadors, other public Ministers and Consuls;—to all Cases of admiralty and maritime Jurisdiction;—to Controversies to which the United States shall be a Party;—to Controversies between two or more States;—*between a State and Citizens of another State,*—between Citizens of different States,—between Citizens of the same State claiming Lands under Grants of different States, and between a State, or the Citizens thereof, and foreign States, Citizens or Subjects.

In all Cases affecting Ambassadors, other public Ministers and Consuls, and those in which a State shall be Party, the supreme Court shall have original Jurisdiction. In all the other Cases before mentioned, the supreme Court shall have appellate Jurisdiction, both as to Law and Fact, with such Exceptions, and under such Regulations as the Congress shall make.

The Trial of all Crimes, except in Cases of Impeachment, shall be by Jury; and such Trial shall be held in the State where the said Crimes shall have been committed; but when not committed within any State, the Trial shall be at such Place or Places as the Congress may by Law have directed.

Section. 3.

Treason against the United States, shall consist only in levying War against them, or in adhering to their Enemies, giving them Aid and Comfort. No Person shall be convicted of Treason unless on the Testimony of two Witnesses to the same overt Act, or on Confession in open Court.

The Congress shall have Power to declare the Punishment of Treason, but no Attainder of Treason shall work Corruption of Blood, or Forfeiture except during the Life of the Person attainted.

Article. IV.

Section. 1.

Full Faith and Credit shall be given in each State to the public Acts, Records, and judicial Proceedings of every other State. And the Congress may by general Laws prescribe the Manner in which such Acts, Records and Proceedings shall be proved, and the Effect thereof.

Section. 2.

The Citizens of each State shall be entitled to all Privileges and Immunities of Citizens in the several States.

A Person charged in any State with Treason, Felony, or other Crime, who shall flee from Justice, and be found in another State, shall on Demand of the executive Authority of the State from which he fled, be delivered up, to be removed to the State having Jurisdiction of the Crime.

No Person held to Service or Labour in one State, under the Laws thereof, escaping into another, shall, in Consequence of any Law or Regulation therein, be discharged from such Service or Labour, but shall be delivered up on Claim of the Party to whom such Service or Labour may be due.

Section. 3.

New States may be admitted by the Congress into this Union; but no new State shall be formed or erected within the Jurisdiction of any other State; nor any State be formed by the Junction of two or more States, or Parts of States, without the Consent of the Legislatures of the States concerned as well as of the Congress.

The Congress shall have Power to dispose of and make all needful Rules and Regulations respecting the Territory or other Property belonging to the United States; and nothing in this Constitution shall be so construed as to Prejudice any Claims of the United States, or of any particular State.

Section. 4.

The United States shall guarantee to every State in this Union a Republican Form of Government, and shall protect each of them against Invasion; and on Application of the Legislature, or of the Executive (when the Legislature cannot be convened), against domestic Violence.

Article. V.

The Congress, whenever two thirds of both Houses shall deem it necessary, shall propose Amendments to this Constitution, or, on the Application of the Legislatures of two thirds of the several States, shall call a Convention for proposing Amendments, which, in either Case, shall be valid to all Intents and Purposes, as Part of this Constitution, when ratified by the Legislatures of three fourths of the several States, or by Conventions in three fourths thereof, as the one or the other Mode of Ratification may be proposed by the Congress; Provided that no Amendment which may be made prior to the Year One thousand eight hundred and eight shall in any Manner affect the first and fourth Clauses in the Ninth Section of the first Article; and that no State, without its Consent, shall be deprived of its equal Suffrage in the Senate.

Article. VI.

All Debts contracted and Engagements entered into, before the Adoption of this Constitution, shall be as valid against the United States under this Constitution, as under the Confederation.

This Constitution, and the Laws of the United States which shall be made in Pursuance thereof; and all Treaties made, or which shall be made, under the Authority of the United States, shall be the supreme Law of the Land; and the Judges in every State shall be bound thereby, any Thing in the Constitution or Laws of any State to the Contrary notwithstanding.

The Senators and Representatives before mentioned, and the Members of the several State Legislatures, and all executive and judicial Officers, both of the United States and of the several States, shall be bound by Oath or Affirmation, to support this Constitution; but no religious Test shall ever be required as a Qualification to any Office or public Trust under the United States.

Article. VII.

The Ratification of the Conventions of nine States, shall be sufficient for the Establishment of this Constitution between the States so ratifying the Same.

The Word, "the," being interlined between the seventh and eighth Lines of the first Page, the Word "Thirty" being partly written on an Erazure in the fifteenth Line of the first Page, The Words "is tried" being interlined between the thirty second and thirty third Lines of the first Page and the Word "the" being interlined between the forty third and forty fourth Lines of the second Page.

Attest William Jackson Secretary

done in Convention by the Unanimous Consent of the States present the Seventeenth Day of September in the Year of our Lord one thousand seven hundred and Eighty seven and of the Independance of the United States of America the Twelfth In witness whereof We have hereunto subscribed our Names,

G°. *Washington*
Presidt and deputy from Virginia

Delaware

Geo: Read
Gunning Bedford jun
John Dickinson
Richard Bassett
Jaco: Broom

Maryland

James McHenry
Dan of St Thos. Jenifer
Danl. Carroll

Virginia

John Blair
James Madison Jr.

North Carolina

Wm. Blount
Richd. Dobbs Spaight
Hu Williamson

South Carolina

J. Rutledge
Charles Cotesworth Pinckney
Charles Pinckney
Pierce Butler

Georgia

William Few
Abr Baldwin

New Hampshire

John Langdon
Nicholas Gilman

Massachusetts
Nathaniel Gorham
Rufus King
Connecticut
Wm. Saml. Johnson
Roger Sherman
New York
Alexander Hamilton
New Jersey
Wil: Livingston
David Brearley
Wm. Paterson
Jona: Dayton
Pennsylvania
B Franklin
Thomas Mifflin
Robt. Morris
Geo. Clymer
Thos. FitzSimons
Jared Ingersoll
James Wilson
Gouv Morris

The Bill of Rights

The Preamble to The Bill of Rights

Congress of the United States begun and held at the City of New-York, on Wednesday the fourth of March, one thousand seven hundred and eighty nine.

THE Conventions of a number of the States, having at the time of their adopting the Constitution, expressed a desire, in order to prevent misconstruction or abuse of its powers, that further declaratory and restrictive clauses should be added: And as extending the ground of public confidence in the Government, will best ensure the beneficent ends of its institution.

RESOLVED by the Senate and House of Representatives of the United States of America, in Congress assembled, two thirds of both Houses concurring, that the following Articles be proposed to the Legislatures of the several States, as amendments to the Constitution of the United States, all, or any of which Articles, when ratified by three fourths of the said Legislatures, to be valid to all intents and purposes, as part of the said Constitution; viz.

ARTICLES in addition to, and Amendment of the Constitution of the United States of America, proposed by Congress, and ratified by the Legislatures of the several States, pursuant to the fifth Article of the original Constitution.

Note: These amendments were ratified December 15, 1791, and form what is known as the "Bill of Rights."

Amendment I

Congress shall make no law respecting an establishment of religion, or prohibiting the free exercise thereof; or abridging the freedom of speech, or of the press; or the right of the people peaceably to assemble, and to petition the Government for a redress of grievances.

Amendment II

A well regulated Militia, being necessary to the security of a free State, the right of the people to keep and bear Arms, shall not be infringed.

Amendment III

No Soldier shall, in time of peace be quartered in any house, without the consent of the Owner, nor in time of war, but in a manner to be prescribed by law.

Amendment IV

The right of the people to be secure in their persons, houses, papers, and effects, against unreasonable searches and seizures, shall not be violated, and no Warrants shall issue, but upon probable cause, supported by Oath or affirmation, and particularly describing the place to be searched, and the persons or things to be seized.

Amendment V

No person shall be held to answer for a capital, or otherwise infamous crime, unless on a presentment or indictment of a Grand Jury, except in cases arising in the land or naval forces, or in the Militia, when in actual service in time of War or public danger; nor shall any person be subject for the same offence to be twice put in jeopardy of life or limb; nor shall be compelled in any criminal case to be a witness against himself, nor be deprived of life, liberty, or property, without due process of law; nor shall private property be taken for public use, without just compensation.

Amendment VI

In all criminal prosecutions, the accused shall enjoy the right to a speedy and public trial, by an impartial jury of the State and district wherein the crime shall have been committed, which district shall have been previously ascertained by law, and to be informed of the nature and cause of the accusation; to be confronted with the witnesses against him; to have compulsory process for obtaining witnesses in his favor, and to have the Assistance of Counsel for his defence.

Amendment VII

In Suits at common law, where the value in controversy shall exceed twenty dollars, the right of trial by jury shall be preserved, and no fact tried by a jury, shall be otherwise re-examined in any Court of the United States, than according to the rules of the common law.

Amendment VIII

Excessive bail shall not be required, nor excessive fines imposed, nor cruel and unusual punishments inflicted.

Amendment IX

The enumeration in the Constitution, of certain rights, shall not be construed to deny or disparage others retained by the people.

Amendment X

The powers not delegated to the United States by the Constitution, nor pro-hibited by it to the States, are reserved to the States respectively, or to the people.

The Constitution: Amendments 11–27

Amendment XI

Passed by Congress March 4, 1794. Ratified February 7, 1795.

Note: Article III, section 2, of the Constitution was modified by the 11th amendment.

The Judicial power of the United States shall not be construed to extend to any suit in law or equity, commenced or prosecuted against one of the United States by Citizens of another State, or by Citizens or Subjects of any Foreign State.

Amendment XII

Passed by Congress December 9, 1803. Ratified June 15, 1804.

Note: A portion of Article II, section 1 of the Constitution was superseded by the 12th amendment.

The Electors shall meet in their respective states and vote by ballot for President and Vice-President, one of whom, at least, shall not be an inhabi-tant of the same state with themselves; they shall name in their ballots the person voted for as President, and in distinct ballots the person voted for as Vice-President, and they shall make distinct lists of all persons voted for as President, and of all persons voted for as Vice-President, and of the number of votes for each, which lists they shall sign and certify, and transmit sealed to the seat of the government of the United States, directed to the President of the Senate;—the President of the Senate shall, in the presence of the Senate and House of Representatives, open all the certificates and the votes shall then be counted;—The person having the greatest number of votes for President, shall be the President, if such number be a majority of the whole number of Electors appointed; and if no person have such majority, then from the per-sons having the highest numbers not exceeding three on the list of those voted for as President, the House of Representatives shall choose immediately, by ballot, the President. But in choosing the President, the votes shall be taken by states, the representation from each state having one vote; a quorum for this purpose shall consist of a member or members from two-thirds of the states, and a majority of all the states shall be necessary to a choice. [And if the House of Representatives shall not choose a President whenever the right of choice shall devolve upon them, before the fourth day of March next following, then the Vice-President shall act as President, as in case of the death or other constitutional disability of the President.—]* The person having the greatest number of votes as Vice-President, shall be the Vice-President, if such number be a majority of the whole number of Electors appointed, and if no person have a majority, then from the two highest numbers on the list, the Senate shall choose the Vice-President; a quorum for the purpose shall consist of two-thirds of the whole number of Senators, and a majority of the whole number shall be necessary to a choice. But no person constitutionally ineligible to the office of President shall be eligible to that of Vice-President of the United States.

*Superseded by section 3 of the 20th amendment.

Amendment XIII
Passed by Congress January 31, 1865. Ratified December 6, 1865.

Note: A portion of Article IV, section 2, of the Constitution was superseded by the 13th amendment.

Section 1.
Neither slavery nor involuntary servitude, except as a punishment for crime whereof the party shall have been duly convicted, shall exist within the United States, or any place subject to their jurisdiction.

Section 2.
Congress shall have power to enforce this article by appropriate legislation.

Amendment XIV
Passed by Congress June 13, 1866. Ratified July 9, 1868.

Note: Article I, section 2, of the Constitution was modified by section 2 of the 14th amendment.

Section 1.

All persons born or naturalized in the United States, and subject to the jurisdiction thereof, are citizens of the United States and of the State wherein they reside. No State shall make or enforce any law which shall abridge the privileges or immunities of citizens of the United States; nor shall any State deprive any person of life, liberty, or property, without due process of law; nor deny to any person within its jurisdiction the equal protection of the laws.

Section 2.

Representatives shall be apportioned among the several States according to their respective numbers, counting the whole number of persons in each State, excluding Indians not taxed. But when the right to vote at any election for the choice of electors for President and Vice-President of the United States, Representatives in Congress, the Executive and Judicial officers of a State, or the members of the Legislature thereof, is denied to any of the male inhabitants of such State, being twenty-one years of age,* and citizens of the United States, or in any way abridged, except for participation in rebellion, or other crime, the basis of representation therein shall be reduced in the proportion which the number of such male citizens shall bear to the whole number of male citizens twenty-one years of age in such State.

Section 3.

No person shall be a Senator or Representative in Congress, or elector of President and Vice-President, or hold any office, civil or military, under the United States, or under any State, who, having previously taken an oath, as a member of Congress, or as an officer of the United States, or as a member of any State legislature, or as an executive or judicial officer of any State, to support the Constitution of the United States, shall have engaged in insurrection or rebellion against the same, or given aid or comfort to the enemies thereof. But Congress may by a vote of two-thirds of each House, remove such disability.

Section 4.

The validity of the public debt of the United States, authorized by law, including debts incurred for payment of pensions and bounties for services in suppressing insurrection or rebellion, shall not be questioned. But neither the United States nor any State shall assume or pay any debt or obligation incurred in aid of insurrection or rebellion against the United States, or any claim for the loss or emancipation of any slave; but all such debts, obligations and claims shall be held illegal and void.

Section 5.

The Congress shall have the power to enforce, by appropriate legislation, the provisions of this article.

Changed by section 1 of the 26th amendment.

Amendment XV

Passed by Congress February 26, 1869. Ratified February 3, 1870.

Section 1.

The right of citizens of the United States to vote shall not be denied or abridged by the United States or by any State on account of race, color, or previous condition of servitude—

Section 2.

The Congress shall have the power to enforce this article by appropriate legislation.

Amendment XVI

Passed by Congress July 2, 1909. Ratified February 3, 1913.
Note: Article I, section 9, of the Constitution was modified by the 16th amendment.

The Congress shall have power to lay and collect taxes on incomes, from whatever source derived, without apportionment among the several States, and without regard to any census or enumeration.

Amendment XVII

Passed by Congress May 13, 1912. Ratified April 8, 1913.
Note: Article I, section 3, of the Constitution was modified by the 17th amendment.

The Senate of the United States shall be composed of two Senators from each State, elected by the people thereof, for six years; and each Senator shall have one vote. The electors in each State shall have the qualifications requisite for electors of the most numerous branch of the State legislatures.

When vacancies happen in the representation of any State in the Senate, the executive authority of such State shall issue writs of election to fill such vacancies: *Provided*, That the legislature of any State may empower the executive thereof to make temporary appointments until the people fill the vacancies by election as the legislature may direct.

This amendment shall not be so construed as to affect the election or term of any Senator chosen before it becomes valid as part of the Constitution.

Amendment XVIII

Passed by Congress December 18, 1917. Ratified January 16, 1919. Repealed by amendment 21.

Section 1.

After one year from the ratification of this article the manufacture, sale, or transportation of intoxicating liquors within, the importation thereof into, or the exportation thereof from the United States and all territory subject to the jurisdiction thereof for beverage purposes is hereby prohibited.

Section 2.

The Congress and the several States shall have concurrent power to enforce this article by appropriate legislation.

Section 3.

This article shall be inoperative unless it shall have been ratified as an amendment to the Constitution by the legislatures of the several States, as provided in the Constitution, within seven years from the date of the submission hereof to the States by the Congress.

Amendment XIX

Passed by Congress June 4, 1919. Ratified August 18, 1920.

The right of citizens of the United States to vote shall not be denied or abridged by the United States or by any State on account of sex.

Congress shall have power to enforce this article by appropriate legislation.

Amendment XX

Passed by Congress March 2, 1932. Ratified January 23, 1933.

Note: Article I, section 4, of the Constitution was modified by section 2 of this amendment. In addition, a portion of the 12th amendment was superseded by section 3.

Section 1.

The terms of the President and the Vice President shall end at noon on the 20th day of January, and the terms of Senators and Representatives at noon on the 3d day of January, of the years in which such terms would have ended if this article had not been ratified; and the terms of their successors shall then begin.

Section 2.

The Congress shall assemble at least once in every year, and such meeting shall begin at noon on the 3d day of January, unless they shall by law appoint a different day.

Section 3.

If, at the time fixed for the beginning of the term of the President, the President elect shall have died, the Vice President elect shall become President. If a President shall not have been chosen before the time fixed for the beginning of his term, or if the President elect shall have failed to qualify, then the Vice President elect shall act as President until a President shall have qualified; and the Congress may by law provide for the case wherein neither a President elect nor a Vice President shall have qualified, declaring who shall then act as President, or the manner in which one who is to act shall be selected, and such person shall act accordingly until a President or Vice President shall have qualified.

Section 4.

The Congress may by law provide for the case of the death of any of the persons from whom the House of Representatives may choose a President whenever the right of choice shall have devolved upon them, and for the case of the death of any of the persons from whom the Senate may choose a Vice President whenever the right of choice shall have devolved upon them.

Section 5.

Sections 1 and 2 shall take effect on the 15th day of October following the ratification of this article.

Section 6.

This article shall be inoperative unless it shall have been ratified as an amendment to the Constitution by the legislatures of three-fourths of the several States within seven years from the date of its submission.

Amendment XXI

Passed by Congress February 20, 1933. Ratified December 5, 1933.

Section 1.

The eighteenth article of amendment to the Constitution of the United States is hereby repealed.

Section 2.

The transportation or importation into any State, Territory, or Possession of the United States for delivery or use therein of intoxicating liquors, in violation of the laws thereof, is hereby prohibited.

Section 3.

This article shall be inoperative unless it shall have been ratified as an amendment to the Constitution by conventions in the several States, as provided in the Constitution, within seven years from the date of the submission hereof to the States by the Congress.

Amendment XXII

   Passed by Congress March 21, 1947. Ratified February 27, 1951.

Section 1.

   No person shall be elected to the office of the President more than twice, and no person who has held the office of President, or acted as President, for more than two years of a term to which some other person was elected President shall be elected to the office of President more than once. But this Article shall not apply to any person holding the office of President when this Article was proposed by Congress, and shall not prevent any person who may be hold-ing the office of President, or acting as President, during the term within which this Article becomes operative from holding the office of President or acting as President during the remainder of such term.

Section 2.

   This article shall be inoperative unless it shall have been ratified as an amendment to the Constitution by the legislatures of three-fourths of the sev-eral States within seven years from the date of its submission to the States by the Congress.

Amendment XXIII

   Passed by Congress June 16, 1960. Ratified March 29, 1961.

Section 1.

   The District constituting the seat of Government of the United States shall appoint in such manner as Congress may direct:

   A number of electors of President and Vice President equal to the whole number of Senators and Representatives in Congress to which the District would be entitled if it were a State, but in no event more than the least pop-ulous State; they shall be in addition to those appointed by the States, but they shall be considered, for the purposes of the election of President and Vice President, to be electors appointed by a State; and they shall meet in the

District and perform such duties as provided by the twelfth article of amendment.

Section 2.

The Congress shall have power to enforce this article by appropriate legislation.

Amendment XXIV

Passed by Congress August 27, 1962. Ratified January 23, 1964.

Section 1.

The right of citizens of the United States to vote in any primary or other election for President or Vice President, for electors for President or Vice President, or for Senator or Representative in Congress, shall not be denied or abridged by the United States or any State by reason of failure to pay poll tax or other tax.

Section 2.

The Congress shall have power to enforce this article by appropriate legislation.

Amendment XXV

Passed by Congress July 6, 1965. Ratified February 10, 1967.
Note: Article II, section 1, of the Constitution was affected by the 25th amendment.

Section 1.

In case of the removal of the President from office or of his death or resignation, the Vice President shall become President.

Section 2.

Whenever there is a vacancy in the office of the Vice President, the President shall nominate a Vice President who shall take office upon confirmation by a majority vote of both Houses of Congress.

Section 3.

Whenever the President transmits to the President pro tempore of the Senate and the Speaker of the House of Representatives his written declaration that he is unable to discharge the powers and duties of his office, and until he transmits to them a written declaration to the contrary, such powers and duties shall be discharged by the Vice President as Acting President.

Section 4.

Whenever the Vice President and a majority of either the principal officers of the executive departments or of such other body as Congress may by law provide, transmit to the President pro tempore of the Senate and the Speaker of the House of Representatives their written declaration that the President is unable to discharge the powers and duties of his office, the Vice President shall immediately assume the powers and duties of the office as Acting President.

Thereafter, when the President transmits to the President pro tempore of the Senate and the Speaker of the House of Representatives his written declaration that no inability exists, he shall resume the powers and duties of his office unless the Vice President and a majority of either the principal officers of the executive department or of such other body as Congress may by law provide, transmit within four days to the President pro tempore of the Senate and the Speaker of the House of Representatives their written declaration that the President is unable to discharge the powers and duties of his office. Thereupon Congress shall decide the issue, assembling within forty-eight hours for that purpose if not in session. If the Congress, within twenty-one days after receipt of the latter written declaration, or, if Congress is not in session, within twenty-one days after Congress is required to assemble, determines by two-thirds vote of both Houses that the President is unable to discharge the powers and duties of his office, the Vice President shall continue to discharge the same as Acting President; otherwise, the President shall resume the powers and duties of his office.

Amendment XXVI

Passed by Congress March 23, 1971. Ratified July 1, 1971.

Note: Amendment 14, section 2, of the Constitution was modified by section 1 of the 26th amendment.

Section 1.

The right of citizens of the United States, who are eighteen years of age or older, to vote shall not be denied or abridged by the United States or by any State on account of age.

Section 2.

The Congress shall have power to enforce this article by appropriate legislation.

Amendment XXVII

Originally proposed Sept. 25, 1789. Ratified May 7, 1992.

No law, varying the compensation for the services of the Senators and Representatives, shall take effect, until an election of representatives shall have intervened.

VII

"Warnings of a parting friend"

GEORGE WASHINGTON'S FAREWELL ADDRESS
(1796)

GEORGE WASHINGTON BEGAN HIS MILITARY CAREER AT THE AGE of twenty, when he was appointed a major in the Virginia militia. He served in the French and Indian War, where he had two horses shot out from under him and four bullets penetrate his clothes. His public service included serving in the Virginia House of Burgesses prior to the American Revolution and as a delegate from Virginia to the Second Continental Congress in Philadelphia.

Washington showed up in Philadelphia wearing his Virginia military uniform. His intent was to show Virginia's willingness to bear arms. At 6-feet, 2-inches, he was taller than most men of his time, who averaged 5-feet, 7-inches. He cut a commanding figure.

Encouraged by John Adams, the Second Continental Congress appointed Washington commander-in-chief in the spring of 1775. At the time he was the only member of the army. Declaring upon acceptance, "I do not think myself equal to the command I am honored with," he served until 1783, when the Treaty of Paris was signed and the Revolutionary War was over. After retiring briefly, Washington returned to public service in 1787, when he presided over the Philadelphia Convention.

Two years later, the Electoral College voted unanimously to elect Washington president. He felt the weight of ensuring that our new form of government—this experimental structure of government by the people— would work. Washington wanted to prove that men could govern themselves and that we were not "made for a master." Washington was unlike modern presidents in that he was not a leader of any party, but focused instead on what he believed was best for the country. His overarching mission was to protect the Constitution and our freedom.

Near the end of his first term, in February 1792, Washington began drafting his farewell speech. For this new system of government to work, the presidency had to transition properly to someone new. Competing for his attention were his thoughts about retirement and the increasingly contentious and divisive dialogue among those with differing views on how the nation should be run.

But Washington was asked to run for a second term by many people. Eliza Powel, a friend and confidante, wrote him, urging him to serve again "for the prosperity of the people for whose happiness you are responsible, for to you their happiness is entrusted."

Bound by obligation to his country, Washington once again accepted the presidency.

As the end of his second term neared and he contemplated his next move, 63-year-old Washington realized that not only was his health failing, but the country was becoming unpleasantly partisan. In December 1795, former Secretary of State Edmund Randolph published "Vindication," a pamphlet on the Jay Treaty. The pamphlet included a description of Washington that "carried strong implications of weakness and indecision," wrote James Thomas Flexner in *Washington: The Indispensible Man*. In its conclusion, Randolph's pamphlet "also stated nastily, for the whole nation to see, what Washington himself suspected and feared: that the President was losing his mental powers."

An early draft of his farewell address, which Madison helped craft, noted,

> As some of the gazettes of the United States have teemed with all the invective that disappointment, ignorance of facts, and malicious falsehoods could invent, to misrepresent my policies and affections—to wound my reputation and feelings—and to weaken, if not destroy the confidence you have been pleased to repose in me; it might be expected at the parting scene of my public life that I should take some notice of such virulent abuse. But, as heretofore, I shall pass them over in utter silence.

Hamilton assisted with the final version, from which the above paragraph was omitted. The final address, released to a Philadelphia newspaper, the *American Daily Advertiser*, was printed on September 19, 1796. The next day, it was reprinted in other newspapers and quickly spread around the country. Praised and admired, it still provides guidance for us more than two centuries later.

Washington notes that his words were the "disinterested warnings of a parting friend." He began by focusing on "the continuance of the union as a primary object of patriotic desire." As the minder of the Constitution, Washington urged "the Constitution which at any time exists, till changed by an explicit and authentic act of the whole people, is sacredly obligatory upon all."

The passion of party, whether geographic or philosophical, weighed heavily on Washington's mind. He noted that, "sooner or later the chief of some prevailing faction, more able or more fortunate than his competitors, turns this disposition to the purposes of his own elevation, on the ruins of public liberty."

He encouraged the building of personal foundations, writing, "Of all the dispositions and habits, which lead to political prosperity, religion and morality are indispensable supports." At the same time, he warned of "the accumulation of debt, not only by shunning occasions of expense, but by vigorous exertions in time of peace to discharge the debts," and further warned "against the mischiefs of foreign intrigue."

Washington's words are as applicable to the nation as they were on the day he uttered them.

—JGC

❧ ❧ ❧

Friends and Fellow Citizens:

The period for a new election of a citizen to administer the executive government of the United States being not far distant, and the time actually arrived when your thoughts must be employed in designating the person who is to be clothed with that important trust, it appears to me proper, especially as it may conduce to a more distinct expression of the public voice, that I should now apprise you of the resolution I have formed, to decline being considered among the number of those out of whom a choice is to be made.

I beg you, at the same time, to do me the justice to be assured that this resolution has not been taken without a strict regard to all the considerations appertaining to the relation which binds a dutiful citizen to his country; and that in withdrawing the tender of service, which silence in my situation might imply, I am influenced by no diminution of zeal for your future interest, no deficiency of grateful respect for your past kindness, but am supported by a full conviction that the step is compatible with both.

The acceptance of, and continuance hitherto in, the office to which your suffrages have twice called me have been a uniform sacrifice of inclination to the opinion of duty and to a deference for what appeared to be your desire. I constantly hoped that it would have been much earlier in my power, consistently with motives which I was not at liberty to disregard, to return to that retirement from which I had been reluctantly drawn. The strength of my inclination to do this, previous to the last election, had even led to the preparation of an address to declare it to you; but mature reflection on the then perplexed and critical posture of our affairs with foreign nations, and the unanimous advice of persons entitled to my confidence, impelled me to abandon the idea.

I rejoice that the state of your concerns, external as well as internal, no longer renders the pursuit of inclination incompatible with the sentiment of duty or propriety, and am persuaded, whatever partiality may be retained for my services, that, in the present circumstances of our country, you will not disapprove my determination to retire.

The impressions with which I first undertook the arduous trust were explained on the proper occasion. In the discharge of this trust, I will only say that I have, with good intentions, contributed towards the organization and administration of the government the best exertions of which a very fallible judgment was capable. Not unconscious in the outset of the inferiority of my qualifications, experience in my own eyes, perhaps still more in the eyes of others, has strengthened the motives to diffidence of myself; and every day the increasing weight of years admonishes me more and more that the shade of retirement is as necessary to me as it will be welcome. Satisfied that if any circumstances have given peculiar value to my services, they were temporary, I have the consolation to believe that, while choice and prudence invite me to quit the political scene, patriotism does not forbid it.

In looking forward to the moment which is intended to terminate the career of my public life, my feelings do not permit me to suspend the deep acknowledgment of that debt of gratitude which I owe to my beloved country for the many honors it has conferred upon me; still more for the steadfast confidence with which it has supported me; and for the opportunities I have thence enjoyed of manifesting my inviolable attachment, by services faithful and persevering, though in usefulness unequal to my zeal. If benefits have resulted to our country from these services, let it always be remembered to your praise, and as an instructive example in our annals, that under circumstances in which the passions, agitated in every direction, were liable to mislead, amidst appearances sometimes dubious, vicissitudes of fortune often discouraging, in situations in which not unfrequently want of success has countenanced the spirit of criticism, the constancy of your support was the essential prop of the efforts, and a guarantee of the plans by which they were effected. Profoundly penetrated with this idea, I shall carry it with me to my grave, as a strong incitement to unceasing vows that heaven may continue to you the choicest tokens of its beneficence; that your union and brotherly affection may be perpetual; that the free Constitution, which is the work of your hands, may be sacredly maintained; that its administration in every department may be stamped with wisdom and virtue; that, in fine, the happiness of the people of these States, under the auspices of liberty, may be made complete by so careful a preservation and so prudent a use of this blessing as will acquire to them the glory of recommending it to the applause, the affection, and adoption of every nation which is yet a stranger to it.

Here, perhaps, I ought to stop. But a solicitude for your welfare, which cannot end but with my life, and the apprehension of danger, natural to that solicitude, urge me, on an occasion like the present, to offer to your solemn contemplation, and to recommend to your frequent review, some sentiments which are the result of much reflection, of no inconsiderable observation, and which appear to me all-important to the permanency of your felicity as a people. These will be offered to you with the more freedom, as you can only see in them the disinterested warnings of a parting friend, who can possibly have no personal motive to bias his counsel. Nor can I forget, as an encouragement to it, your indulgent reception of my sentiments on a former and not dissimilar occasion.

Interwoven as is the love of liberty with every ligament of your hearts, no recommendation of mine is necessary to fortify or confirm the attachment.

The unity of government which constitutes you one people is also now dear to you. It is justly so, for it is a main pillar in the edifice of your real independence, the support of your tranquility at home, your peace abroad; of your safety; of your prosperity; of that very liberty which you so highly prize. But as it is easy to foresee that, from different causes and from different quarters, much pains will be taken, many artifices employed to weaken in your minds the conviction of this truth; as this is the point in your political fortress against which the batteries of internal and external enemies will be most constantly and actively (though often covertly and insidiously) directed, it is of infinite moment that you should properly estimate the immense value of your national union to your collective and individual happiness; that you should cherish a cordial, habitual, and immovable attachment to it; accustoming yourselves to think and speak of it as of the palladium of your political safety and prosperity; watching for its preservation with jealous anxiety; discountenancing whatever may suggest even a suspicion that it can in any event be abandoned; and indignantly frowning upon the first dawning of every attempt to alienate any portion of our country from the rest, or to enfeeble the sacred ties which now link together the various parts.

For this you have every inducement of sympathy and interest. Citizens, by birth or choice, of a common country, that country has a right to concentrate your affections. The name of American, which belongs to you in your national capacity, must always exalt the just pride of patriotism more than any appellation derived from local discriminations. With slight shades of difference, you have the same religion, manners, habits, and political principles. You have in a common cause fought and triumphed together; the independence and liberty you possess are the work of joint counsels, and joint efforts of common dangers, sufferings, and successes.

But these considerations, however powerfully they address themselves to your sensibility, are greatly outweighed by those which apply more immediately to your interest. Here every portion of our country finds the most commanding motives for carefully guarding and preserving the union of the whole.

The North, in an unrestrained intercourse with the South, protected by the equal laws of a common government, finds in the productions of the latter great additional resources of maritime and commercial enterprise and precious materials of manufacturing industry. The South, in the same intercourse, benefiting by the agency of the North, sees its agriculture grow and its commerce expand. Turning partly into its own channels the seamen of the North, it finds its particular navigation invigorated; and, while it contributes, in different ways, to nourish and increase the general mass of the national navigation, it looks forward to the protection of a maritime strength, to which itself is unequally adapted. The East, in a like intercourse with the West, already finds, and in the progressive improvement of interior communications by land and water, will more and more find a valuable vent for the commodities which it brings from abroad, or manufactures at home. The West derives from the East supplies requisite to its growth and comfort, and, what is perhaps of still greater consequence, it must of necessity owe the secure enjoyment of indispensable outlets for its own productions to the weight, influence, and the future maritime strength of the Atlantic side of the Union, directed by an indissoluble community of interest as one nation. Any other tenure by which the West can hold this essential advantage, whether derived from its own separate strength, or from an apostate and unnatural connection with any foreign power, must be intrinsically precarious.

While, then, every part of our country thus feels an immediate and particular interest in union, all the parts combined cannot fail to find in the united mass of means and efforts greater strength, greater resource, proportionably greater security from external danger, a less frequent interruption of their peace by foreign nations; and, what is of inestimable value, they must derive from union an exemption from those broils and wars between themselves, which so frequently afflict neighboring countries not tied together by the same governments, which their own rival ships alone would be sufficient to produce, but which opposite foreign alliances, attachments, and intrigues would stimulate and embitter. Hence, likewise, they will avoid the necessity of those overgrown military establishments which, under any form of government, are inauspicious to liberty, and which are to be regarded as particularly hostile to republican liberty. In this sense it is that your union ought to be considered as a main prop of your liberty, and that the love of the one ought to endear to you the preservation of the other.

These considerations speak a persuasive language to every reflecting and virtuous mind, and exhibit the continuance of the Union as a primary object of patriotic desire. Is there a doubt whether a common government can embrace so large a sphere? Let experience solve it. To listen to mere speculation in such a case were criminal. We are authorized to hope that a proper organization of the whole with the auxiliary agency of governments for the respective subdivisions, will afford a happy issue to the experiment. It is well worth a fair and full experiment. With such powerful and obvious motives to union, affecting all parts of our country, while experience shall not have demonstrated its impracticability, there will always be reason to distrust the patriotism of those who in any quarter may endeavor to weaken its bands.

In contemplating the causes which may disturb our Union, it occurs as matter of serious concern that any ground should have been furnished for characterizing parties by geographical discriminations, Northern and Southern, Atlantic and Western; whence designing men may endeavor to excite a belief that there is a real difference of local interests and views. One of the expedients of party to acquire influence within particular districts is to misrepresent the opinions and aims of other districts. You cannot shield yourselves too much against the jealousies and heartburnings which spring from these misrepresentations; they tend to render alien to each other those who ought to be bound together by fraternal affection. The inhabitants of our Western country have lately had a useful lesson on this head; they have seen, in the negotiation by the Executive, and in the unanimous ratification by the Senate, of the treaty with Spain, and in the universal satisfaction at that event, throughout the United States, a decisive proof how unfounded were the suspicions propagated among them of a policy in the General Government and in the Atlantic States unfriendly to their interests in regard to the Mississippi; they have been witnesses to the formation of two treaties, that with Great Britain, and that with Spain, which secure to them everything they could desire, in respect to our foreign relations, towards confirming their prosperity. Will it not be their wisdom to rely for the preservation of these advantages on the Union by which they were procured? Will they not henceforth be deaf to those advisers, if such there are, who would sever them from their brethren and connect them with aliens?

To the efficacy and permanency of your Union, a government for the whole is indispensable. No alliance, however strict, between the parts can be an adequate substitute; they must inevitably experience the infractions and interruptions which all alliances in all times have experienced. Sensible of this momentous truth, you have improved upon your first essay, by the adoption of a constitution of government better calculated than your former for an intimate union, and for the efficacious management of your common concerns.

This government, the offspring of our own choice, uninfluenced and unawed, adopted upon full investigation and mature deliberation, completely free in its principles, in the distribution of its powers, uniting security with energy, and containing within itself a provision for its own amendment, has a just claim to your confidence and your support. Respect for its authority, compliance with its laws, acquiescence in its measures, are duties enjoined by the fundamental maxims of true liberty. The basis of our political systems is the right of the people to make and to alter their constitutions of government. But the Constitution which at any time exists, till changed by an explicit and authentic act of the whole people, is sacredly obligatory upon all. The very idea of the power and the right of the people to establish government presupposes the duty of every individual to obey the established government.

All obstructions to the execution of the laws, all combinations and associations, under whatever plausible character, with the real design to direct, control, counteract, or awe the regular deliberation and action of the constituted authorities, are destructive of this fundamental principle, and of fatal tendency. They serve to organize faction, to give it an artificial and extraordinary force; to put, in the place of the delegated will of the nation the will of a party, often a small but artful and enterprising minority of the community; and, according to the alternate triumphs of different parties, to make the public administration the mirror of the ill-concerted and incongruous projects of faction, rather than the organ of consistent and wholesome plans digested by common counsels and modified by mutual interests.

However combinations or associations of the above description may now and then answer popular ends, they are likely, in the course of time and things, to become potent engines, by which cunning, ambitious, and unprincipled men will be enabled to subvert the power of the people and to usurp for themselves the reins of government, destroying afterwards the very engines which have lifted them to unjust dominion.

Towards the preservation of your government, and the permanency of your present happy state, it is requisite, not only that you steadily discountenance irregular oppositions to its acknowledged authority, but also that you resist with care the spirit of innovation upon its principles, however specious the pretexts. One method of assault may be to effect, in the forms of the Constitution, alterations which will impair the energy of the system, and thus to undermine what cannot be directly overthrown. In all the changes to which you may be invited, remember that time and habit are at least as necessary to fix the true character of governments as of other human institutions; that experience is the surest standard by which to test the real tendency of the existing constitution of a country; that facility in changes, upon the credit of mere hypothesis and opinion, exposes to perpetual change, from the endless variety of hypothesis and opinion; and remember, especially, that for the efficient management of your common interests, in a country so extensive as ours, a government of as much vigor as is consistent with the perfect security of liberty is indispensable. Liberty itself will find in such a government, with powers properly distributed and adjusted, its surest guardian. It is, indeed, little else than a name, where the government is too feeble to withstand the enterprises of faction, to confine each member of the society within the limits prescribed by the laws, and to maintain all in the secure and tranquil enjoyment of the rights of person and property.

I have already intimated to you the danger of parties in the State, with particular reference to the founding of them on geographical discriminations. Let me now take a more comprehensive view, and warn you in the most solemn manner against the baneful effects of the spirit of party generally.

This spirit, unfortunately, is inseparable from our nature, having its root in the strongest passions of the human mind. It exists under different shapes in all governments, more or less stifled, controlled, or repressed; but, in those of the popular form, it is seen in its greatest rankness, and is truly their worst enemy.

The alternate domination of one faction over another, sharpened by the spirit of revenge, natural to party dissension, which in different ages and countries has perpetrated the most horrid enormities, is itself a frightful despotism. But this leads at length to a more formal and permanent despotism. The disorders and miseries which result gradually incline the minds of men to seek security and repose in the absolute power of an individual; and sooner or later the chief of some prevailing faction, more able or more fortunate than his competitors, turns this disposition to the purposes of his own elevation, on the ruins of public liberty.

Without looking forward to an extremity of this kind (which nevertheless ought not to be entirely out of sight), the common and continual mischiefs of the spirit of party are sufficient to make it the interest and duty of a wise people to discourage and restrain it.

It serves always to distract the public councils and enfeeble the public administration. It agitates the community with ill-founded jealousies and false alarms, kindles the animosity of one part against another, foments occasionally riot and insurrection. It opens the door to foreign influence and corruption, which finds a facilitated access to the government itself through the channels of party passions. Thus the policy and the will of one country are subjected to the policy and will of another.

There is an opinion that parties in free countries are useful checks upon the administration of the government and serve to keep alive the spirit of liberty. This within certain limits is probably true; and in governments of a monarchical cast, patriotism may look with indulgence, if not with favor, upon the spirit of party. But in those of the popular character, in governments purely elective, it is a spirit not to be encouraged. From their natural tendency, it is certain there will always be enough of that spirit for every salutary purpose. And there being constant danger of excess, the effort ought to be by force of public opinion, to mitigate and assuage it. A fire not to be quenched, it demands a uniform vigilance to prevent its bursting into a flame, lest, instead of warming, it should consume.

It is important, likewise, that the habits of thinking in a free country should inspire caution in those entrusted with its administration, to confine themselves within their respective constitutional spheres, avoiding in the exercise of the powers of one department to encroach upon another. The spirit of encroachment tends to consolidate the powers of all the departments in one, and thus to create, whatever the form of government, a real despotism. A just estimate of that love of power, and proneness to abuse it, which predominates in the human heart, is sufficient to satisfy us of the truth of this position. The necessity of reciprocal checks in the exercise of political power, by dividing and distributing it into different depositaries, and constituting each the guardian of the public weal against invasions by the others, has been evinced by experiments ancient and modern; some of them in our country and under our own eyes. To preserve them must be as necessary as to institute them. If, in the opinion of the people, the distribution or modification of the constitutional powers be in any particular wrong, let it be corrected by an amendment in the way which the Constitution designates. But let there be no change by usurpation; for though this, in one instance, may be the instrument of good, it is the customary weapon by which free governments are destroyed. The precedent must always greatly overbalance in permanent evil any partial or transient benefit, which the use can at any time yield.

Of all the dispositions and habits which lead to political prosperity, religion and morality are indispensable supports. In vain would that man claim the tribute of patriotism, who should labor to subvert these great pillars of human happiness, these firmest props of the duties of men and citizens. The mere politician, equally with the pious man, ought to respect and to cherish them. A volume could not trace all their connections with private and public felicity. Let it simply be asked: Where is the security for property, for reputation, for life, if the sense of religious obligation desert the oaths which are the instruments of investigation in courts of justice ? And let us with caution indulge the supposition that morality can be maintained without religion. Whatever may be conceded to the influence of refined education on minds of peculiar structure, reason and experience both forbid us to expect that national morality can prevail in exclusion of religious principle.

It is substantially true that virtue or morality is a necessary spring of popular government. The rule, indeed, extends with more or less force to every species of free government. Who that is a sincere friend to it can look with indifference upon attempts to shake the foundation of the fabric?

Promote then, as an object of primary importance, institutions for the general diffusion of knowledge. In proportion as the structure of a government gives force to public opinion, it is essential that public opinion should be enlightened.

As a very important source of strength and security, cherish public credit. One method of preserving it is to use it as sparingly as possible, avoiding occasions of expense by cultivating peace, but remembering also that timely disbursements to prepare for danger frequently prevent much greater disbursements to repel it, avoiding likewise the accumulation of debt, not only by shunning occasions of expense, but by vigorous exertion in time of peace to discharge the debts which unavoidable wars may have occasioned, not ungenerously throwing upon posterity the burden which we ourselves ought to bear. The execution of these maxims belongs to your representatives, but it is necessary that public opinion should co-operate. To facilitate to them the performance of their duty, it is essential that you should practically bear in mind that towards the payment of debts there must be revenue; that to have revenue there must be taxes; that no taxes can be devised which are not more or less inconvenient and unpleasant; that the intrinsic embarrassment, inseparable from the selection of the proper objects (which is always a choice of difficulties), ought to be a decisive motive for a candid construction of the conduct of the government in making it, and for a spirit of acquiescence in the measures for obtaining revenue, which the public exigencies may at any time dictate.

Observe good faith and justice towards all nations; cultivate peace and harmony with all. Religion and morality enjoin this conduct; and can it be, that good policy does not equally enjoin it? It will be worthy of a free, enlightened, and at no distant period, a great nation, to give to mankind the magnanimous and too novel example of a people always guided by an exalted justice and benevolence. Who can doubt that, in the course of time and things, the fruits of such a plan would richly repay any temporary advantages which might be lost by a steady adherence to it ? Can it be that Providence has not connected the permanent felicity of a nation with its virtue ? The experiment, at least, is recommended by every sentiment which ennobles human nature. Alas! is it rendered impossible by its vices?

In the execution of such a plan, nothing is more essential than that permanent, inveterate antipathies against particular nations, and passionate attachments for others, should be excluded; and that, in place of them, just and amicable feelings towards all should be cultivated. The nation which indulges towards another a habitual hatred or a habitual fondness is in some degree a slave. It is a slave to its animosity or to its affection, either of which is sufficient to lead it astray from its duty and its interest. Antipathy in one nation against another disposes each more readily to offer insult and injury, to lay hold of slight causes of umbrage, and to be haughty and intractable, when accidental or trifling occasions of dispute occur. Hence, frequent collisions, obstinate, envenomed, and bloody contests. The nation, prompted by ill-will and resentment, sometimes impels to war the government, contrary to the best calculations of policy. The government sometimes participates in the national propensity, and adopts through passion what reason would reject; at other times it makes the animosity of the nation subservient to projects of hostility instigated by pride, ambition, and other sinister and pernicious motives. The peace often, sometimes perhaps the liberty, of nations, has been the victim.

So likewise, a passionate attachment of one nation for another produces a variety of evils. Sympathy for the favorite nation, facilitating the illusion of an imaginary common interest in cases where no real common interest exists, and infusing into one the enmities of the other, betrays the former into a participation in the quarrels and wars of the latter without adequate inducement or justification. It leads also to concessions to the favorite nation of privileges denied to others which is apt doubly to injure the nation making the concessions; by unnecessarily parting with what ought to have been retained, and by exciting jealousy, ill-will, and a disposition to retaliate, in the parties from whom equal privileges are withheld. And it gives to ambitious, corrupted, or deluded citizens (who devote themselves to the favorite nation), facility to betray or sacrifice the interests of their own country, without odium, sometimes even with popularity; gilding, with the appearances of a virtuous sense of obligation, a commendable deference for public opinion, or a laudable zeal for public good, the base or foolish compliances of ambition, corruption, or infatuation.

As avenues to foreign influence in innumerable ways, such attachments are particularly alarming to the truly enlightened and independent patriot. How many opportunities do they afford to tamper with domestic factions, to practice the arts of seduction, to mislead public opinion, to influence or awe the public councils? Such an attachment of a small or weak towards a great and powerful nation dooms the former to be the satellite of the latter.

Against the insidious wiles of foreign influence (I conjure you to believe me, fellow-citizens) the jealousy of a free people ought to be constantly awake, since history and experience prove that foreign influence is one of the most baneful foes of republican government. But that jealousy to be useful must be impartial; else it becomes the instrument of the very influence to be avoided, instead of a defense against it. Excessive partiality for one foreign nation and excessive dislike of another cause those whom they actuate to see danger only on one side, and serve to veil and even second the arts of influence on the other. Real patriots who may resist the intrigues of the favorite are liable to become suspected and odious, while its tools and dupes usurp the applause and confidence of the people, to surrender their interests.

The great rule of conduct for us in regard to foreign nations is in extending our commercial relations, to have with them as little political connection as possible. So far as we have already formed engagements, let them be fulfilled with perfect good faith. Here let us stop. Europe has a set of primary interests which to us have none; or a very remote relation. Hence she must be engaged in frequent controversies, the causes of which are essentially foreign to our concerns. Hence, therefore, it must be unwise in us to implicate ourselves by artificial ties in the ordinary vicissitudes of her politics, or the ordinary combinations and collisions of her friendships or enmities.

Our detached and distant situation invites and enables us to pursue a different course. If we remain one people under an efficient government. the period is not far off when we may defy material injury from external annoyance; when we may take such an attitude as will cause the neutrality we may at any time resolve upon to be scrupulously respected; when belligerent nations, under the impossibility of making acquisitions upon us, will not lightly hazard the giving us provocation; when we may choose peace or war, as our interest, guided by justice, shall counsel.

Why forego the advantages of so peculiar a situation? Why quit our own to stand upon foreign ground? Why, by interweaving our destiny with that of any part of Europe, entangle our peace and prosperity in the toils of European ambition, rivalship, interest, humor or caprice?

It is our true policy to steer clear of permanent alliances with any portion of the foreign world; so far, I mean, as we are now at liberty to do it; for let me not be understood as capable of patronizing infidelity to existing engagements. I hold the maxim no less applicable to public than to private affairs, that honesty is always the best policy. I repeat it, therefore, let those engagements be observed in their genuine sense. But, in my opinion, it is unnecessary and would be unwise to extend them.

Taking care always to keep ourselves by suitable establishments on a respectable defensive posture, we may safely trust to temporary alliances for extraordinary emergencies.

Harmony, liberal intercourse with all nations, are recommended by policy, humanity, and interest. But even our commercial policy should hold an equal and impartial hand; neither seeking nor granting exclusive favors or preferences; consulting the natural course of things; diffusing and diversifying by gentle means the streams of commerce, but forcing nothing; establishing (with powers so disposed, in order to give trade a stable course, to define the rights of our merchants, and to enable the government to support them) conventional rules of intercourse, the best that present circumstances and mutual opinion will permit, but temporary, and liable to be from time to time abandoned or varied, as experience and circumstances shall dictate; constantly keeping in view that it is folly in one nation to look for disinterested favors from another; that it must pay with a portion of its independence for whatever it may accept under that character; that, by such acceptance, it may place itself in the condition of having given equivalents for nominal favors, and yet of being reproached with ingratitude for not giving more. There can be no greater error than to expect or calculate upon real favors from nation to nation. It is an illusion, which experience must cure, which a just pride ought to discard.

In offering to you, my countrymen, these counsels of an old and affectionate friend, I dare not hope they will make the strong and lasting impression I could wish; that they will control the usual current of the passions, or prevent our nation from running the course which has hitherto marked the destiny of nations. But, if I may even flatter myself that they may be productive of some partial benefit, some occasional good; that they may now and then recur to moderate the fury of party spirit, to warn against the mischiefs of foreign intrigue, to guard against the impostures of pretended patriotism; this hope will be a full recompense for the solicitude for your welfare, by which they have been dictated.

How far in the discharge of my official duties I have been guided by the principles which have been delineated, the public records and other evidences of my conduct must witness to you and to the world. To myself, the assurance of my own conscience is, that I have at least believed myself to be guided by them.

In relation to the still subsisting war in Europe, my proclamation of the twenty-second of April, 1793, is the index of my plan. Sanctioned by your approving voice, and by that of your representatives in both houses of Congress, the spirit of that measure has continually governed me, uninfluenced by any attempts to deter or divert me from it.

After deliberate examination, with the aid of the best lights I could obtain, I was well satisfied that our country, under all the circumstances of the case, had a right to take, and was bound in duty and interest to take, a neutral position. Having taken it, I determined, as far as should depend upon me, to maintain it, with moderation, perseverance, and firmness.

The considerations which respect the right to hold this conduct, it is not necessary on this occasion to detail. I will only observe that, according to my understanding of the matter, that right, so far from being denied by any of the belligerent powers, has been virtually admitted by all.

The duty of holding a neutral conduct may be inferred, without anything more, from the obligation which justice and humanity impose on every nation, in cases in which it is free to act, to maintain inviolate the relations of peace and amity towards other nations.

The inducements of interest for observing that conduct will best be referred to your own reflections and experience. With me a predominant motive has been to endeavor to gain time to our country to settle and mature its yet recent institutions, and to progress without interruption to that degree of strength and consistency which is necessary to give it, humanly speaking, the command of its own fortunes.

Though, in reviewing the incidents of my administration, I am unconscious of intentional error, I am nevertheless too sensible of my defects not to think it probable that I may have committed many errors. Whatever they may be, I fervently beseech the Almighty to avert or mitigate the evils to which they may tend. I shall also carry with me the hope that my country will never cease to view them with indulgence; and that, after forty five years of my life dedicated to its service with an upright zeal, the faults of incompetent abilities will be consigned to oblivion, as myself must soon be to the mansions of rest.

Relying on its kindness in this as in other things, and actuated by that fervent love towards it, which is so natural to a man who views in it the native soil of himself and his progenitors for several generations, I anticipate with pleasing expectation that retreat in which I promise myself to realize, without alloy, the sweet enjoyment of partaking, in the midst of my fellow-citizens, the benign influence of good laws under a free government, the ever-favorite object of my heart, and the happy reward, as I trust, of our mutual cares, labors, and dangers.

United States 19ᵗʰ September, 1796

Geo. Washington

VIII

"We are all republicans; we are all federalists"

Thomas Jefferson's
First Inaugural Address
(1801)

IN 1796, WHEN GEORGE WASHINGTON ANNOUNCED THAT HE WOULD not seek a third term as president, the nation was forced to find a new leader. John Adams and Thomas Jefferson vied for the presidency.

Under the rules at the time, the candidate who received the most electoral votes became president, and the person with the second-most became vice president. Adams received seventy-one electoral votes, and Thomas Jefferson received sixty-eight. With the election came the transition from President Washington to President Adams. This handoff of power, from one president to another, proved that Americans could transition leadership peacefully.

America was not a monarchy.

While Adams' election represented the first time the presidency had passed from one man to anther, the transition from Adams (a Federalist) to Jefferson (a Republican) in 1801 was even more important. It represented a peaceful transition from one political party to another. Power between parties could shift according to the will of the people and without war.

This transition did not come easily. Jefferson and Aaron Burr had amassed an equal number of electoral votes, so the decision fell to the lame-duck House of Representatives, which was controlled by the Federalists, Adams' party. After thirty-six ballots, Jefferson was elected president and Burr his vice president. Jefferson's election came after he had served his country in varying capacities for thirty-one years.

Jefferson was the son of Peter Jefferson and Jane Randolph, a member of the prominent Randolph family. His father died when he was fourteen and, as the eldest son, he inherited most of his father's estate. Jefferson attended the College of William & Mary where he met George Wythe, who became one of Jefferson's mentors. After graduation, Jefferson read law under Wythe, who guided his studies toward parliamentary law and shaped Jefferson's passion for life-long learning.

Beginning in 1769, Jefferson served in the Virginia House of Burgesses and then as a delegate to the Second Continental Congress. It was there that he met Washington and Adams. When a committee of five delegates, including Adams and Jefferson, was chosen to draft a declaration of independence, Adams noted that Jefferson had a "happy talent for composition and singular felicity of expression." Jefferson was tapped to write the first draft.

Jefferson served as the second governor of Virginia, after Patrick Henry, from 1779 to 1781. Afterward, he served as ambassador to France. Under President Washington, Jefferson served as our nation's first Secretary of State.

Jefferson, along with James Madison, began to organize supporters in 1792, and their party members came to be known as Republicans (and, to contemporary historians, Democratic-Republicans). Jefferson and his allies believed that the American Revolution was the first of what would be a number of democratic revolutions that would spread across the globe, transforming the world. He strongly believed in states' rights and republicanism, the ability of the people to rule themselves. In his inaugural address, he stated his belief that America is "the world's best hope."

Jefferson was a complex man. He believed that the government would be best served by being debt-free and self-sufficient but was deeply in debt himself. After his presidency, he sold his library to the nation to create the Library of Congress, as well as to raise the money he needed to pay off his personal debts.

Jefferson, the third president of the United States, was sworn into office on March 4, 1801. After having endured a difficult election, he asked those in attendance to understand that part of the strength of our nation is our ability to hold personal opinions and speak about them freely. "Every difference of opinion is not a difference of principle," he said. "We have called by different names brethren of the same principle. We are all Republicans, we are all Federalists."

Jefferson is remembered for his Republican beliefs as well as his life-long practice of putting his country first.

—JGC

🙞 🙞 🙞

Friends & Fellow Citizens,

Called upon to undertake the duties of the first Executive office of our country, I avail myself of the presence of that portion of my fellow citizens which is here assembled to express my grateful thanks for the favor with which they have been pleased to look towards me, to declare a sincere consciousness that the task is above my talents, and that I approach it with those anxious and awful presentiments which the greatness of the charge, and the weakness of my powers so justly inspire. A rising nation, spread over a wide and fruitful land, traversing all the seas with the rich productions of their industry, engaged in commerce with nations who feel power and forget right, advancing rapidly to destinies beyond the reach of mortal eye; when I contemplate these transcendent objects, and see the honour, the happiness, and the hopes of this beloved country committed to the issue and the auspices of this day, I shrink from the contemplation & humble myself before the magnitude of the undertaking. Utterly indeed should I despair, did not the presence of many, whom I here see, remind me, that, in the other high authorities provided by our constitution, I shall find resources of wisdom, of virtue, and of zeal, on which to rely under all difficulties. To you, then, gentlemen, who are charged with the sovereign functions of legislation, and to those associated with you, I look with encouragement for that guidance and support which may enable us to steer with safety the vessel in which we are all embarked, amidst the conflicting elements of a troubled world.

During the contest of opinion through which we have past, the animation of discusions and of exertions has sometimes worn an aspect which might impose on strangers unused to think freely, and to speak and to write what they think; but this being now decided by the voice of the nation, announced according to the rules of the constitution all will of course arrange themselves under the will of the law, and unite in common efforts for the common good. All too will bear in mind this sacred principle, that though the will of the majority is in all cases to prevail, that will, to be rightful, must be reasonable; that the minority possess their equal rights, which equal laws must protect, and to violate would be oppression. Let us then, fellow citizens, unite with one heart and one mind, let us restore to social intercourse that harmony and affection without which liberty, and even life itself, are but dreary things. And let us reflect that having banished from our land that religious intolerance under which mankind so long bled and suffered, we have yet gained little if we countenance a political intolerance, as despotic, as wicked, and capable of as bitter and bloody persecutions. During the throes and convulsions of the ancient world, during the agonising spasms of infuriated man, seeking through blood and slaughter his long lost liberty, it was not wonderful that the agitation of the billows should reach even this distant and peaceful shore; that this should be more felt and feared by some and less by others; and should divide opinions as to measures of safety; but every difference of opinion is not a difference of principle. We have called by different names brethren of the same principle. We are all republicans: we are all federalists. If there be any among us who would wish to dissolve this Union, or to change its republican form, let them stand undisturbed as monuments of the safety with which error of opinion may be tolerated, where reason is left free to combat it. I know indeed that some honest men fear that a republican government cannot be strong; that this government is not strong enough. But would the honest patriot, in the full tide of successful experiment, abandon a government which has so far kept us free and firm, on the theoretic and visionary fear, that this government, the world's best hope, may, by possibility, want energy to preserve itself? I trust not. I believe this, on the contrary, the strongest government on earth. I believe it the only one, where every man, at the call of the law, would fly to the standard of the law, and would meet invasions of the public order as his own personal concern.— Sometimes it is said that man cannot be trusted with the government of himself. Can he then be trusted with the government of others? Or have we found angels, in the form of kings, to govern him? Let history answer this question.

Let us then, with courage and confidence, pursue our own federal and republican principles; our attachment to union and representative government. Kindly separated by nature and a wide ocean from the exterminating havoc of one quarter of the globe; too high minded to endure the degradations of the others, possessing a chosen country, with room enough for our descendants to the thousandth and thousandth generation, entertaining a due sense of our equal right to the use of our own faculties, to the acquisitions of our own industry, to honor and confidence from our fellow citizens, resulting not from birth, but from our actions and their sense of them, enlightened by a benign religion, professed indeed and practised in various forms, yet all of them inculcating honesty, truth, temperance, gratitude and the love of man, acknowledging and adoring an overruling providence, which by all its dispensations proves that it delights in the happiness of man here, and his greater happiness hereafter; with all these blessings, what more is necessary to make us a happy and a prosperous people? Still one thing more, fellow citizens, a wise and frugal government, which shall restrain men from injuring one another, shall leave them otherwise free to regulate their own pursuits of industry and improvement, and shall not take from the mouth of labor the bread it has earned. This is the sum of good government; and this is necessary to close the circle of our felicities.

About to enter, fellow citizens, on the exercise of duties which comprehend every thing dear and valuable to you, it is proper you should understand what I deem the essential principles of our government, and consequently those which ought to shape its administration. I will compress them within the narrowest compass they will bear, stating the general principle, but not all its limitations.—Equal and exact justice to all men, of whatever state or persuasion, religious or political:—peace, commerce, and honest friendship with all nations, entangling alliances with none:—the support of the state governments in all their rights, as the most competent administrations for our domestic concerns, and the surest bulwarks against anti-republican tendencies:—the preservation of the General government in its whole constitutional vigor, as the sheet anchor of our peace at home, and safety abroad: a jealous care of the right of election by the people, a mild and safe corrective of abuses which are lopped by the sword of revolution where peaceable remedies are unprovided:— absolute acquiescence in the decisions of the majority, the vital principle of republics, from which is no appeal but to force, the vital principle and immediate parent of the despotism:—a well disciplined militia, our best reliance in peace, and for the first moments of war, till regulars may relieve them:—the supremacy of the civil over the military authority:—economy in the public expence, that labor may be lightly burthened:—the honest payment of our debts and sacred preservation of the public faith:—encouragement of agriculture, and of commerce as its handmaid:—the diffusion of information, and arraignment of all abuses at the bar of the public reason:—freedom of religion; freedom of the press; and freedom of person, under the protection of the Habeas Corpus:—and trial by juries impartially selected. These principles form the bright constellation, which has gone before us and guided our steps through an age of revolution and reformation. The wisdom of our sages, and blood of our heroes have been devoted to their attainment:—they should be the creed of our political faith; the text of civic instruction, the touchstone by which to try the services of those we trust; and should we wander from them in moments of error or of alarm, let us hasten to retrace our steps, and to regain the road which alone leads to peace, liberty and safety.

I repair then, fellow citizens, to the post you have assigned me. With experience enough in subordinate offices to have seen the difficulties of this the greatest of all, I have learnt to expect that it will rarely fall to the lot of imperfect man to retire from this station with the reputation, and the favor, which bring him into it. Without pretensions to that high confidence you reposed in our first and greatest revolutionary character, whose pre-eminent services had entitled him to the first place in his country's love, and destined for him the fairest page in the volume of faithful history, I ask so much confidence only as may give firmness and effect to the legal administration of your affairs. I shall often go wrong through defect of judgment. When right, I shall often be thought wrong by those whose positions will not command a view of the whole ground. I ask your indulgence for my own errors, which will never be intentional; and your support against the errors of others, who may condemn what they would not if seen in all its parts. The approbation implied by your suffrage, is a great consolation to me for the past; and my future solicitude will be, to retain the good opinion of those who have bestowed it in advance, to conciliate that of others by doing them all the good in my power, and to be instrumental to the happiness and freedom of all.

Relying then on the patronage of your good will, I advance with obedience to the work, ready to retire from it whenever you become sensible how much better choices it is in your power to make. And may that infinite power, which rules the destinies of the universe, lead our councils to what is best, and give them a favorable issue for your peace and prosperity.

IX

"Advance, then, ye future generations!"

DANIEL WEBSTER'S DISCOURSE, DELIVERED AT PLYMOUTH (1820)

D ANIEL WEBSTER STEPPED FORWARD ON DECEMBER 22, 1820, TO deliver the Plymouth Oration, celebrating the 200th anniversary of the Pilgrims landing on Plymouth Rock in the current state of Massachusetts. One of the most famous speechmakers of his day, he was also a former congressman, respected lawyer, and statesman.

Webster was born in 1782, after our nation had declared its independence, but before our independence was secured. His parents were Ebenezer Webster, a former captain in the American Revolutionary War, and Abigail Eastman, Ebenezer's second wife. He came from a simple family: His father had no formal education, but understood its value. He made sure that Daniel was able to attend school.

Webster attended Phillips Exeter Academy, in Exeter, New Hampshire, studied with a tutor to prepare for college entrance exams, and then progressed to Dartmouth College a little over 100 miles away. In college he began giving speeches, and joined a debating society, the United Fraternity. His first recorded public speaking event was in 1800, when he spoke at Hanover for New Hampshire's Independence Day celebration, while he was still in college.

"We are now assembled to celebrate an anniversary, ever to be held in dear remembrance by the sons of freedom," Webster began. "Nothing less than the birth of a nation, nothing less than the emancipation of three millions of people, from the degrading chains of foreign domination, is the event we commemorate."

After reflecting on the men who fought for freedom, and the peaceful transition from the Articles of Confederation to the Constitution, Webster ended with a call to preserve freedom: "Let us, who are this day free . . . assemble before the hallowed temple of Columbian Freedom, and swear, to the God of our Fathers, to preserve it secure, or die at its portals!"

His first public speech contained many of the same traits that his other speeches would hold: a focus on the Founding Fathers and tradition as well as praise of country and liberty. "The enduring work which Mr. Webster did in the world, and his meaning and influence in American history, are all summed up in the principles enunciated in that boyish speech at Hanover." He "preached love of country, the grandeur of American nationality, fidelity to the constitution as the bulwark of nationality, and the necessity and the nobility of the union of the states," Henry Cabot Lodge wrote in his biography, *Daniel Webster*.

Webster graduated from Dartmouth in 1805 and began practicing law that same year. Elected to Congress from Massachusetts as a Federalist in 1812, he served for four years before retiring to return to the practice of law and to earn money. He won national legal and speaking fame when arguing a case in front of the Supreme Court for his alma mater, Dartmouth, in 1818. The New Hampshire State Legislature had attempted to take control over the college, and the college protested via lawsuit.

Webster combined his knowledge of the legalities of the case with simple words, clear logic, illustrations, and emotions. He was known for stirring the heart as well as informing the mind.

"Sir, you may destroy this little institution," he said in wrapping up the case. "It is weak; it is in your hands! You may put it out; but if you do, you must carry on your work! You must extinguish one after another, all those great lights of science, which, for more than a century, have thrown their radiance over the land . . . It is, sir, as I have said a small college—and yet there are those who love it."

His defense was based on facts and law, but from the standpoint of the audience, it was also part performance. "The whole audience had been wrought up to the highest excitement; many were dissolved in tears," according to Justice Joseph Story. Chief Justice John Marshall's majority opinion for the college closely followed Webster's arguments and logic.

Two years later, Webster stepped up to deliver the Plymouth Oration. His delivery was said to have been as great as the content. A performance might have been a better term, as Webster used not only words, but gestures and emotions to move his audience.

Afterward, he revised and edited a version that was printed and distributed. When it was complete, Webster sent a copy to former President John Adams, who replied it was "the effort of a great mind. . . . If there be an American who can read it without tears, I am not that American." Adams noted that Webster earned the title "the most consummate orator of modern times. "This oration will be read five hundred years hence with as much rapture, as it was heard. It ought to be read at the end of every century, and indeed at the end of every year, for ever and ever."

Webster's political career continued.

In 1830, as a senator from Massachusetts, Webster spoke out against the idea of nullification, the idea that a state may invalidate any federal law it deems unconstitutional, and provided support to a single federal union. "To begin with nullification with the avowed intent, nevertheless, not to proceed to secession, dismemberment, and general revolution, is as if one were to take the plunge of Niagara, and cry out that he would stop halfway down. In the one case, as in the other, the rash adventurer must go to the bottom of the dark abyss below, were it not that the abyss has no discovered bottom."

In 1850, Webster delivered "The Seventh of March Speech" in support of Senator Henry Clay's Compromise of 1850 which resolved an impasse between southern slave states and free northern states.

"Mr. President, I wish to speak today, not as a Massachusetts man, nor as a Northern man, but as an American, and a member of the Senate of the United States.... I speak for the preservation of the Union." His appeal for support was quickly spread via telegraph. His constituents were unhappy due to the speech, and he soon resigned and served as secretary of state until his death in 1852 at the age of seventy.

As we read Webster's Discourse, we should remember that hearts as well as minds impact the decisions of those who have come before us. Their stories remind us of the foundation of our national values. Our Pilgrim forefathers fled religious persecution. We believe in freedom of religion. They held the first Thanksgiving and gave thanks to their Creator. We have a tradition of belief in God. We also value hard work—because without hard work the Pilgrims would have died.

We, like Webster, should remember and give thanks for our Pilgrim fore-fathers.

—JGC

∾ ∾ ∾

Let us rejoice that we behold this day. Let us be thankful that we have lived to see the bright and happy breaking of the auspicious morn, which commences the third century of the history of New England. Auspicious, indeed,—bringing a happiness beyond the common allotment of Providence to men,—full of present joy, and gilding with bright beams the prospect of futurity, is the dawn that awakens us to the commemoration of the landing of the Pilgrims.

Living at an epoch which naturally marks the progress of the history of our native land, we have come hither to celebrate the great event with which that history commenced. For ever honored be this, the place of our fathers' refuge! For ever remembered the day which saw them, weary and distressed, broken in everything but spirit, poor in all but faith and courage, at last secure from the dangers of wintry seas, and impressing this shore with the first footsteps of civilized man!

It is a noble faculty of our nature which enables us to connect our thoughts, our sympathies, and our happiness with what is distant in place or time; and, looking before and after, to hold communion at once with our ancestors and our posterity. Human and mortal although we are, we are nevertheless not mere insulated beings, without relation to the past or the future. Neither the point of time, nor the spot of earth, in which we physically live, bounds our rational and intellectual enjoyments. We live in the past by a knowledge of its history; and in the future, by hope and anticipation. By ascending to an association with our ancestors; by contemplating their example and studying their character; by partaking their sentiments, and imbibing their spirit; by accompanying them in their toils, by sympathizing in their sufferings, and rejoicing in their successes and their triumphs; we seem to belong to their age, and to mingle our own existence with theirs. We become their contemporaries, live the lives which they lived, endure what they endured, and partake in the rewards which they enjoyed. And in like manner, by running along the line of future time, by contemplating the probable fortunes of those who are coming after us, by attempting something which may promote their happiness, and leave some not dishonorable memorial of ourselves for their regard, when we shall sleep with the fathers, we protract our own earthly being, and seem to crowd whatever is future, as well as all that is past, into the narrow compass of our earthly existence. As it is not a vain and false, but an exalted and religious imagination, which leads us to raise our thoughts from the orb, which, amidst this universe of worlds, the Creator has given us to inhabit, and to send them with something of the feeling which nature prompts, and teaches to be proper among children of the same Eternal Parent, to the contemplation of the myriads of fellow-beings with which his goodness has peopled the infinite of space; so neither is it false or vain to consider ourselves as interested and connected with our whole race, through all time; allied to our ancestors; allied to our posterity; closely compacted on all sides with others; ourselves being but links in the great chain of being, which begins with the origin of our race, runs onward through its successive generations, binding together the past, the present, and the future, and terminating at last, with the consummation of all things earthly, at the throne of God.

There may be, and there often is, indeed, a regard for ancestry, which nourishes only a weak pride; as there is also a care for posterity, which only disguises an habitual avarice, or hides the workings of a low and grovelling [sic] vanity. But there is also a moral and philosophical respect for our ancestors, which elevates the character and improves the heart. Next to the sense of religious duty and moral feeling, I hardly know what should bear with stronger obligation on a liberal and enlightened mind, than a consciousness of alliance with excellence which is departed; and a consciousness, too, that in its acts and conduct, and even in its sentiments and thoughts, it may be actively operating on the happiness of those who come after it. Poetry is found to have few stronger conceptions, by which it would affect or overwhelm the mind, than those in which it presents the moving and speaking image of the departed dead to the senses of the living. This belongs to poetry, only because it is congenial to our nature. Poetry is, in this respect, but the handmaid of true philosophy and morality; it deals with us as human beings, naturally reverencing those whose visible connection with this state of existence is severed, and who may yet exercise we know not what sympathy with ourselves; and when it carries us forward, also, and shows us the long continued result of all the good we do, in the prosperity of those who follow us, till it bears us from ourselves, and absorbs us in an intense interest for what shall happen to the generations after us, it speaks only in the language of our nature, and affects us with sentiments which belong to us as human beings.

Standing in this relation to our ancestors and our posterity, we are assembled on this memorable spot, to perform the duties which that relation and the present occasion impose upon us. We have come to this Rock, to record here our homage for our Pilgrim Fathers; our sympathy in their sufferings; our gratitude for their labors; our admiration of their virtues; our veneration for their piety; and our attachment to those principles of civil and religious liberty, which they encountered the dangers of the ocean, the storms of heaven, the violence of savages, disease, exile, and famine, to enjoy and to establish. And we would leave here, also, for the generations which are rising up rapidly to fill our places, some proof that we have endeavored to transmit the great inheritance unimpaired; that in our estimate of public principles and private virtue, in our veneration of religion and piety, in our devotion to civil and religious liberty, in our regard for whatever advances human knowledge or improves human happiness, we are not altogether unworthy of our origin.

There is a local feeling connected with this occasion, too strong to be resisted; a sort of *genius of the place*, which inspires and awes us. We feel that we are on the spot where the first scene of our history was laid; where the hearths and altars of New England were first placed; where Christianity, and civilization, and letters made their first lodgement, in a vast extent of country, covered with a wilderness, and peopled by roving barbarians. We are here, at the season of the year at which the event took place. The imagination irresistibly and rapidly draws around us the principal features and the leading characters in the original scene. We cast our eyes abroad on the ocean, and we see where the little bark, with the interesting group upon its deck, made its slow progress to the shore. We look around us, and behold the hills and promontories where the anxious eyes of our fathers first saw the places of habitation and of rest. We feel the cold which benumbed, and listen to the winds which pierced them. Beneath us is the Rock, on which New England received the feet of the Pilgrims. We seem even to behold them, as they struggle with the elements, and, with toilsome efforts, gain the shore. We listen to the chiefs in council; we see the unexampled exhibition of female fortitude and resignation; we hear the whisperings of youthful impatience, and we see, what a painter of our own has also represented by his pencil, chilled and shivering childhood, houseless, but for a mother's arms, couchless, but for a mother's breast, till our own blood almost freezes. The mild dignity of Carver and of Bradford; the decisive and soldierlike air and manner of Standish; the devout Brewster; the enterprising Allerton; the general firmness and thoughtfulness of the whole band; their conscious joy for dangers escaped; their deep solicitude about dangers to come; their trust in Heaven; their high religious faith, full of confidence and anticipation; all of these seem to belong to this place, and to be present upon this occasion, to fill us with reverence and admiration.

The settlement of New England by the colony which landed here on the twenty-second of December, sixteen hundred and twenty, although not the first European establishment in what now constitutes the United States, was yet so peculiar in its causes and character, and has been followed and must still be followed by such consequences, as to give it a high claim to lasting commemoration. On these causes and consequences, more than on its immediately attendant circumstances, its importance, as an historical event, depends. Great actions and striking occurrences, having excited a temporary admiration, often pass away and are forgotten, because they leave no lasting results, affecting the prosperity and happiness of communities. Such is frequently the fortune of the most brilliant military achievements. Of the ten thousand battles which have been fought, of all the fields fertilized with carnage, of the banners which have been bathed in blood, of the warriors who have hoped that they had risen from the field of conquest to a glory as bright and as durable as the stars, how few that continue long to interest mankind! The victory of yesterday is reversed by the defeat of to-day; the star of military glory, rising like a meteor, like a meteor has fallen; disgrace and disaster hang on the heels of conquest and renown; victor and vanquished presently pass away to oblivion, and the world goes on in its course, with the loss only of so many lives and so much treasure.

But if this be frequently, or generally, the fortune of military achievements, it is not always so. There are enterprises, military as well as civil, which sometimes check the current of events, give a new turn to human affairs, and transmit their consequences through ages. We see their importance in their results, and call them great, because great things follow. There have been battles which have fixed the fate of nations. These come down to us in history with a solid and permanent interest, not created by a display of glittering armor, the rush of adverse battalions, the sinking and rising of pennons, the flight, the pursuit, and the victory; but by their effect in advancing or retarding human knowledge, in overthrowing or establishing despotism, in extending or destroying human happiness. When the traveller pauses on the plain of Marathon, what are the emotions which most strongly agitate his breast? What is that glorious recollection, which thrills through his frame, and suffuses his eyes? Not, I imagine, that Grecian skill and Grecian valor were here most signally displayed; but that Greece herself was saved. It is because to this spot, and to the event which has rendered it immortal, he refers all the succeeding glories of the republic. It is because, if that day had gone otherwise, Greece had perished. It is because he perceives that her philosophers and orators, her poets and painters, her sculptors and architects, her governments and free institutions, point backward to Marathon, and that their future existence seems to have been suspended on the contingency, whether the Persian or the Grecian banner should wave victorious in the beams of that day's setting sun. And, as his imagination kindles at the retrospect, he is transported back to the interesting moment; he counts the fearful odds of the contending hosts; his interest for the result overwhelms him; he trembles, as if it were still uncertain, and seems to doubt whether he may consider Socrates and Plato, Demosthenes, Sophocles, and Phidias, as secure, yet, to himself and to the world.

"If we conquer," said the Athenian commander on the approach of that decisive day, "if we conquer, we shall make Athens the greatest city of Greece." A prophecy how well fulfilled! "If God prosper us," might have been the more appropriate language of our fathers, when they landed upon this Rock, "if God prosper us, we shall here begin a work which shall last for ages; we shall plant here a new society, in the principles of the fullest liberty and the purest religion; we shall subdue this wilderness which is before us; we shall fill this region of the great continent, which stretches almost from pole to pole, with civilization and Christianity; the temples of the true God shall rise, where now ascends the smoke of idolatrous sacrifice; fields and gardens, the flowers of summer, and the waving and golden harvest of autumn, shall spread over a thousand hills, and stretch along a thousand valleys, never yet, since the creation, reclaimed to the use of civilized man. We shall whiten this coast with the canvas of a prosperous commerce; we shall stud the long and winding shore with a hundred cities. That which we sow in weakness shall be raised in strength. From our sincere, but houseless worship, there shall spring splendid temples to record God's goodness; from the simplicity of our social union, there shall arise wise and politic constitutions of government, full of the liberty which we ourselves bring and breathe; from our zeal for learning, institutions shall spring which shall scatter the light of knowledge throughout the land, and, in time, paying back where they have borrowed, shall contribute their part to the great aggregate of human knowledge; and our descendants, through all generations, shall look back to this spot, and to this hour, with unabated affection and regard."

A brief remembrance of the causes which led to the settlement of this place; some account of the peculiarities and characteristic qualities of that settlement, as distinguished from other instances of colonization; a short notice of the progress of New England in the great interests of society, during the century which is now elapsed; with a few observations on the principles upon which society and government are established in this country; comprise all that can be attempted, and much more than can be satisfactorily performed, on the present occasion.

Of the motives which influenced the first settlers to a voluntary exile, induced them to relinquish their native country, and to seek an asylum in this then unexplored wilderness, the first and principal, no doubt, were connected with religion. They sought to enjoy a higher degree of religious freedom, and what they esteemed a purer form of religious worship, than was allowed to their choice, or presented to their imitation, in the Old World. The love of religious liberty is a stronger sentiment, when fully excited, than an attachment to civil or political freedom. That freedom which the conscience demands, and which men feel bound by their hope of salvation to contend for, can hardly fail to be attained. Conscience, in the cause of religion and the worship of the Deity, prepares the mind to act and to suffer beyond almost all other causes. It sometimes gives an impulse so irresistible, that no fetters of power or of opinion can withstand it. History instructs us that this love of religious liberty, a compound sentiment in the breast of man, made up of the clearest sense of right and the highest conviction of duty, is able to look the sternest despotism in the face, and, with means apparently most inadequate, to shake principalities and powers. There is a boldness, a spirit of daring, in religious reformers, not to be measured by the general rules which control men's purposes and actions. If the hand of power be laid upon it, this only seems to augment its force and its elasticity, and to cause its action to be more formidable and violent. Human invention has devised nothing, human power has compassed nothing, that can forcibly restrain it, when it breaks forth. Nothing can stop it, but to give way to it; nothing can check it, but indulgence. It loses its power only when it has gained its object. The principle of toleration, to which the world has come so slowly, is at once the most just and the most wise of all principles. Even when religious feeling takes a character of extravagance and enthusiasm, and seems to threaten the order of society and shake the columns of the social edifice, its principal danger is in its restraint. If it be allowed indulgence and expansion, like the elemental fires, it only agitates, and perhaps purifies, the atmosphere; while its efforts to throw off restraint would burst the world asunder.

It is certain, that, although many of them were republicans in principle, we have no evidence that our New England ancestors would have emigrated, as they did, from their own native country, would have become wanderers in Europe, and finally would have undertaken the establishment of a colony here, merely from their dislike of the political systems of Europe. They fled not so much from the civil government, as from the hierarchy, and the laws which enforced conformity to the church establishment. Mr. Robinson had left England as early as 1608, on account of the persecutions for non-conformity, and had retired to Holland. He left England from no disappointed ambition in affairs of state, from no regrets at the want of preferment in the church, nor from any motive of distinction or of gain. Uniformity in matters of religion was pressed with such extreme rigor, that a voluntary exile seemed the most eligible mode of escaping from the penalties of non-compliance. The accession of Elizabeth had, it is true, quenched the fires of Smithfield, and put an end to the easy acquisition of the crown of martyrdom. Her long reign had established the Reformation, but toleration was a virtue beyond her conception, and beyond the age. She left no example of it to her successor; and he was not of a character which rendered a sentiment either so wise or so liberal would originate with him. At the present period it seems incredible that the learned, accomplished, unassuming, and inoffensive Robinson should neither be tolerated in his peaceable mode of worship in his own country, nor suffered quietly to depart from it. Yet such was the fact. He left his country by stealth, that he might elsewhere enjoy those rights which ought to belong to men in all countries. The departure of the Pilgrims for Holland is deeply interesting, from its circumstances, and also as it marks the character of the times, independently of its connection with names now incorporated with the history of empire. The embarkation was intended to be made in such a manner that it might escape the notice of the officers of government. Great pains had been taken to secure boats, which should come undiscovered to the shore, and receive the fugitives; and frequent disappointments had been experienced in this respect.

At length the appointed time came, bringing with it unusual severity of cold and rain. An unfrequented and barren heath, on the shores of Lincolnshire, was the selected spot, where the feet of the Pilgrims were to tread, for the last time, the land of their fathers. The vessel which was to receive them did not come until the next day, and in the mean time the little band was collected, and men and women and children and baggage were crowded together, in melancholy and distressed confusion. The sea was rough, and the women and children were already sick, from their passage down the river to the place of embarkation on the sea. At length the wished-for boat silently and fearfully approaches the shore, and men and women and children, shaking with fear and with cold, as many as the small vessel could bear, venture off on a dangerous sea. Immediately the advance of horses is heard from behind, armed men appear, and those not yet embarked are seized and taken into custody. In the hurry of the moment, the first parties had been sent on board without any attempt to keep members of the same family together, and on account of the appearance of the horsemen, the boat never returned for the residue. Those who had got away, and those who had not, were in equal distress. A storm, of great violence and long duration, arose at sea, which not only protracted the voyage, rendered distressing by the want of all those accommodations which the interruption of the embarkation had occasioned, but also forced the vessel out of her course, and menaced immediate shipwreck; while those on shore, when they were dismissed from the custody of the officers of justice, having no longer homes or houses to retire to, and their friends and protectors being already gone, became objects of necessary charity, as well as of deep commiseration.

As this scene passes before us, we can hardly forbear asking whether this be a band of malefactors and felons flying from justice. What are their crimes, that they hide themselves in darkness? To what punishment are they exposed, that, to avoid it, men, and women, and children, thus encounter the surf of the North Sea and the terrors of a night storm? What induces this armed pursuit, and this arrest of fugitives, of all ages and both sexes? Truth does not allow us to answer these inquiries in a manner that does credit to the wisdom or the justice of the times. This was not the flight of guilt, but of virtue. It was an humble and peaceable religion, flying from causeless oppression. It was conscience, attempting to escape from the arbitrary rule of the Stuarts. It was Robinson and Brewster, leading off their little band from their native soil, at first to find shelter on the shore of the neighboring continent, but ultimately to come hither; and having surmounted all difficulties and braved a thousand dangers, to find here a place of refuge and of rest. Thanks be to God, that this spot was honored as the asylum of religious liberty! May its standard, reared here, remain for ever! May it rise up as high as heaven, till its banner shall fan the air of both continents, and wave as a glorious ensign of peace and security to the nations!

The peculiar character, condition, and circumstances of the colonies which introduced civilization and an English race into New England, afford a most interesting and extensive topic of discussion. On these, much of our subsequent character and fortune has depended. Their influence has essentially affected our whole history, through the two centuries which have elapsed; and as they have become intimately connected with government, laws, and property, as well as with our opinions on the subjects of religion and civil liberty, that influence is likely to continue to be felt through the centuries which shall succeed. Emigration from one region to another, and the emission of colonies to people countries more or less distant from the residence of the parent stock, are common incidents in the history of mankind; but it has not often, perhaps never, happened, that the establishment of colonies should be attempted under circumstances, however beset with present difficulties and dangers, yet so favorable to ultimate success, and so conducive to magnificent results, as those which attended the first settlements on this part of the American continent. In other instances, emigration has proceeded from a less exalted purpose, in periods of less general intelligence, or more without plan and by accident; or under circumstances, physical and moral, less favorable to the expectation of laying a foundation for great public prosperity and future empire.

A great resemblance exists, obviously, between all the English colonies established within the present limits of the United States; but the occasion attracts our attention more immediately to those which took possession of New England, and the peculiarities of these furnish a strong contrast with most other instances of colonization.

Among the ancient nations, the Greeks, no doubt, sent forth from their territories the greatest number of colonies. So numerous, indeed, were they, and so great the extent of space over which they were spread, that the parent country fondly and naturally persuaded herself, that by means of them she had laid a sure foundation for the universal civilization of the world. These establishments, from obvious causes, were most numerous in places most contiguous; yet they were found on the coasts of France, on the shores of the Euxine Sea, in Africa, and even, as is alleged, on the borders of India. These emigrations appear to have been sometimes voluntary and sometimes compulsory; arising from the spontaneous enterprise of individuals, or the order and regulation of government. It was a common opinion with ancient writers, that they were undertaken in religious obedience to the commands of oracles, and it is probable that impressions of this sort might have had more or less influence; but it is probable, also, that on these occasions the oracles did not speak a language dissonant from the views and purposes of the state.

Political science among the Greeks seems never to have extended to the comprehension of a system, which should be adequate to the government of a great nation upon principles of liberty. They were accustomed only to the contemplation of small republics, and were led to consider an augmented population as incompatible with free institutions. The desire of a remedy for this supposed evil, and the wish to establish marts for trade, led the governments often to undertake the establishment of colonies as an affair of state expediency. Colonization and commerce, indeed, would naturally become objects of interest to an ingenious and enterprising people, inhabiting a territory closely circumscribed in its limits, and in no small part mountainous and sterile; while the islands of the adjacent seas, and the promontories and coasts of the neighboring continents, by their mere proximity, strongly solicited the excited spirit of emigration. Such was this proximity, in many instances, that the new settlements appeared rather to be the mere extension of population over contiguous territory, than the establishment of distant colonies. In proportion as they were near to the parent state, they would be under its authority, and partake of its fortunes. The colony at Marseilles might perceive lightly, or not at all, the sway of Phocis; while the islands in the Aegean Sea could hardly attain to independence of their Athenian origin. Many of these establishments took place at an early age; and if there were defects in the governments of the parent states, the colonists did not possess philosophy or experience sufficient to correct such evils in their own institutions, even if they had not been, by other causes, deprived of the power. An immediate necessity, connected with the support of life, was the main and direct inducement to these undertakings, and there could hardly exist more than the hope of a successful imitation of institutions with which they were already acquainted, and of holding an equality with their neighbors in the course of improvement. The laws and customs, both political and municipal, as well as the religious worship of the parent city, were transferred to the colony; and the parent city herself, with all such of her colonies as were not too far remote for frequent intercourse and common sentiments, would appear like a family of cities, more or less dependent, and more or less connected. We know how imperfect this system was, as a system of general politics, and what scope it gave to those mutual dissensions and conflicts which proved so fatal to Greece.

But it is more pertinent to our present purpose to observe, that nothing existed in the character of Grecian emigrations, or in the spirit and intelligence of the emigrants, likely to give a new and important direction to human affairs, or a new impulse to the human mind. Their motives were not high enough, their views were not sufficiently large and prospective. They went not forth, like our ancestors, to erect systems of more perfect civil liberty, or to enjoy a higher degree of religious freedom. Above all, there was nothing in the religion and learning of the age, that could either inspire high purposes, or give the ability to execute them. Whatever restraints on civil liberty, or whatever abuses in religious worship, existed at the time of our fathers' emigration, yet even then all was light in the moral and mental world, in comparison with its condition in most periods of the ancient states. The settlement of a new continent, in an age of progressive knowledge and improvement, could not but do more than merely enlarge the natural boundaries of the habitable world. It could not but do much more even than extend commerce and increase wealth among the human race. We see how this event has acted, how it must have acted, and wonder only why it did not act sooner, in the production of moral effects, on the state of human knowledge, the general tone of human sentiments, and the prospects of human happiness. It gave to civilized man not only a new continent to be inhabited and cultivated, and new seas to be explored; but it gave him also a new range for his thoughts, new objects for curiosity, and new excitements to knowledge and improvement.

Roman colonization resembled, far less than that of the Greeks, the original settlements of this country. Power and dominion were the objects of Rome, even in her colonial establishments. Her whole exterior aspect was for centuries hostile and terrific. She grasped at dominion, from India to Britain, and her measures of colonization partook of the character of her general system. Her policy was military, because her objects were power, ascendency, and subjugation. Detachments of emigrants from Rome incorporated themselves with, and governed, the original inhabitants of conquered countries. She sent citizens where she had first sent soldiers; her law followed her sword. Her colonies were a sort of military establishment; so many advanced posts in the career of her dominion. A governor from Rome ruled the new colony with absolute sway, and often with unbounded rapacity. In Sicily, in Gaul, in Spain, and in Asia, the power of Rome prevailed, not nominally only, but really and effectually. Those who immediately exercised it were Roman; the tone and tendency of its administration, Roman. Rome herself continued to be the heart and centre of the great system which she had established. Extortion and rapacity, finding a wide and often rich field of action in the provinces, looked nevertheless to the banks of the Tiber, as the scene in which their ill-gotten treasures should be displayed; or, if a spirit of more honest acquisition prevailed, the object, nevertheless, was ultimate enjoyment in Rome itself. If our own history and our own times did not sufficiently expose the inherent and incurable evils of provincial government, we might see them portrayed, to our amazement, in the desolated and ruined provinces of the Roman empire. We might hear them, in a voice that terrifies us, in those strains of complaint and accusation, which the advocates of the provinces poured forth in the Roman Forum:—"Quas res luxuries in flagitiis, crudelitas in suppliciis, avaritia in rapinis, superbia in contumeliis, efficere potuisset, eas omnes sese pertulisse."

As was to be expected, the Roman Provinces partook of the fortunes, as well as of the sentiments and general character, of the seat of empire. They lived together with her, they flourished with her, and fell with her. The branches were lopped away even before the vast and venerable trunk itself fell prostrate to the earth. Nothing had proceeded from her which could support itself, and bear up the name of its origin, when her own sustaining arm should be enfeebled or withdrawn. It was not given to Rome to see, either at her zenith or in her decline, a child of her own, distant, indeed, and independent of her control, yet speaking her language and inheriting her blood, springing forward to a competition with her own power, and a comparison with her own great renown. She saw not a vast region of the earth peopled from her stock, full of states and political communities, improving upon the models of her institutions, and breathing in fuller measure the spirit which she had breathed in the best periods of her existence; enjoying and extending her arts and her literature; rising rapidly from political childhood to manly strength and independence; her offspring, yet now her equal; unconnected with the causes which might affect the duration of her own power and greatness; of common origin, but not linked to a common fate; giving ample pledge, that her name should not be forgotten, that her language should not cease to be used among men; that whatsoever she had done for human knowledge and human happiness should be treasured up and preserved; that the record of her existence and her achievements should not be obscured, although, in the inscrutable purposes of Providence, it might be her destiny to fall from opulence and splendor; although the time might come, when darkness should settle on all her hills; when foreign or domestic violence should overturn her altars and her temples; when ignorance and despotism should fill the places where Laws, and Arts, and Liberty had flourished; when the feet of barbarism should trample on the tombs of her consuls, and the walls of her senate-house and forum echo only to the voice of savage triumph. She saw not this glorious vision, to inspire and fortify her against the possible decay or downfall of her power. Happy are they who in our day may behold it, if they shall contemplate it with the sentiments which it ought to inspire!

The New England Colonies differ quite as widely from the Asiatic establishments of the modern European nations, as from the models of the ancient states. The sole object of those establishments was originally trade; although we have seen, in one of them, the anomaly of a mere trading company attaining a political character, disbursing revenues, and maintaining armies and fortresses, until it has extended its control over seventy millions of people. Differing from these, and still more from the New England and North American Colonies, are the European settlements in the West India Islands. It is not strange, that, when men's minds were turned to the settlement of America, different objects should be proposed by those who emigrated to the different regions of so vast a country. Climate, soil, and condition were not all equally favorable to all pursuits. In the West Indies, the purpose of those who went thither was to engage in that species of agriculture, suited to the soil and climate, which seems to bear more resemblance to commerce than to the hard and plain tillage of New England. The great staples of these countries, being partly an agricultural and partly a manufactured product, and not being of the necessaries of life, become the object of calculation, with respect to a profitable investment of capital, like any other enterprise of trade or manufacture. The more especially, as, requiring, by necessity or habit, slave labor for their production, the capital necessary to carry on the work of this production is very considerable. The West Indies are resorted to, therefore, rather for the investment of capital than for the purpose of sustaining life by personal labor. Such as possess a considerable amount of capital, or such as choose to adventure in commercial speculations without capital, can alone be fitted to be emigrants to the islands. The agriculture of these regions, as before observed, is a sort of commerce; and it is a species of employment in which labor seems to form an inconsiderable ingredient in the productive causes, since the portion of white labor is exceedingly small, and slave labor is rather more like profit on stock or capital than *labor* properly so called. The individual who undertakes an establishment of this kind takes into the account the cost of the necessary number of slaves, in the same manner as he calculates the cost of the land. The uncertainty, too, of this species of employment, affords another ground of resemblance to commerce. Although gainful on the whole, and in a series of years, it is often very disastrous for a single year, and, as the capital is not readily invested in other pursuits, bad crops or bad markets not only affect the profits, but the capital itself. Hence the sudden depressions which take place in the value of such estates.

But the great and leading observation, relative to these establishments, remains to be made. It is, that the owners of the soil and of the capital seldom consider themselves *at home* in the colony. A very great portion of the soil itself is usually owned in the mother country; a still greater is mortgaged for capital obtained there; and, in general, those who are to derive an interest from the products look to the parent country as the place for enjoyment of their wealth. The population is therefore constantly fluctuating. Nobody comes but to return. A constant succession of owners, agents, and factors takes place. Whatsoever the soil, forced by the unmitigated toil of slavery, can yield, is sent home to defray rents, and interest, and agencies, or to give the means of living in a better society. In such a state, it is evident that no spirit of permanent improvement is likely to spring up. Profits will not be invested with a distant view of benefiting posterity. Roads and canals will hardly be built; schools will not be founded; colleges will not be endowed. There will be few fixtures in society; no principles of utility or of elegance, planted now, with the hope of being developed and expanded hereafter. Profit, immediate profit, must be the principal active spring in the social system. There may be many particular exceptions to these general remarks, but the outline of the whole is such as is here drawn.

Another most important consequence of such a state of things is, that no idea of independence of the parent country is likely to arise; unless, indeed, it should spring up in a form that would threaten universal desolation. The inhabitants have no strong attachment to the place which they inhabit. The hope of a great portion of them is to leave it; and their great desire, to leave it soon. However useful they may be to the parent state, how much soever they may add to the conveniences and luxuries of life, these colonies are not favored spots for the expansion of the human mind, for the progress of permanent improvement, or for sowing the seeds of future independent empire.

Different, indeed, most widely different, from all these instances of emigration and plantation, were the condition, the purposes, and the prospects of our fathers, when they established their infant colony upon this spot. They came hither to a land from which they were never to return. Hither they had brought, and here they were to fix, their hopes, their attachments, and their objects in life. Some natural tears they shed, as they left the pleasant abodes of their fathers, and some emotions they suppressed, when the white cliffs of their native country, now seen for the last time, grew dim to their sight. They were acting, however, upon a resolution not to be daunted. With whatever stifled regrets, with whatever occasional hesitation, with whatever appalling apprehensions, which might sometimes arise with force to shake the firmest purpose, they had yet committed themselves to Heaven and the elements; and a thousand leagues of water soon interposed to separate them for ever from the region which gave them birth. A new existence awaited them here; and when they saw these shores, rough, cold, barbarous, and barren, as then they were, they beheld their country. That mixed and strong feeling, which we call love of country, and which is, in general, never extinguished in the heart of man, grasped and embraced its proper object here. Whatever constitutes *country*, except the earth and the sun, all the moral causes of affection and attachment which operate upon the heart, they had brought with them to their new abode. Here were now their families and friends, their homes, and their property. Before they reached the shore, they had established the elements of a social system, and at a much earlier period had settled their forms of religious worship. At the moment of their landing, therefore, they possessed institutions of government, and institutions of religion: and friends and families, and social and religious institutions, framed by consent, founded on choice and preference, how nearly do these fill up our whole idea of country! The morning that beamed on the first night of their repose saw the Pilgrims already *at home* in their country. There were political institutions, and civil liberty, and religious worship. Poetry has fancied nothing, in the wanderings of heroes, so distinct and characteristic. Here was man, indeed, unprotected, and unprovided for, on the shore of a rude and fearful wilderness; but it was politic, intelligent, and educated man. Every thing was civilized but the physical world. Institutions, containing in substance all that ages had done for human government, were organized in a forest. Cultivated mind was to act on uncultivated nature; and, more than all, a government and a country were to commence, with the very first foundations laid under the divine light of the Christian religion. Happy auspices of a happy futurity! Who would wish that his country's existence had otherwise begun? Who would desire the power of going back to the ages of fable? Who would wish for an origin obscured in the darkness of antiquity? Who would wish for other emblazoning of his country's heraldry, or other ornaments of her genealogy, than to be able to say, that her first existence was with intelligence, her first breath the inspiration of liberty, her first principle the truth of divine religion?

Local attachments and sympathies would ere long spring up in the breasts of our ancestors, endearing to them the place of their refuge. Whatever natural objects are associated with interesting scenes and high efforts obtain a hold on human feeling, and demand from the heart a sort of recognition and regard. This Rock soon became hallowed in the esteem of the Pilgrims, and these hills grateful to their sight. Neither they nor their children were again to till the soil of England, nor again to traverse the seas which surround her. But here was a new sea, now open to their enterprise, and a new soil, which had not failed to respond gratefully to their laborious industry, and which was already assuming a robe of verdure. Hardly had they provided shelter for the living, ere they were summoned to erect sepulchres for the dead. The ground had become sacred, by enclosing the remains of some of their companions and connections. A parent, a child, a husband, or a wife, had gone the way of all flesh, and mingled with the dust of New England. We naturally look with strong emotions to the spot, though it be a wilderness, where the ashes of those we have loved repose. Where the heart has laid down what it loved most, there it is desirous of laying itself down. No sculptured marble, no enduring monument, no honorable inscription, no ever-burning taper that would drive away the darkness of the tomb, can soften our sense of the reality of death, and hallow to our feelings the ground which is to cover us, like the consciousness that we shall sleep, dust to dust, with the objects of our affections.

In a short time other causes sprung up to bind the Pilgrims with new cords to their chosen land. Children were born, and the hopes of future generations arose, in the spot of their new habitation. The second generation found this the land of their nativity, and saw that they were bound to its fortunes. They beheld their fathers' graves around them, and while they read the memorials of their toils and labors, they rejoiced in the inheritance which they found bequeathed to them.

Under the influence of these causes, it was to be expected that an interest and a feeling should arise here, entirely different from the interest and feeling of mere Englishmen; and all the subsequent history of the Colonies proves this to have actually and gradually taken place. With a general acknowledgment of the supremacy of the British crown, there was, from the first, a repugnance to an entire submission to the control of British legislation. The Colonies stood upon their charters, which, as they contended, exempted them from the ordinary power of the British Parliament, and authorized them to conduct their own concerns by their own counsels. They utterly resisted the notion that they were to be ruled by the mere authority of the government at home, and would not endure even that their own charter governments should be established on the other side of the Atlantic. It was not a controlling or protecting board in England, but a government of their own, and existing immediately within their limits, which could satisfy their wishes. It was easy to foresee, what we know also to have happened, that the first great cause of collision and jealousy would be, under the notion of political economy then and still prevalent in Europe, an attempt on the part of the mother country to monopolize the trade of the Colonies. Whoever has looked deeply into the causes which produced our Revolution has found, if I mistake not, the original principle far back in this claim, on the part of England, to monopolize our trade, and a continued effort on the part of the Colonies to resist or evade that monopoly; if, indeed, it be not still more just and philosophical to go farther back, and to consider it decided, that an independent government must arise here, the moment it was ascertained that an English colony, such as landed in this place, could sustain itself against the dangers which surrounded it, and, with other similar establishments, overspread the land with an English population. Accidental causes retarded at times, and at times accelerated, the progress of the controversy. The Colonies wanted strength, and time gave it to them. They required measures of strong and palpable injustice, on the part of the mother country, to justify resistance; the early part of the late king's reign furnished them. They needed spirits of high order, of great daring, of long foresight, and of commanding power, to seize the favoring occasion to strike a blow, which should sever, for all time, the tie of colonial dependence; and these spirits were found, in all the extent which that or any crisis could demand, in Otis, Adams, Hancock, and the other immediate authors of our independence.

Still, it is true that, for a century, causes had been in operation tending to prepare things for this great result. In the year 1660 the English Act of Navigation was passed; the first and grand object of which seems to have been, to secure to England the whole trade with her plantations. It was provided by that act, that none but English ships should transport American produce over the ocean, and that the principal articles of that produce should be allowed to be sold only in the markets of the mother country. Three years afterwards another law was passed, which enacted, that such commodities as the Colonies might wish to purchase should be bought only in the markets of the mother country. Severe rules were prescribed to enforce the provisions of these laws, and heavy penalties imposed on all who should violate them. In the subsequent years of the same reign, other statutes were enacted to re-enforce these statutes, and other rules prescribed to secure a compliance with these rules. In this manner was the trade to and from the Colonies restricted, almost to the exclusive advantage of the parent country. But laws, which rendered the interest of a whole people subordinate to that of another people, were not likely to execute themselves, nor was it easy to find many on the spot, who could be depended upon for carrying them into execution. In fact, these laws were more or less evaded or resisted, in all the Colonies. To enforce them was the constant endeavor of the government at home; to prevent or elude their operation, the perpetual object here. "The laws of navigation," says a living British writer, "were nowhere so openly disobeyed and contemned as in New England." "The people of Massachusetts Bay," he adds, "were from the first disposed to act as if independent of the mother country, and having a governor and magistrates of their own choice, it was difficult to enforce any regulation which came from the English Parliament, adverse to their interests." To provide more effectually for the execution of these laws, we know that courts of admiralty were afterwards established by the crown, with power to try revenue causes, as questions of admiralty, upon the construction given by the crown lawyers to an act of Parliament; a great departure from the ordinary principles of English jurisprudence, but which has been maintained, nevertheless, by the force of habit and precedent, and is adopted in our own existing systems of government.

"There lie," says another English writer, whose connection with the Board of Trade has enabled him to ascertain many facts connected with Colonial history, "There lie among the documents in the board of trade and state-paper office, the most satisfactory proofs, from the epoch of the English Revolution in 1688, throughout every reign, and during every administration, of the settled purpose of the Colonies to acquire direct independence and positive sovereignty." Perhaps this may be stated somewhat too strongly; but it cannot be denied, that, from the very nature of the establishments here, and from the general character of the measures respecting their concerns early adopted and steadily pursued by the English government, a division of the empire was the natural and necessary result to which every thing tended.

I have dwelt on this topic, because it seems to me, that the peculiar original character of the New England Colonies, and certain causes coeval with their existence, have had a strong and decided influence on all their subsequent history, and especially on the great event of the Revolution. Whoever would write our history, and would understand and explain early transactions, should comprehend the nature and force of the feeling which I have endeavored to describe. As a son, leaving the house of his father for his own, finds, by the order of nature, and the very law of his being, nearer and dearer objects around which his affections circle, while his attachment to the parental roof becomes moderated, by degrees, to a composed regard and an affectionate remembrance; so our ancestors, leaving their native land, not without some violence to the feelings of nature and affection, yet, in time, found here a new circle of engagements, interests, and affections; a feeling, which more and more encroached upon the old, till an undivided sentiment, *that this was their country*, occupied the heart; and patriotism, shutting out from its embraces the parent realm, became *local* to America.

Some retrospect of the century which has now elapsed is among the duties of the occasion. It must, however, necessarily be imperfect, to be compressed within the limits of a single discourse. I shall content myself, therefore, with taking notice of a few of the leading and most important occurrences which have distinguished the period.

When the first century closed, the progress of the country appeared to have been considerable; notwithstanding that, in comparison with its subsequent advancement, it now seems otherwise. A broad and lasting foundation had been laid; excellent institutions had been established; many of the prejudices of former times had been removed; a more liberal and catholic spirit on subjects of religious concern had begun to extend itself, and many things conspired to give promise of increasing future prosperity. Great men had arisen in public life, and the liberal professions. The Mathers, father and son, were then sinking low in the western horizon; Leverett, the learned, the accomplished, the excellent Leverett, was about to withdraw his brilliant and useful light. In Pemberton great hopes had been suddenly extinguished, but Prince and Colman were in our

sky; and along the east had begun to flash the crepuscular light of a great lumi-
nary which was about to appear, and which was to stamp the age with his own
name, as the age of Franklin.

The bloody Indian wars, which harassed the people for a part of the first
century; the restrictions on the trade of the Colonies, added to the discouragements inherently belonging to all forms of colonial government; the distance
from Europe, and the small hope of immediate profit to adventurers, are among
the causes which had contributed to retard the progress of population. Perhaps
it may be added, also, that during the period of the civil wars in England, and
the reign of Cromwell, many persons, whose religious opinions and religious
temper might, under other circumstances, have induced them to join the New
England colonists, found reasons to remain in England; either on account of
active occupation in the scenes which were passing, or of an anticipation of the
enjoyment, in their own country, of a form of government, civil and religious,
accommodated to their views and principles. The violent measures, too, pursued against the Colonies in the reign of Charles the Second, the mockery of
a trial, and the forfeiture of the charters, were serious evils. And during the open
violences of the short reign of James the Second, and the tyranny of Andros,
as the venerable historian of Connecticut observes, "All the motives to great
actions, to industry, economy, enterprise, wealth, and population, were in a
manner annihilated. A general inactivity and languishment pervaded the public body. Liberty, property, and every thing which ought to be dear to men, every
day grew more and more insecure."

With the Revolution in England, a better prospect had opened on this
country, as well as on that. The joy had been as great at that event, and far more
universal, in New than in Old England. A new charter had been granted to
Massachusetts, which, although it did not confirm to her inhabitants all their
former privileges, yet relieved them from great evils and embarrassments, and
promised future security. More than all, perhaps, the Revolution in England
had done good to the general cause of liberty and justice. A blow had been
struck in favor of the rights and liberties, not of England alone, but of descendants and kinsmen of England all over the world. Great political truths had

been established. The champions of liberty had been successful in a fearful and perilous conflict. Somers, and Cavendish, and Jekyl, and Howard, had triumphed in one of the most noble causes ever undertaken by men. A revolution had been made upon principle. A monarch had been dethroned for violating the original compact between king and people. The rights of the people to partake in the government, and to limit the monarch by fundamental rules of government, had been maintained; and however unjust the government of England might afterwards be towards other governments or towards her colonies, she had ceased to be governed herself by the arbitrary maxims of the Stuarts.

New England had submitted to the violence of James the Second not longer than Old England. Not only was it reserved to Massachusetts, that on her soil should be acted the first scene of that great revolutionary drama, which was to take place near a century afterwards, but the English Revolution itself, as far as the Colonies were concerned, commenced in Boston. The seizure and imprisonment of Andros, in April, 1689, were acts of direct and forcible resistance to the authority of James the Second. The pulse of liberty beat as high in the extremities as at the heart. The vigorous feeling of the Colony burst out before it was known how the parent country would finally conduct herself. The king's representative, Sir Edmund Andros, was a prisoner in the castle at Boston, before it was or could be known that the king himself had ceased to exercise his full dominion on the English throne.

Before it was known here whether the invasion of the Prince of Orange would or could prove successful, as soon as it was known that it had been undertaken, the people of Massachusetts, at the imminent hazard of their lives and fortunes, had accomplished the Revolution as far as respected themselves. It is probable that, reasoning on general principles and the known attachment of the English people to their constitution and liberties, and their deep and fixed dislike of the king's religion and politics, the people of New England expected a catastrophe fatal to the power of the reigning prince. Yet it was neither certain enough, nor near enough, to come to their aid against the authority of the crown, in that crisis which had arrived, and in which they trusted to put themselves, relying on God and their own courage. There were spirits in

Massachusetts congenial with the spirits of the distinguished friends of the Revolution in England. There were those who were fit to associate with the boldest asserters of civil liberty; and Mather himself, then in England, was not unworthy to be ranked with those sons of the Church, whose firmness and spirit in resisting kingly encroachments in matters of religion, entitled them to the gratitude of their own and succeeding ages.

The second century opened upon New England under circumstances which evinced that much had already been accomplished, and that still better prospects and brighter hopes were before her. She had laid, deep and strong, the foundations of her society. Her religious principles were firm, and her moral habits exemplary. Her public schools had begun to diffuse widely the elements of knowledge; and the College, under the excellent and acceptable administration of Leverett, had been raised to a high degree of credit and usefulness.

The commercial character of the country, notwithstanding all discouragements, had begun to display itself, and *five hundred vessels*, then belonging to Massachusetts, placed her, in relation to commerce, thus early at the head of the Colonies. An author who wrote very near the close of the first century says:—"New England is almost deserving that *noble name*, so mightily hath it increased; and from a small settlement at first, is now become a *very populous* and *flourishing* government. The *capital city*, Boston, is a place of *great wealth and trade*; and by much the largest of any in the English empire of America; and not exceeded but by few cities, perhaps two or three, in all the American world."

But if our ancestors at the close of the first century could look back with joy and even admiration, at the progress of the country, what emotions must we not feel, when, from the point on which we stand, we also look back and run along the events of the century which has now closed! The country which then, as we have seen, was thought deserving of a "noble name,"—which then had "mightily increased," and become "very populous,"—what was it, in comparison with what our eyes behold it? At that period, a very great proportion of its inhabitants lived in the eastern section of Massachusetts proper, and in Plymouth Colony. In Connecticut, there were towns along the coast, some of them respectable, but in the interior all was a wilderness beyond Hartford. On Connecticut River, settlements had proceeded as far up as Deerfield, and Fort Dummer had been built near where is now the south line of New Hampshire. In New Hampshire no settlement was then begun thirty miles from the mouth of Piscataqua River, and in what is now Maine the inhabitants were confined to the coast. The aggregate of the whole population of New England did not exceed one hundred and sixty thousand. Its present amount (1820) is probably one million seven hundred thousand. Instead of being confined to its former limits, her population has rolled backward, and filled up the spaces included within her actual local boundaries. Not this only, but it has overflowed those boundaries, and the waves of emigration have pressed farther and farther toward the West. The Alleghany has not checked it; the banks of the Ohio have been covered with it. New England farms, houses, villages, and churches spread over and adorn the immense extent from the Ohio to Lake Erie, and stretch along from the Alleghany onwards, beyond the Miamis, and toward the Falls of St. Anthony. Two thousand miles westward from the rock where their fathers landed, may now be found the sons of the Pilgrims, cultivating smiling fields, rearing towns and villages, and cherishing, we trust, the patrimonial blessings of wise institutions, of liberty, and religion. The world has seen nothing like this. Regions large enough to be empires, and which, half a century ago, were known only as remote and unexplored wildernesses, are now teeming with population, and prosperous in all the great concerns of life; in good governments, the means of subsistence, and social happiness. It may be safely asserted, that there are now more than a million of people, descendants of New England ancestry, living, free and happy, in regions which scarce sixty years ago were tracts of unpenetrated forest. Nor do rivers, or mountains, or seas resist the progress of industry and enterprise. Erelong, the sons of the Pilgrims will be on the shores of the Pacific. The imagination hardly keeps pace with the progress of population, improvement, and civilization.

It is now five-and-forty years since the growth and rising glory of America were portrayed in the English Parliament, with inimitable beauty, by the most consummate orator of modern times. Going back somewhat more than half a century, and describing our progress as foreseen from that point by his amiable friend Lord Bathurst, then living, he spoke of the wonderful progress which America had made during the period of a single human life. There is no American heart, I imagine, that does not glow, both with conscious, patriotic pride, and admiration for one of the happiest efforts of eloquence, so often as the vision of "that little speck, scarce visible in the mass of national interest, a small seminal principle, rather than a formed body," and the progress of its astonishing development and growth, are recalled to the recollection. But a stronger feeling might be produced, if we were able to take up this prophetic description where he left it, and, placing ourselves at the point of time in which he was speaking, to set forth with equal felicity the subsequent progress of the country. There is yet among the living a most distinguished and venerable name, a descendant of the Pilgrims; one who has been attended through life by a great and fortunate genius; a man illustrious by his own great merits, and favored of Heaven in the long continuation of his years. The time when the English orator was thus speaking of America preceded but by a few days the actual opening of the revolutionary drama at Lexington. He to whom I have alluded, then at the age of forty, was among the most zealous and able defenders of the violated rights of his country. He seemed already to have filled a full measure of public service, and attained an honorable fame. The moment was full of difficulty and danger, and big with events of immeasurable importance. The country was on the very brink of a civil war, of which no man could foretell the duration or the result. Something more than a courageous hope, or characteristic ardor, would have been necessary to impress the glorious prospect on his belief, if, at that moment, before the sound of the first shock of actual war had reached his ears, some attendant spirit had opened to him the vision of the future;—if it had said to him, "The blow is struck, and America is severed from England for ever!"—if it had informed him, that he himself, during the next annual revolution of the sun, should put his own hand to the great instrument of independence, and write his name where all nations should behold it and all time should not efface it; that erelong he himself should maintain the interests and represent the sovereignty of his newborn country in the proudest courts of Europe; that he should one day exercise her supreme magistracy;

that he should yet live to behold ten millions of fellow-citizens paying him the homage of their deepest gratitude and kindest affections; that he should see distinguished talent and high public trust resting where his name rested; that he should even see with his own unclouded eyes the close of the second century of New England, who had begun life almost with its commencement, and lived through nearly half the whole history of his country; and that on the morning of this auspicious day he should be found in the political councils of his native State, revising, by the light of experience, that system of government which forty years before he had assisted to frame and establish; and, great and happy as he should then behold his country, there should be nothing in prospect to cloud the scene, nothing to check the ardor of that confident and patriotic hope which should glow in his bosom to the end of his long protracted and happy life.

It would far exceed the limits of this discourse even to mention the principal events in the civil and political history of New England during the century; the more so, as for the last half of the period that history has, most happily, been closely interwoven with the general history of the United States. New England bore an honorable part in the wars which took place between England and France. The capture of Louisburg gave her a character for military achievement; and in the war which terminated with the peace of 1763, her exertions on the frontiers wore of most essential service, as well to the mother country as to all the Colonies.

In New England the war of the Revolution commenced. I address those who remember the memorable 19th of April, 1775; who shortly after saw the burning spires of Charlestown; who beheld the deeds of Prescott, and heard the voice of Putnam amidst the storm of war, and saw the generous Warren fall, the first distinguished victim in the cause of liberty. It would be superfluous to say, that no portion of the country did more than the States of New England to bring the Revolutionary struggle to a successful issue. It is scarcely less to her credit, that she saw early the necessity of a closer union of the States, and gave an efficient and indispensable aid to the establishment and organization of the Federal government.

Perhaps we might safely say, that a new spirit and a new excitement began to exist here about the middle of the last century. To whatever causes it may be imputed, there seems then to have commenced a more rapid improvement. The Colonies had attracted more of the attention of the mother country, and some renown in arms had been acquired. Lord Chatham was the first English minister who attached high importance to these possessions of the crown, and who foresaw any thing of their future growth and extension. His opinion was, that the great rival of England was chiefly to be feared as a maritime and commercial power, and to drive her out of North America and deprive her of her West Indian possessions was a leading object in his policy. He dwelt often on the fisheries, as nurseries for British seamen, and the colonial trade, as furnishing them employment. The war, conducted by him with so much vigor, terminated in a peace, by which Canada was ceded to England. The effect of this was immediately visible in the New England Colonies; for, the fear of Indian hostilities on the frontiers being now happily removed, settlements went on with an activity before that time altogether unprecedented, and public affairs wore a new and encouraging aspect. Shortly after this fortunate termination of the French war, the interesting topics connected with the taxation of America by the British Parliament began to be discussed, and the attention and all the faculties of the people drawn towards them. There is perhaps no portion of our history more full of interest than the period from 1760 to the actual commencement of the war. The progress of opinion in this period, though less known, is not less important than the progress of arms afterwards. Nothing deserves more consideration than those events and discussions which affected the public sentiment and settled the Revolution in men's minds, before hostilities openly broke out.

Internal improvement followed the establishment and prosperous commencement of the present government. More has been done for roads, canals, and other public works, within the last thirty years, than in all our former history. In the first of these particulars, few countries excel the New England States. The astonishing increase of their navigation and trade is known to every one, and now belongs to the history of our national wealth.

We may flatter ourselves, too, that literature and taste have not been stationary, and that some advancement has been made in the elegant, as well as in the useful arts.

The nature and constitution of society and government in this country are interesting topics, to which I would devote what remains of the time allowed to this occasion. Of our system of government the first thing to be said is, that it is really and practically a free system. It originates entirely with the people, and rests on no other foundation than their assent. To judge of its actual operation, it is not enough to look merely at the form of its construction. The practical character of government depends often on a variety of considerations, besides the abstract frame of its constitutional organization. Among these are the condition and tenure of property; the laws regulating its alienation and descent; the presence or absence of a military power; an armed or unarmed yeomanry; the spirit of the age, and the degree of general intelligence. In these respects it cannot be denied that the circumstances of this country are most favorable to the hope of maintaining the government of a great nation on principles entirely popular. In the absence of military power, the nature of government must essentially depend on the manner in which property is holden and distributed. There is a natural influence belonging to property, whether it exists in many hands or few; and it is on the rights of property that both despotism and unrestrained popular violence ordinarily commence their attacks. Our ancestors began their system of government here under a condition of comparative equality in regard to wealth, and their early laws were of a nature to favor and continue this equality.

A republican form of government rests not more on political constitutions, than on those laws which regulate the descent and transmission of property. Governments like ours could not have been maintained, where property was holden according to the principles of the feudal system; nor, on the other hand, could the feudal constitution possibly exist with us. Our New England ancestors brought hither no great capitals from Europe; and if they had, there was nothing productive in which they could have been invested. They left behind them the whole feudal policy of the other continent. They broke away at once from the system of military service established in the Dark Ages, and which continues, down even to the present time, more or less to affect the condition of property all over Europe. They came to a new country. There were, as yet, no lands yielding rent, and no tenants rendering service. The whole soil was unreclaimed from barbarism. They were themselves, either from their original condition, or from the necessity of their common interest, nearly on a general level in respect to property. Their situation demanded a parcelling out and division of the lands, and it may be fairly said, that this necessary act *fixed the future frame and form of their government.* The character of their political institutions was determined by the fundamental laws respecting property. The laws rendered estates divisible among sons and daughters. The right of primogeniture, at first limited and curtailed, was afterwards abolished. The property was all freehold. The entailment of estates, long trusts, and the other processes for fettering and tying up inheritances, were not applicable to the condition of society, and seldom made use of. On the contrary, alienation of the land was every way facilitated, even to the subjecting of it to every species of debt. The establishment of public registries, and the simplicity of our forms of conveyance, have greatly facilitated the change of real estate from one proprietor to another. The consequence of all these causes has been a great subdivision of the soil, and a great equality of condition; the true basis, most certainly, of a popular government. "If the people," says Harrington, "hold three parts in four of the territory, it is plain there can neither be any single person nor nobility able to dispute the government with them; in this case, therefore, *except force be interposed,* they govern themselves."

The history of other nations may teach us how favorable to public liberty are the division of the soil into small freeholds, and a system of laws, of which the tendency is, without violence or injustice, to produce and to preserve a degree of equality of property. It has been estimated, if I mistake not, that about the time of Henry the Seventh four fifths of the land in England was holden by the great barons and ecclesiastics. The effects of a growing commerce soon afterwards began to break in on this state of things, and before the Revolution, in 1688, a vast change had been wrought. It may be thought probable, that, for the last half-century, the process of subdivision in England has been retarded, if not reversed; that the great weight of taxation has compelled many of the lesser freeholders to dispose of their estates, and to seek employment in the army and navy, in the professions of civil life, in commerce, or in the colonies. The effect of this on the British constitution cannot but be most unfavorable. A few large estates grow larger; but the number of those who have no estates also increases; and there may be danger, lest the inequality of property become so great, that those who possess it may be dispossessed by force; in other words, that the government may be overturned.

A most interesting experiment of the effect of a subdivision of property on government is now making in France. It is understood, that the law regulating the transmission of property in that country, now divides it, real and personal, among all the children equally, both sons and daughters; and that there is, also, a very great restraint on the power of making dispositions of property by will. It has been supposed, that the effects of this might probably be, in time, to break up the soil into such small subdivisions, that the proprietors would be too poor to resist the encroachments of executive power. I think far otherwise. What is lost in individual wealth will be more than gained in numbers, in intelligence, and in a sympathy of sentiment. If, indeed, only one or a few landholders were to resist the crown, like the barons of England, they must, of course, be great and powerful landholders, with multitudes of retainers, to promise success. But if the proprietors of a given extent of territory are summoned to resistance, there is no reason to believe that such resistance would be less forcible, or less successful, because the number of such proprietors happened to be great. Each would perceive his own importance, and his own interest, and would feel that natural elevation of character which the consciousness of property inspires. A common sentiment would unite all, and numbers would not only add strength, but excite enthusiasm. It is true, that France possesses a vast military force, under the direction of an hereditary executive government; and military power, it is possible, may overthrow any government. It is in vain, however, in this period of the world, to look for security against military power to the arm of the great landholders. That notion is derived from a state of things long since past; a state in which a feudal baron, with his retainers, might stand against the sovereign and his retainers, himself but the greatest baron. But at present, what could the richest landholder do, against one regiment of disciplined troops? Other securities, therefore, against the prevalence of military power must be provided. Happily for us, we are not so situated as that any purpose of national defence requires, ordinarily and constantly, such a military force as might seriously endanger our liberties.

In respect, however, to the recent law of succession in France, to which I have alluded, I would, presumptuously perhaps, hazard a conjecture, that, if the government do not change the law, the law in half a century will change the government; and that this change will be, not in favor of the power of the crown, as some European writers have supposed, but against it. Those writers only reason upon what they think correct general principles, in relation to this subject. They acknowledge a want of experience. Here we have had that experience; and we know that a multitude of small proprietors, acting with intelligence, and that enthusiasm which a common cause inspires, constitute not only a formidable, but an invincible power.

The true principle of a free and popular government would seem to be, so to construct it as to give to all, or at least to a very great majority, an interest in its preservation; to found it, as other things are founded, on men's interest. The stability of government demands that those who desire its continuance should be more powerful than those who desire its dissolution. This power, of course, is not always to be measured by mere numbers. Education, wealth, talents, are all parts and elements of the general aggregate of power; but numbers, nevertheless, constitute ordinarily the most important consideration, unless, indeed, there be *a military force* in the hands of the few, by which they can control the many. In this country we have actually existing systems of government, in the maintenance of which, it should seem, a great majority, both in numbers and in other means of power and influence, must see their interest. But this state of things is not brought about solely by written political constitutions, or the mere manner of organizing the government; but also by the laws which regulate the descent and transmission of property. The freest government, if it could exist, would not be long acceptable, if the tendency of the laws were to create a rapid accumulation of property in few hands, and to render the great mass of the population dependent and penniless. In such a case, the popular power would be likely to break in upon the rights of property, or else the influence of property to limit and control the exercise of popular power. Universal suffrage, for example, could not long exist in a community where there was great inequality of property. The holders of estates would be obliged, in such case, in some way to restrain the right of suffrage, or else such right of suffrage would, before long, divide the property. In the nature of things, those who have not property, and see their neighbors possess much more than they think them to need, cannot be favorable to laws made for the protection of property. When this class becomes numerous, it grows clamorous. It looks on property as its prey and plunder, and is naturally ready, at all times, for violence and revolution.

It would seem, then, to be the part of political wisdom to found government on property; and to establish such distribution of property, by the laws which regulate its transmission and alienation, as to interest the great majority of society in the support of the government. This is, I imagine, the true theory and the actual practice of our republican institutions. With property divided as we have it, no other government than that of a republic could be maintained, even were we foolish enough to desire it. There is reason, therefore, to expect a long continuance of our system. Party and passion, doubtless, may prevail at times, and much temporary mischief be done. Even modes and forms may be changed, and perhaps for the worse. But a great revolution in regard to property must take place, before our governments can be moved from their republican basis, unless they be violently struck off by military power. The people possess the property, more emphatically than it could ever be said of the people of any other country, and they can have no interest to overturn a government which protects that property by equal laws.

Let it not be supposed, that this state of things possesses too strong tendencies towards the production of a dead and uninteresting level in society. Such tendencies are sufficiently counteracted by the infinite diversities in the characters and fortunes of individuals. Talent, activity, industry, and enterprise tend at all times to produce inequality and distinction; and there is room still for the accumulation of wealth, with its great advantages, to all reasonable and useful extent. It has been often urged against the state of society in America, that it furnishes no class of men of fortune and leisure. This may be partly true, but it is not entirely so, and the evil, if it be one, would affect rather the progress of taste and literature, than the general prosperity of the people. But the promotion of taste and literature cannot be primary objects of political institutions; and if they could, it might be doubted whether, in the long course of things, as much is not gained by a wide diffusion of general knowledge, as is lost by diminishing the number of those who are enabled by fortune and leisure to devote themselves exclusively to scientific and literary pursuits. However this may be, it is to be considered that it is the spirit of our system to be equal and general, and if there be particular disadvantages incident to this, they are far more than counterbalanced by the benefits which weigh against them. The important concerns of society are generally conducted, in all countries, by the men of business and practical ability; and even in matters of taste and literature, the advantages of mere leisure are liable to be overrated. If there exist adequate means of education and a love of letters be excited, that love will find its way to the object of its desire, through the crowd and pressure of the most busy society.

Connected with this division of property, and the consequent participation of the great mass of people in its possession and enjoyments, is the system of representation, which is admirably accommodated to our condition, better understood among us, and more familiarly and extensively practised, in the higher and in the lower departments of government, than it has been by any other people. Great facility has been given to this in New England by the early division of the country into townships or small districts, in which all concerns of local police are regulated, and in which representatives to the legislature are elected. Nothing can exceed the utility of these little bodies. They are so many councils or parliaments, in which common interests are discussed, and useful knowledge acquired and communicated.

The division of governments into departments, and the division, again, of the legislative department into two chambers, are essential provisions in our system. This last, although not new in itself, yet seems to be new in its application to governments wholly popular. The Grecian republics, it is plain, knew nothing of it; and in Rome, the check and balance of legislative power, such as it was, lay between the people and the senate. Indeed, few things are more difficult than to ascertain accurately the true nature and construction of the Roman commonwealth. The relative power of the senate and the people, of the consuls and the tribunes, appears not to have been at all times the same, nor at any time accurately defined or strictly observed. Cicero, indeed, describes to us an admirable arrangement of political power, and a balance of the constitution, in that beautiful passage, in which he compares the democracies of Greece with the Roman commonwealth. *"O morem preclarum, disciplinamque, quam a majoribus accepimus, si quidem teneremus! sed nescio quo pacto jam de manibus elabitur. Nullam enim illi nostri sapientissimi et sanctissimi viri vim concionis esse voluerunt, quae scisseret plebs, aut quae populus juberet; summota concione, distributis partibus, tributim et centuriatim descriptis ordinibus, classibus, aetatibus, auditis auctoribus, re multos dies promulgata et cognita, juberi vetarique voluerunt. Graecorum autem totae respublicae sedentis concionis temeritate administrantur."*

But at what time this wise system existed in this perfection at Rome, no proofs remain to show. Her constitution, originally framed for a monarchy, never seemed to be adjusted in its several parts after the expulsion of the kings. Liberty there was, but it was a disputatious, an uncertain, an ill-secured liberty. The patrician and plebeian orders, instead of being matched and joined, each in its just place and proportion, to sustain the fabric of the state, were rather like hostile powers, in perpetual conflict. With us, an attempt has been made, and so far not without success, to divide representation into chambers, and, by difference of age, character, qualification, or mode of election, to establish salutary checks, in governments altogether elective.

Having detained you so long with these observations, I must yet advert to another most interesting topic,—the Free Schools. In this particular, New England may be allowed to claim, I think, a merit of a peculiar character. She early adopted, and has constantly maintained the principle, that it is the undoubted right and the bounden duty of government to provide for the instruction of all youth. That which is elsewhere left to chance or to charity, we secure by law. For the purpose of public instruction, we hold every man subject to taxation in proportion to his property, and we look not to the question, whether he himself have, or have not, children to be benefited by the education for which he pays. We regard it as a wise and liberal system of police, by which property, and life, and the peace of society are secured. We seek to prevent in some measure the extension of the penal code, by inspiring a salutary and conservative principle of virtue and of knowledge in an early age. We strive to excite a feeling of respectability, and a sense of character, by enlarging the capacity and increasing the sphere of intellectual enjoyment. By general instruction, we seek, as far as possible, to purify the whole moral atmosphere; to keep good sentiments uppermost, and to turn the strong current of feeling and opinion, as well as the censures of the law and the denunciations of religion, against immorality and crime. We hope for a security beyond the law, and above the law, in the prevalence of an enlightened and well-principled moral sentiment. We hope to continue and prolong the time, when, in the villages and farm-houses of New England, there may be undisturbed sleep within unbarred doors. And knowing that our government rests directly on the public will, in order that we may preserve it we endeavor to give a safe and proper direction to that public will. We do not, indeed, expect all men to be philosophers or statesmen; but we confidently trust, and our expectation of the duration of our system of government rests on that trust, that, by the diffusion of general knowledge and good and virtuous sentiments, the political fabric may be secure, as well against open violence and overthrow, as against the slow, but sure, undermining of licentiousness.

We know that, at the present time, an attempt is making in the English Parliament to provide by law for the education of the poor, and that a gentleman of distinguished character (Mr. Brougham) has taken the lead in presenting a plan to government for carrying that purpose into effect. And yet, although the representatives of the three kingdoms listened to him with astonishment as well as delight, we hear no principles with which we ourselves have not been familiar from youth; we see nothing in the plan but an approach towards that system which has been established in New England for more than a century and a half. It is said that in England not more than *one child in fifteen* possesses the means of being taught to read and write; in Wales, *one in twenty*; in France, until lately, when some improvement was made, not more than *one in thirty-five*. Now, it is hardly too strong to say, that in New England *every child possesses* such means. It would be difficult to find an instance to the contrary, unless where it should be owing to the negligence of the parent; and, in truth, the means are actually used and enjoyed by nearly every one. A youth of fifteen, of either sex, who cannot both read and write, is very seldom to be found. Who can make this comparison, or contemplate this spectacle, without delight and a feeling of just pride? Does any history show property more beneficently applied? Did any government ever subject the property of those who have estates to a burden, for a purpose more favorable to the poor, or more useful to the whole community?

A conviction of the importance of public instruction was one of the earliest sentiments of our ancestors. No lawgiver of ancient or modern times has expressed more just opinions, or adopted wiser measures, than the early records of the Colony of Plymouth show to have prevailed here. Assembled on this very spot, a hundred and fifty-three years ago, the legislature of this Colony declared, "Forasmuch as the maintenance of good literature doth much tend to the advancement of the weal and flourishing state of societies and republics, this Court doth therefore order, that in whatever township in this government, consisting of fifty families or upwards, any meet man shall be obtained to teach a grammar school, such township shall allow at least twelve pounds, to be raised by rate on all the inhabitants."

Having provided that all youth should be instructed in the elements of learning by the institution of free schools, our ancestors had yet another duty to perform. Men were to be educated for the professions and the public. For this purpose they founded the University, and with incredible zeal and perseverance they cherished and supported it, through all trials and discouragements. On the subject of the University, it is not possible for a son of New England to think without pleasure, or to speak without emotion. Nothing confers more honor on the State where it is established, or more utility on the country at large. A respectable university is an establishment which must be the work of time. If pecuniary means were not wanting, no new institution could possess character and respectability at once. We owe deep obligation to our ancestors, who began, almost on the moment of their arrival, the work of building up this institution.

Although established in a different government, the Colony of Plymouth manifested warm friendship for Harvard College. At an early period, its government took measures to promote a general subscription throughout all the towns in this Colony, in aid of its small funds. Other colleges were subsequently founded and endowed, in other places, as the ability of the people allowed; and we may flatter ourselves, that the means of education at present enjoyed in New England are not only adequate to the diffusion of the elements of knowledge among all classes, but sufficient also for respectable attainments in literature and the sciences.

Lastly, our ancestors established their system of government on morality and religious sentiment. Moral habits, they believed, cannot safely be trusted on any other foundation than religious principle, nor any government be secure which is not supported by moral habits. Living under the heavenly light of revelation, they hoped to find all the social dispositions, all the duties which men owe to each other and to society, enforced and performed. Whatever makes men good Christians, makes them good citizens. Our fathers came here to enjoy their religion free and unmolested; and, at the end of two centuries, there is nothing upon which we can pronounce more confidently, nothing of which we can express a more deep and earnest conviction, than of the inestimable importance of that religion to man, both in regard to this life and that which is to come.

If the blessings of our political and social condition have not been too highly estimated, we cannot well overrate the responsibility and duty which they impose upon us. We hold these institutions of government, religion, and learning, to be transmitted, as well as enjoyed. We are in the line of conveyance, through which whatever has been obtained by the spirit and efforts of our ancestors is to be communicated to our children.

We are bound to maintain public liberty, and, by the example of our own systems, to convince the world that order and law, religion and morality, the rights of conscience, the rights of persons, and the rights of property, may all be preserved and secured, in the most perfect manner, by a government entirely and purely elective. If we fail in this, our disaster will be signal, and will furnish an argument, stronger than has yet been found, in support of those opinions which maintain that government can rest safely on nothing but power and coercion. As far as experience may show errors in our establishments, we are bound to correct them; and if any practices exist contrary to the principles of justice and humanity within the reach of our laws or our influence, we are inexcusable if we do not exert ourselves to restrain and abolish them.

I deem it my duty on this occasion to suggest, that the land is not yet wholly free from the contamination of a traffic, at which every feeling of humanity must for ever revolt,—I mean the African slave-trade. Neither public sentiment, nor the law, has hitherto been able entirely to put an end to this odious and abominable trade. At the moment when God in his mercy has blessed the Christian world with a universal peace, there is reason to fear, that, to the disgrace of the Christian name and character, new efforts are making for the extension of this trade by subjects and citizens of Christian states, in whose hearts there dwell no sentiments of humanity or of justice, and over whom neither the fear of God nor the fear of man exercises a control. In the sight of our law, the African slave-trader is a pirate and a felon; and in the sight of Heaven, an offender far beyond the ordinary depth of human guilt. There is no brighter page of our history, than that which records the measures which have been adopted by the government at an early day, and at different times since, for the suppression of this traffic; and I would call on all the true sons of New England to co-operate with the laws of man, and the justice of Heaven. If there be, within the extent of our knowledge or influence, any participation in this traffic, let us pledge ourselves here, upon the rock of Plymouth, to extirpate and destroy it. It is not fit that the land of the Pilgrims should bear the shame longer. I hear the sound of the hammer, I see the smoke of the furnaces where manacles and fetters are still forged for human limbs. I see the visages of those who by stealth and at midnight labor in this work of hell, foul and dark, as may become the artificers of such instruments of misery and torture. Let that spot be purified, or let it cease to be of New England. Let it be purified, or let it be set aside from the Christian world; let it be put out of the circle of human sympathies and human regards, and let civilized man henceforth have no communion with it.

I would invoke those who fill the seats of justice, and all who minister at her altar, that they execute the wholesome and necessary severity of the law. I invoke the ministers of our religion, that they proclaim its denunciation of these crimes, and add its solemn sanctions to the authority of human laws. If the pulpit be silent whenever or wherever there may be a sinner bloody with this guilt within the hearing of its voice, the pulpit is false to its trust. I call on the fair merchant, who has reaped his harvest upon the seas, that he assist in scourging from those seas the worst pirates that ever infested them. That ocean, which seems to wave with a gentle magnificence to waft the burden of an honest commerce, and to roll along its treasures with a conscious pride,—that ocean, which hardy industry regards, even when the winds have ruffled its surface, as a field of grateful toil,—what is it to the victim of this oppression, when he is brought to its shores, and looks forth upon it, for the first time, loaded with chains, and bleeding with stripes? What is it to him but a wide-spread prospect of suffering, anguish, and death? Nor do the skies smile longer, nor is the air longer fragrant to him. The sun is cast down from heaven. An inhuman and accursed traffic has cut him off in his manhood, or in his youth, from every enjoyment belonging to his being, and every blessing which his Creator intended for him.

The Christian communities send forth their emissaries of religion and letters, who stop, here and there, along the coast of the vast continent of Africa, and with painful and tedious efforts make some almost imperceptible progress in the communication of knowledge, and in the general improvement of the natives who are immediately about them. Not thus slow and imperceptible is the transmission of the vices and bad passions which the subjects of Christian states carry to the land. The slave-trade having touched the coast, its influence and its evils spread, like a pestilence, over the whole continent, making savage wars more savage and more frequent, and adding new and fierce passions to the contests of barbarians.

I pursue this topic no further, except again to say, that all Christendom, being now blessed with peace, is bound by every thing which belongs to its character, and to the character of the present age, to put a stop to this inhuman and disgraceful traffic.

We are bound, not only to maintain the general principles of public liberty, but to support also those existing forms of government which have so well secured its enjoyment, and so highly promoted the public prosperity. It is now more than thirty years that these States have been united under the Federal Constitution, and whatever fortune may await them hereafter, it is impossible that this period of their history should not be regarded as distinguished by signal prosperity and success. They must be sanguine indeed, who can hope for benefit from change. Whatever division of the public judgment may have existed in relation to particular measures of the government, all must agree, one should think, in the opinion, that in its general course it has been eminently productive of public happiness. Its most ardent friends could not well have hoped from it more than it has accomplished; and those who disbelieved or doubted ought to feel less concern about predictions which the event has not verified, than pleasure in the good which has been obtained. Whoever shall hereafter write this part of our history, although he may see occasional errors or defects, will be able to record no great failure in the ends and objects of government. Still less will he be able to record any series of lawless and despotic acts, or any successful usurpation. His page will contain no exhibition of provinces depopulated, of civil authority habitually trampled down by military power, or of a community crushed by the burden of taxation. He will speak, rather, of public liberty protected, and public happiness advanced; of increased revenue, and population augmented beyond all example; of the growth of commerce, manufactures, and the arts; and of that happy condition, in which the restraint and coercion of government are almost invisible and imperceptible, and its influence felt only in the benefits which it confers. We can entertain no better wish for our country, than that this government may be preserved; nor have a clearer duty than to maintain and support it in the full exercise of all its just constitutional powers.

The cause of science and literature also imposes upon us an important and delicate trust. The wealth and population of the country are now so far advanced, as to authorize the expectation of a correct literature and a well formed taste, as well as respectable progress in the abstruse sciences. The country has risen from a state of colonial subjection; it has established an independent government, and is now in the undisturbed enjoyment of peace and political security. The elements of knowledge are universally diffused, and the reading portion of the community is large. Let us hope that the present may be an auspicious era of literature. If, almost on the day of their landing, our ancestors founded schools and endowed colleges, what obligations do not rest upon us, living under circumstances so much more favorable both for providing and for using the means of education? Literature becomes free institutions. It is the graceful ornament of civil liberty, and a happy restraint on the asperities which political controversies sometimes occasion. Just taste is not only an embellishment of society, but it rises almost to the rank of the virtues, and diffuses positive good throughout the whole extent of its influence. There is a connection between right feeling and right principles, and truth in taste is allied with truth in morality. With nothing in our past history to discourage us, and with something in our present condition and prospects to animate us, let us hope, that, as it is our fortune to live in an age when we may behold a wonderful advancement of the country in all its other great interests, we may see also equal progress and success attend the cause of letters.

Finally, let us not forget the religious character of our origin. Our fathers were brought hither by their high veneration for the Christian religion. They journeyed by its light, and labored in its hope. They sought to incorporate its principles with the elements of their society, and to diffuse its influence through all their institutions, civil, political, or literary. Let us cherish these sentiments, and extend this influence still more widely; in the full conviction, that that is the happiest society which partakes in the highest degree of the mild and peaceful spirit of Christianity.

The hours of this day are rapidly flying, and this occasion will soon be passed. Neither we nor our children can expect to behold its return. They are in the distant regions of futurity, they exist only in the all-creating power of God, who shall stand here a hundred years hence, to trace, through us, their descent from the Pilgrims, and to survey, as we have now surveyed, the progress of their country, during the lapse of a century. We would anticipate their concurrence with us in our sentiments of deep regard for our common ancestors. We would anticipate and partake the pleasure with which they will then recount the steps of New England's advancement. On the morning of that day, although it will not disturb us in our repose, the voice of acclamation and gratitude, commencing on the Rock of Plymouth, shall be transmitted through millions of the sons of the Pilgrims, till it lose itself in the murmurs of the Pacific seas.

We would leave for the consideration of those who shall then occupy our places, some proof that we hold the blessings transmitted from our fathers in just estimation; some proof of our attachment to the cause of good government, and of civil and religious liberty; some proof of a sincere and ardent desire to promote every thing which may enlarge the understandings and improve the hearts of men. And when, from the long distance of a hundred years, they shall look back upon us, they shall know, at least, that we possessed affections, which, running backward and warming with gratitude for what our ancestors have done for our happiness, run forward also to our posterity, and meet them with cordial salutation, ere yet they have arrived on the shore of being.

Advance, then, ye future generations! We would hail you, as you rise in your long succession, to fill the places which we now fill, and to taste the blessings of existence where we are passing, and soon shall have passed, our own human duration. We bid you welcome to this pleasant land of the fathers. We bid you welcome to the healthful skies and the verdant fields of New England. We greet your accession to the great inheritance which we have enjoyed. We welcome you to the blessings of good government and religious liberty. We welcome you to the treasures of science and the delights of learning. We welcome you to the transcendent sweets of domestic life, to the happiness of kindred, and parents, and children. We welcome you to the immeasurable blessings of rational existence, the immortal hope of Christianity, and the light of everlasting truth!

X

"Remember the Alamo!"

CAPTAIN MOSLEY BAKER'S SPEECH AT SAN JACINTO
(1836)

To UNDERSTAND THE INDEPENDENT NATURE OF MOST TEXANS TODAY, it helps to understand the history of Texas and its path to statehood. Unlike other territories, it was not purchased, settled, and admitted to statehood. Instead, Texans fought for their freedom several times before deciding to join the United States. Texas was part of Mexico when it won its independence from Spain in 1821. Mexico adopted a constitution in 1824 that included guarantees of certain liberties, though not freedom of religion, and restrictions on the federal government.

In 1822, in an effort to increase population and economic activity, Mexico offered to sell foreigners land in the Texas territory for ten cents an acre. Groups of families emigrated from the United States to Mexican Texas during this period.

Less than a decade later, there were many more Americans than Mexicans in the Texas territory. The Mexican government became concerned that the American population might have an overwhelming influence on the territory. In 1830, Mexico banned immigration from America.

In 1833, Mexican General Antonio Lopez de Santa Anna took control of the Mexican government. He began to strip away the liberties of the people, centralizing control. Santa Anna basically supplanted the 1824 constitution with the Siete Leyes, a much more dictatorial body of laws, in December 1835. Many of the people in Texas were unhappy that their liberties were being taken away. Above all, they were people who loved freedom and liberty.

This led to the Consultation in San Felipe, Texas, in November 1835, where fifty-five people from thirteen municipalities throughout Texas came together to determine how to proceed, even though fighting had already begun on October 2, 1835, at the Battle of Gonzales. They did not want to declare independence at that time, but wanted to put the Mexican government and the rest of the world on notice that they would not allow a Mexican despot to strip away their liberties and dictate how they lived their lives. They communicated to the Mexican government that either the 1824 constitution had to be restored or Texans would fight for their independence.

At this same time, General Sam Houston was named the commander of the Texas troops. As the friction between the Mexican Government and the Texas people intensified, men from the United States and its territories traveled to Texas to help it fight for independence.

Houston ordered Captain Jim Bowie to remove the artillery from the Alamo, a garrison near San Antonio, and destroy the structure. But Bowie could not move the artillery due to lack of draft animals, and instead decided to defend the Alamo. At the same time—on March 2, 1836—the war aim changed from restoring the 1824 constitution, when Texas officially declared its independence.

After laying siege for thirteen days, Santa Anna's men stormed the Alamo on March 6, 1836. Not content to win, the Mexican soldiers killed every Texas soldier in the Alamo in less than two hours, sparing only women, children, and slaves. The Texan death toll was 180 to 200 men; the Mexican casualties numbered approximately 600.

Not long afterward, Texas soldier Colonel James Fannin surrendered to the Mexican Army outside Goliad. Instead of being treated humanely, Fannin and his wounded men were shot inside a church, while the rest of the almost 400 captives were marched out and slaughtered on the same day, Palm Sunday. Only a few survived the massacre.

Soon after, thousands of Texans fled the area in what was later termed the Runaway Scrape.

Houston knew that the independent Texans needed a victory, but he also knew that he first had to rebuild his army and train his troops.

Santa Anna, emboldened by his army's recent wins at the Alamo and Goliad, assumed that he and his army would continue to be victorious. He became more confident and less cautious.

Captain Moseley Baker was one of Houston's troops. Born in Virginia, he had lived in Alabama before moving west to the Texas territory. Baker had served in the 1835 Consultation, and recruited soldiers for Texas' fight for independence. Many of his men were from outside of Texas, places as far-flung as Georgia, Alabama, and Louisiana.

In order to win, Santa Anna had to not only drive back, but also crush the resistance to ensure no thought of independence remained. Instead, however, he focused on capturing the seat of government.

After weeks of following each other, by April 21, the two armies were close enough to engage in the Battle of San Jacinto. Houston delayed attacking Santa Anna that morning. Convinced that Houston would not attack at all that day, Santa Anna allowed his troops to rest in the early afternoon, and no sentries were posted. When Houston's forces attacked around 4 p.m., they were met with little Mexican resistance.

Before the attack on Santa Anna's army, Baker provided a rousing, inspirational talk to his men. There exists no verbatim transcript of the talk; what follows was pieced together from witness recollections. Baker reminded the men that they were fighting for liberty from a tyrannical Santa Anna; that they were the last best hope for Texas, a phrase we find echoed in other historic speeches.

What we do know is that Houston's army won the battle in eighteen minutes; Santa Anna's overconfidence had led to bad planning.

During the battle, Houston had two horses shot from under him. The Texans continued to kill the Mexican soldiers for more than an hour. What made the battle the turning point was the capture the next day of Santa Anna, who had changed clothes, except for his shirt with diamond-encrusted studs, and was trying to escape. His capture forever changed the sovereignty of the West.

Santa Anna's surrender led to the signing of the Treaty of Velasco between him and Texas President David Burnet. The fighting drew to an end when Mexican Commander Vicente Filisola left Texas under orders from Santa Anna.

Texas had won its freedom.

Texas' independence led to the Mexican-American War and eventually to the annexation by the United States of Arizona, California, Nevada, New Mexico, Texas, Utah and parts of Colorado, Kansas, Oklahoma and Wyoming—almost a million square miles.

The story of liberty-loving Texans fighting for independence—first from Spain and then from a Mexican dictator—illustrates why Americans are willing to die for their freedom and liberty.

—JGC

✇ ✇ ✇

You are now paraded to go in battle. For the past few weeks our greatest desire has been to meet our foes in mortal combat, and that desire is about to be gratified. I have confidence to believe that you will do your duty and act like men worthy of freedom, but if there be one who is not fully satisfied that he can face death unfalteringly he is at liberty to remain at camp, for I do not wish my company disgraced by a single act of cowardice.

Yonder, within less than a mile is the tyrant, Santa Anna, with his myrmidons, who have overrun our country, destroyed our property, put to flight our families and butchered in cold blood many of our brave men.

Remember, comrades, that we this day fight for all that is dear to us on earth, our homes, our families and our liberty. He who would not fight for these is not worthy of the name of man.

Remember that this little army of less than 800 men is the last hope of Texas, and with its defeat or dispersion, dies the cause of freedom here and we will be regarded by the world as rash adventurers, but should victory crown our efforts, of which I have but little doubt, we can anticipate a riddance to the country of the oppressors, followed by peace and prosperity, and in the further years when this broad, beautiful and fertile land shall be occupied by millions of intelligent and thrifty people who can appreciate the value of liberty, we will be honored as the founders of a republic.

Remember that Travis, Crockett, Bowie and their companions, numbering one hundred and eighty-three of the bravest of brave men, stood a siege of ten days against twenty times their number and fought till the last man was killed, not one being left to tell the news or tell the tale.

Remember that Fannin and four hundred volunteers were basely murdered after they had capitulated as prisoners of war and sent to the United States.

Remember you fight an enemy who gives no quarter, and regards neither age nor sex. Recollect that your homes are destroyed; imagine your wives and daughters trudging mud and water, and your children crying for bread, and then remember that the author of all this woe is within a short distance of us; that the arch fiend is now within our grasp; and that the time has come at last for us to avenge the blood of our fallen heroes and to teach the haughty dictator that Texans can not be conquered and that they can and will be free. Then nerve yourselves for the battle, knowing that our cause is just and we are in the hands of an All-wise Creator and as you strike the murderous blow let your watchwords be "Remember Goliad! Remember the Alamo!"

XI

"The Union is unbroken"

ABRAHAM LINCOLN'S FIRST INAUGURAL ADDRESS (1861)

ABRAHAM LINCOLN, THE FIRST REPUBLICAN PRESIDENT, WAS ELECTED the sixteenth president of the United States on November 6, 1860. The campaign had been impassioned and contentious. More than 80 percent of eligible voters turned out. Lincoln received 59 percent of the electoral votes, but less than 40 percent of the popular vote. Republicans did not win either the House or Senate chamber. South Carolina was the only southern state to include Lincoln on its ballot. There, he received less than one percent of the vote.

In the seventeen weeks between Lincoln's election and his inaugural address, seven states—South Carolina, Mississippi, Georgia, Florida, Alabama, Louisiana and Texas—seceded from the Union. This untenable start led him to focus his inaugural address on conciliation. Lincoln's talent for mediation had been developed while he was a circuit lawyer. He knew that once the legal battle was over, fractious neighbors would still have to live next to each other. He often encouraged his clients to settle.

He hoped this would be the case with the Union, peace without war, but he was determined to keep the nation united.

On February 11, 1861, when leaving Springfield to travel to Washington, Lincoln said to the crowd that had gathered at the train station to send him off,

> I now leave, not knowing when, or whether ever, I may return, with a task before me greater than that which rested upon Washington. Without the assistance of that Divine Being, who ever attended him, I cannot succeed. With that assistance, I cannot fail. Trusting in him, who can go with me, and remain with you and be everywhere for good, let us confidently hope that all will yet be well. To his care commending you, as I hope in your prayers you will commend me.

During the months he worked on his inaugural speech, Lincoln asked others for input. William Seward, another Republican candidate for the 1860 presidential nomination who would become Lincoln's secretary of state, provided Lincoln with a seven-page letter containing forty-nine suggestions. Lincoln rewrote twenty-seven of his passages based on Seward's recommendations.

In the address, he placed the onus for potential war on the southern states, "In your hands, my dissatisfied countrymen, and not in mine, is the momentous issue of civil war."

The first two drafts of his address included the closing sentence, "With you and not with me is the solemn question, 'Shall it be peace or a sword?'"

Seward's comments and Lincoln's revision resulted in the close:

> I am loath to close. We are not enemies, but friends. We must not be enemies. Though passion may have strained it must not break our bonds of affection. The mystic chords of memory, stretching from every battlefield and patriot grave to every living heart and hearthstone

all over this broad land, will yet swell the chorus of the Union, when again touched, as surely they will be, by the better angels of our nature.

Most of the northern pundits lauded the speech, while the southern pundits were either silent or panned it. Noted orator and politician, Edward Everett, wrote that the English press viewed the address as "almost universally spoken if as feeble, equivocal, and temporizing. It has evidently disappointed public expectation.... the truth is the president's situation is impossible."

Montgomery Meigs, a Democrat who became quartermaster general of the Union army during the Civil War, wrote to his brother, John, after hearing the address. Prior to the address, he had worried that "some shilly-shally policy would prevail," but afterwards he wrote that Lincoln had "put into every patriotic heart new strength and hope."

The day after his inauguration, March 5, 1861, Lincoln was informed that, unless resupplied, Fort Sumter, a Union garrison in Charleston, South Carolina, would be forced to surrender in six weeks. Lincoln decided to hold the garrison. Confederate gunners in Charleston fired the first shots of the Civil War on April 12, 1861.

Lincoln's attempt to bridge the chasm between the north and south reminds us that we should always try to work toward peaceful resolutions. His steadfast determination to retain hope while upholding the foundations of our country should inspire us to always reach out toward others while keeping our own feet firmly planted on the bedrock of our nation—the Declaration of Independence and the Constitution.

—JGC

⁂ ⁂ ⁂

In compliance with a custom as old as the government itself, I appear before you to address you briefly, and to take, in your presence, the oath prescribed by the Constitution of the United States, to be taken by the President "before he enters on the execution of his office."

I do not consider it necessary, at present, for me to discuss those matters of administration about which there is no special anxiety, or excitement.

Apprehension seems to exist among the people of the Southern States, that by the accession of a Republican Administration, their property, and their peace, and personal security, are to be endangered. There has never been any reasonable cause for such apprehension. Indeed, the most ample evidence to the contrary has all the while existed, and been open to their inspection. It is found in nearly all the published speeches of him who now addresses you. I do but quote from one of those speeches when I declare that "I have no purpose, directly or indirectly, to interfere with the institution of slavery in the States where it exists. I believe I have no lawful right to do so, and I have no inclination to do so." Those who nominated and elected me did so with full knowledge that I had made this, and many similar declarations, and had never recanted them. And more than this, they placed in the platform, for my acceptance, and as a law to themselves, and to me, the clear and emphatic resolution which I now read:

"Resolved, That the maintenance inviolate of the rights of the States, and especially the right of each State to order and control its own domestic institutions according to its own judgment exclusively, is essential to that balance of power on which the perfection and endurance of our political fabric depend; and we denounce the lawless invasion by armed force of the soil of any State or Territory, no matter under what pretext, as among the gravest of crimes."

I now reiterate these sentiments: and in doing so, I only press upon the public attention the most conclusive evidence of which the case is susceptible, that the property, peace and security of no section are to be in anywise endangered by the now incoming Administration. I add too, that all the protection which, consistently with the Constitution and the laws, can be given, will be cheerfully given to all the States when lawfully demanded, for whatever cause—as cheerfully to one section, as to another.

There is much controversy about the delivering up of fugitives from service or labor. The clause I now read is as plainly written in the Constitution as any other of its provisions:

"No person held to service or labor in one State, under the laws thereof, escaping into another, shall, in consequence of any law or regulation therein, be discharged from such service or labor, but shall be delivered up on claim of the party to whom such service or labor may be due."

It is scarcely questioned that this provision was intended by those who made it, for the reclaiming of what we call fugitive slaves; and the intention of the law-giver is the law. All members of Congress swear their support to the whole Constitution—to this provision as much as to any other. To the proposition, then, that slaves whose cases come within the terms of this clause, "shall be delivered up," their oaths are unanimous. Now, if they would make the effort in good temper, could they not, with nearly equal unanimity, frame and pass a law, by means of which to keep good that unanimous oath?

There is some difference of opinion whether this clause should be enforced by national or by state authority; but surely that difference is not a very mate-rial one. If the slave is to be surrendered, it can be of but little consequence to him, or to others, by which authority it is done. And should any one, in any case, be content that his oath shall go unkept, on a merely unsubstantial controversy as to how it shall be kept?

Again, in any law upon this subject, ought not all the safeguards of liberty known in civilized and humane jurisprudence to be introduced, so that a free man be not, in any case, surrendered as a slave? And might it not be well, at the same time, to provide by law for the enforcement of that clause in the Consti-tution which guarranties that "The citizens of each State shall be entitled to all previleges [sic] and immunities of citizens in the several States"?

I take the official oath to-day, with no mental reservations, and with no pur-pose to construe the Constitution or laws, by any hypercritical rules. And while I do not choose now to specify particular acts of Congress as proper to be enforced, I do suggest, that it will be much safer for all, both in official and pri-vate stations, to conform to, and abide by, all those acts which stand unrepealed, than to violate any of them, trusting to find impunity in having them held to be unconstitutional.

It is seventy-two years since the first inauguration of a President under our national Constitution. During that period fifteen different and greatly distinguished citizens, have, in succession, administered the executive branch of the government. They have conducted it through many perils; and, generally, with great success. Yet, with all this scope for precedent, I now enter upon the same task for the brief constitutional term of four years, under great and peculiar difficulty. A disruption of the Federal Union heretofore only menaced, is now formidably attempted.

I hold, that in contemplation of universal law, and of the Constitution, the Union of these States is perpetual. Perpetuity is implied, if not expressed, in the fundamental law of all national governments. It is safe to assert that no government proper, ever had a provision in its organic law for its own termination. Continue to execute all the express provisions of our national Constitution, and the Union will endure forever—it being impossible to destroy it, except by some action not provided for in the instrument itself.

Again, if the United States be not a government proper, but an association of States in the nature of contract merely, can it, as a contract, be peaceably unmade, by less than all the parties who made it? One party to a contract may violate it—break it, so to speak; but does it not require all to lawfully rescind it?

Descending from these general principles, we find the proposition that, in legal contemplation, the Union is perpetual, confirmed by the history of the Union itself. The Union is much older than the Constitution. It was formed in fact, by the Articles of Association in 1774. It was matured and continued by the Declaration of Independence in 1776. It was further matured and the faith of all the then thirteen States expressly plighted and engaged that it should be perpetual, by the Articles of Confederation in 1778. And finally, in 1787, one of the declared objects for ordaining and establishing the Constitution, was "to form a more perfect union."

But if destruction of the Union, by one, or by a part only, of the States, be lawfully possible, the Union is less perfect than before the Constitution, having lost the vital element of perpetuity—

It follows from these views that no State, upon its own mere motion, can lawfully get out of the Union,—that resolves and ordinances to that effect are legally revolutionary, according to circumstances.

I therefore consider that, in view of the constitution and the laws, the Union is unbroken; and, to the extent of my ability, I shall take care, as the constitution itself expressly enjoins upon me, that the laws of the Union be faithfully executed in all the states. Doing this I deem to be only a simple duty on my part; and I shall perform it, so far as practicable, unless my rightful masters, the American people, shall withhold the requisite means, or, in some authoritative manner, direct the contrary. I trust this will not be regarded as a menace, but only as the declared purpose of the Union that it will constitutionally defend, and maintain itself—

In doing this there needs to be no bloodshed or violence; and there shall be none, unless it be forced upon the national authority. The power confided to me, will be used to hold, occupy, and possess the property, and places belonging to the government, and to collect the duties and imposts; but beyond what may be necessary for these objects, there will be no invasion—no using of force against, or among the people anywhere—Where hostility to the United States, in any interior locality, shall be so great and so universal, as to prevent competent resident citizens from holding the Federal offices, there will be no attempt to force obnoxious strangers among the people for that object. While the strict legal right may exist in the government to enforce the exercise of these offices, the attempt to do so would be so irritating, and so nearly impracticable with all, that I deem it better to forego, for the time, the uses of such offices.

The mails, unless repelled, will continue to be furnished in all parts of the Union. So far as possible, the people everywhere shall have that sense of perfect security which is most favorable to calm thought and reflection. The course here indicated will be followed, unless current events, and experience, shall show a modification, or change, to be proper; and in every case and exigency, my best discretion will be exercised, according to circumstances actually existing, and with a view and a hope of a peaceful solution of the national troubles, and the restoration of fraternal sympathies and, affections.

That there are persons in one section, or another who seek to destroy the Union at all events, and are glad of any pretext to do it, I will neither affirm or deny; but if there be such, I need address no word to them. To those, however, who really love the Union, may I not speak?

Before entering upon so grave a matter as the destruction of our national fabric, with all its benefits, it's memories, and it's hopes, would it not be wise to ascertain precisely why we do it? Will you hazard so desperate a step, while there is any possibility that any portion of the ills you fly from, have no real existence? Will you, while the certain ills you fly to, are greater than all the real ones you fly from? Will you risk the commission of so fearful a mistake?

All profess to be content in the Union, if all constitutional rights can be maintained. Is it true, then, that any right, plainly written in the Constitution, has been denied? I think not. Happily the human mind is so constituted, that no party can reach to the audacity of doing this. Think, if you can, of a single instance in which a plainly written provision of the Constitution has ever been denied. If, by the mere force of numbers, a majority should deprive a minority of any clearly written constitutional right, it might, in a moral point of view, justify revolution—certainly would, if such right were a vital one. But such is not our case. All the vital rights of minorities, and of individuals, are so plainly assured to them, by affirmations and negations guaranties [sic] and prohibitions, in the Constitution, that controversies never arise concerning them. But no organic law can ever be framed with a provision specifically applicable to every question which may occur in practical administration. No foresight can anticipate, nor any document of reasonable length contain express provisions for all possible questions. Shall fugitives from labor be surrendered by national or by State authority? The Constitution does not expressly say. May Congress prohibit slavery in the territories? The Constitution does not expressly say. Must Congress protect slavery in the territories? The Constitution does not expressly say.

From questions of this class spring all our constitutional controversies, and we divide upon them into majorities and minorities. If the minority will not acquiesce, the majority must, or the government must cease. There is no other alternative; for continuing the government, is acquiescence on one side or the other. If a minority, in such case, will secede rather than acquiesce, they make a precedent which, in turn, will divide and ruin them; for a minority of their own number will secede from them, whenever a majority refuses to be controlled by such minority. For instance, why may not any portion of a new confederacy, a year or two hence, arbitrarily secede again, precisely as portions of the present Union now claim to secede from it. All who cherish disunion sentiments are now being educated to the exact temper of doing this. Is there such perfect identity of interests among the States to compose a new Union, as to produce harmony only, and prevent renewed secession?

Plainly, the central idea of secession, is the essence of anarchy. A majority, held in restraint by constitutional checks, and limitations, and always changing easily, with deliberate changes of popular opinions and sentiments, is the only true sovereign of a free people. Whoever rejects it, does, of necessity, fly to anarchy or to despotism. Unanimity is impossible; the rule of a minority, as a permanent arrangement, is wholly inadmissible [sic]; so that, rejecting the majority principle, anarchy, or despotism in some form, is all that is left.

I do not forget the position assumed by some, that constitutional questions are to be decided by the Supreme Court; nor do I deny that such decisions must be binding in any case, upon the parties to a suit, as to the object of that suit, while they are also entitled to a very high respect and consideration, in all parallel [sic] cases, by all other departments of the government—And while it is obviously possible that such decision may be erroneous in any given case, still the evil effect following it, being limited to that particular case, with the chance that it may be over-ruled, and never become a precedent for other cases, can better be borne than could the evils of a different practice. At the same time the candid citizen must confess, that if the policy of the government, upon vital questions, affecting the whole people, is to be irrevocably fixed by decisions of the Supreme Court, the instant they are made, in ordinary litigation between parties, in personal actions, the people will have ceased, to be their own rulers, having, to that extent, practically resigned their government, into the hands of that eminent tribunal. Nor is there, in this view, any assault upon the Court, or the judges—It is a duty, from which they may not shrink, to decide cases properly brought before them; and it is no fault of theirs, if others seek to turn their decisions to political purposes.

One section of our country believes slavery is right, and ought to be extended, while the other believes it is wrong, and ought not to be extended. This is the only substantial dispute. The fugitive slave clause of the Constitution, and the law for the suppression of the foreign slave trade, are each as well enforced, perhaps as any law can ever be in a community where the moral sense of the people imperfectly supports the law itself. The great body of the people abide by the dry legal obligation in both cases, and a few break over in each This, I think, cannot be perfectly cured; and it would be worse in both cases after the separation of the sections, than before. The foreign slave trade, now imperfectly suppressed, would be ultimately revived without restriction, in one section; while fugitive slaves, now only partially surrendered, would not be surrendered at all, by the other.

Physically speaking, we cannot separate. We cannot remove our respective sections from each other, nor build an impassable wall between them. A husband and wife may be divorced, and go out of the presence, and beyond the reach of each other; but the different parts of our country cannot do this. They cannot but remain face to face; and intercourse, either amicable or hostile, must continue between them. Is it possible then to make that intercourse more advantageous, or more satisfactory, after separation than before? Can aliens make treaties easier than friends can make laws? Can treaties be more faithfully enforced between aliens, than laws can among friends? Suppose you go to war, you cannot fight always; and when, after much loss on both sides, and no gain on either, you cease fighting, the identical old questions, as to terms of intercourse, are again upon you.

This country, with its institutions, belongs to the people who inhabit it. Whenever they shall grow weary of the existing government, they can exercise their constitutional right of amending it, or their revolutionary right to dismember, or overthrow [it.] I can not be ignorant of the fact that many worthy, and patriotic citizens are desirous of having the national constitution amended.

While I make no recommendation of amendments, I fully recognize the rightful authority of the people over the whole subject, to be exercised in either of the modes prescribed in the instrument itself; and I should, under existing circumstances, favor, rather than oppose, a fair oppertunity [sic] being afforded the people to act upon it—

I will venture to add that, to me, the Convention mode seems preferable, in that it allows amendments to originate with the people themselves, instead of only permitting them to take, or reject, propositions, originated by others, not especially chosen for the purpose, and which might not be precisely such, as they would wish to either accept or refuse.48 I understand a proposed amendment to the constitution which amendment, however, I have not seen, has passed Congress, to the effect that the federal government, shall never interfere with the domestic institutions of the States, including that of persons held to service—To avoid misconstruction of what I have said, I depart from my purpose not to speak of particular amendments, so far as to say that, holding such a provision to now be implied Constitutional law, I have no objection to it's being made express, and irrevocable—

The Chief Magistrate derives all his authority from the people, and they have conferred none upon him to fix terms for the separation of the States. The people themselves can do this also if they choose; but the executive, as such, has nothing to do with it. His duty is to administer the present government, as it came to his hands, and to transmit it, unimpaired by him, to his successor.

Why should there not be a patient confidence in the ultimate justice of the people? Is there any better, or equal hope, in the world? In our present differences, is either party without faith of being in the right? If the Almighty Ruler of nations, with his eternal truth and justice, be on your side of the North, or on yours of the South, that truth, and that justice, will surely prevail, by the judgment of this great tribunal, the American people.

By the frame of the government under which we live, this same people have wisely given their public servants but little power for mischief: and have, with equal wisdom, provided for the return of that little to their own hands at very short intervals.

While the people retain their virtue, and vigilance [sic], no administration, by any extreme of wickedness or folly, can very seriously injure the government, in the short space of four years.

My countrymen, one and all, think calmly and well, upon this whole subject. Nothing valuable can be lost by taking time. If there be an object to hurry any of you, in hot haste, to a step which you would never take deliberately, that object will be frustrated by taking time; but no good object can be frustrated by it. Such of you as are now dissatisfied, still have the old Constitution unimpaired, and, on the sensitive point, the laws of your own framing under it; while the new administration will have no immediate power, if it would, to change either. If it were admitted that you who are dissatisfied, hold the right side in the dispute, there still is no single good reason for precipitate action. Intelligence, patriotism, Christianity, and a firm reliance on Him, who has never yet forsaken this favored land, are still competent to adjust, in the best way, all our present difficulty.

In your hands, my dissatisfied fellow countrymen, and not in mine, is the momentous issue of civil war. The government will not assail you. You can have no conflict, without being yourselves the aggressors. You have no oath registered in Heaven to destroy the government, while I shall have the most solemn one to "preserve, protect and defend" it.

I am loath to close. We are not enemies, but friends—We must not be enemies. Though passion may have strained, it must not break our bonds of affection. The mystic chords of memory s, streching from every battlefield, and patriot grave, to every living heart and hearthstone, all over this broad land, will yet swell the chorus of the Union, when again touched, as surely they will be, by the better angels of our nature.

XII

"And henceforth shall be free"

EMANCIPATION PROCLAMATION
(1862)

ABRAHAM LINCOLN, WHILE OPPOSING SLAVERY PERSONALLY, DID NOT support emancipation at the beginning of the Civil War. He did not mention it in his first inaugural address, nor in his July 4, 1861 address to Congress. Lincoln's focus was saving the Union through the enforcement of the Constitution and laws.

His attitude began to change through the spring and summer of 1862. As the war grew more bloody and bitter, support for bolder steps grew stronger.

He first read a draft of the proclamation to his cabinet on July 22, 1862. He specified that he was not asking approval, but providing information on what might be coming.

Secretary of War Edwin Stanton, not wanting the proclamation to appear as a move of desperation, freeing slaves in the hope they would rebel, urged

Lincoln to wait until Union forces had achieved a significant victory before announcing the emancipation.

Lincoln decided to wait.

On August 19 of that year, Horace Greeley, (the editor of the *New York Tribune*) published an open letter to Lincoln championing emancipation and implying a lack of leadership on the president's part.

Lincoln, aware of the importance of public sentiment, wrote a response to Greeley's letter, trying to address Greeley's leadership complaints. Lincoln noted in his letter that his main goal was to save the union, not to defend nor to abolish slavery, saying of his policy that, "I would save the Union. I would save it the shortest way under the Constitution." He concluded, "I have stated my purpose according to my official duty, and I intend no modification of my oft-expressed personal wish that all men everywhere could be free."

What Greeley and the general public did not know was that, even as Lincoln wrote that response, he already possessed a draft of the proclamation.

The Union victory Lincoln was waiting for came on September 18, with the Battle of Antietam. Four days later, Lincoln called his Cabinet together and provided them with his reason for issuing the proclamation at that time.

Diaries of two of the Cabinet members, Salmon Chase and Gideon Welles, provide corroborating narratives of Lincoln stating that he had promised God that if the rebels were driven from Maryland, he would issue the Emancipation Proclamation. Welles recorded Lincoln's conclusion, "God has decided this question in favor of the slaves."

On September 22, 1862, Lincoln released the Emancipation Proclamation with an effective date of January 1, 1863. This changed the focus of the Civil War from restoring the union to creating a new union free of slavery.

Lincoln's second annual message, delivered to Congress on December 1, 1862, communicated this transition and its importance to the American people. "The dogmas of the quiet past are inadequate to the stormy present," he said. "The occasion is piled high with difficulty, and we must rise with the occasion. As our case is new, so we must think anew, and act anew."

Thinking anew meant contemplating a future in which slaves were emancipated.

"In giving freedom to the slave, we assure freedom to the free—honorable alike in what we give and what we preserve," noted Lincoln. "We shall nobly save, or meanly lose, the last best, hope of earth."

The Emancipation Proclamation freed the slaves in states that were "in rebellion," meaning that they were not part of the Union when it was signed. Slavery was not outlawed throughout the nation until the passage of the 13th Amendment in January 1865.

The Emancipation Proclamation was an extraordinary step in freeing people and ending a terrible institution. It earned Lincoln the title "the Great Emancipator."

—JGC

❧ ❧ ❧

By the president of the United States of America:

A Proclamation.

Whereas, on the twenty-second day of September, in the year of our Lord one thousand eight hundred and sixty-two, a proclamation was issued by the President of the United States, containing, among other things, the following, to wit:

"That on the first day of January, in the year of our Lord one thousand eight hundred and sixty-three, all persons held as slaves within any State or designated part of a State, the people whereof shall then be in rebellion against the United States, shall be then, thenceforward, and forever free; and the Executive Government of the United States, including the military and naval authority thereof, will recognize and maintain the freedom of such persons, and will do no act or acts to repress such persons, or any of them, in any efforts they may make for their actual freedom.

"That the Executive will, on the first day of January aforesaid, by proclamation, designate the States and parts of States, if any, in which the people thereof, respectively, shall then be in rebellion against the United States; and the fact that any State, or the people thereof, shall on that day be, in good faith, represented in the Congress of the United States by members chosen thereto at elections wherein a majority of the qualified voters of such State shall have participated, shall, in the absence of strong countervailing testimony, be deemed conclusive evidence that such State, and the people thereof, are not then in rebellion against the United States.

"Now, therefore I, Abraham Lincoln, president of the United States, by virtue of the power in me vested as Commander-in-Chief, of the Army and Navy of the United States in time of actual armed rebellion against the authority and government of the United States, and as a fit and necessary war measure for suppressing said rebellion, do, on this first day of January, in the year of our Lord one thousand eight hundred and sixty-three, and in accordance with my purpose so to do publicly proclaimed for the full period of one hundred days, from the day first above mentioned, order and designate as the States and parts of States wherein the people thereof respectively, are this day in rebellion against the United States, the following, to wit:

"Arkansas, Texas, Louisiana, (except the Parishes of St. Bernard, Plaquemines, Jefferson, St. John, St. Charles, St. James Ascension, Assumption, Terrebonne, Lafourche, St. Mary, St. Martin, and Orleans, including the City of New Orleans) Mississippi, Alabama, Florida, Georgia, South Carolina, North Carolina, and Virginia, (except the forty-eight counties designated as West Virginia, and also the counties of Berkley, Accomac, Northampton, Elizabeth City, York, Princess Ann, and Norfolk, including the cities of Norfolk and Portsmouth[)], and which excepted parts, are for the present, left precisely as if this proclamation were not issued.

"And by virtue of the power, and for the purpose aforesaid, I do order and declare that all persons held as slaves within said designated States, and parts of States, are, and henceforward shall be free; and that the Executive government of the United States, including the military and naval authorities thereof, will recognize and maintain the freedom of said persons.

"And I hereby enjoin upon the people so declared to be free to abstain from all violence, unless in necessary self-defence; and I recommend to them that, in all cases when allowed, they labor faithfully for reasonable wages.

"And I further declare and make known, that such persons of suitable condition, will be received into the armed service of the United States to garrison forts, positions, stations, and other places, and to man vessels of all sorts in said service.

"And upon this act, sincerely believed to be an act of justice, warranted by the Constitution, upon military necessity, I invoke the considerate judgment of mankind, and the gracious favor of Almighty God.

"In witness whereof, I have hereunto set my hand and caused the seal of the United States to be affixed.

"Done at the City of Washington, this first day of January, in the year of our Lord one thousand eight hundred and sixty three, and of the Independence of the United States of America the eighty-seventh."

By the president: ABRAHAM LINCOLN

WILLIAM H. SEWARD, Secretary of State.

XIII

"Engaged in a great civil war"

ABRAHAM LINCOLN'S ADDRESS AT GETTYSBURG, PENNSYLVANIA (1863)

THE FIRST SHOT IN THE BATTLE OF GETTYSBURG WAS FIRED BY UNION soldier Lieutenant Marcellus Jones of the 8th Illinois Volunteer Cavalry at 7:30 a.m. on July 1, 1863. Neither side had planned on fighting at Gettysburg, but the battle broke out when they stumbled upon each other.

More than 170,000 soldiers participated in the three-day battle. At the end of the fighting, there were nearly 50,000 American casualties. Almost 8,000 of them lay dead. It was the biggest single battle of the Civil War. While it did not end the war, it was the decisive Union victory that made the end apparent.

By the evening of July 3, the Union army had driven back the Confederate soldiers. Confederate General Robert E. Lee had pulled his troops back to Seminary Ridge. General Gordon Meade issued a declaration of congratulations on July 4, noting "the commanding general looks to the army for greater efforts to drive from our soil every vestige of the presence of the invader."

Meade wanted to drive out the rebels; Lincoln wanted his army to destroy the rebellion. This difference in approach would lead Lincoln to place General Ulysses S. Grant over Meade in March 1864.

In Washington on July 4, Lincoln announced the costly Union victory at Gettysburg with deep gratitude, "He whose will, not ours, should ever be done, be everywhere remembered and reverenced with profoundest gratitude," he said.

A memorial service for the battle, and dedication for the Soldiers' National Cemetery at Gettysburg, was planned by David Wills, an attorney who had championed the idea of a National Soldiers' Cemetery. In addition to acting as an agent of the State of Pennsylvania to purchase the land, Wills planned the dedication ceremony to include the nationally renowned orator, Edward Everett, a former senator from Massachusetts and governor. The ceremony was pushed back to November 19, as Everett required more than a month to prepare.

Almost as an afterthought, on November 2, Wills invited President Lincoln to speak briefly at the November 19 event. He accepted.

The event was held outdoors, and over 15,000 people attended.

Everett spoke for more than two hours.

Once Everett was finished, Lincoln rose and delivered his address in a few minutes. His talk was so short that the photographer was still setting up his camera when Lincoln sat down.

Everett wrote a note to Lincoln afterwards, recognizing the value of Lincoln's address, "I should be glad, if I could flatter myself that I came as near to the central idea of the occasion in two hours, as you did in two minutes."

Never once does Lincoln use "I" or "me." In 278 words, he takes his audience from the past to the present, then provides a glimpse into the future of our nation and the role of its citizens in its development. He reminds us that, as the beneficiaries of others' sacrifices, our job is to ensure their sacrifice will be remembered through our actions. "That we here highly resolve that these dead shall not have died in vain—that this nation, under God, shall have a new birth of freedom."

The *Chicago Times* panned the speech, writing, "The cheek of every American must tingle with shame as he reads the silly, flat and dishwatery utterances of the man who has to be pointed out to intelligent foreigners as the President of the United States." The *Springfield Republican* and *Chicago Tribune* summed up the effect quite well, "Half a century hence, to have lived in this age will be fame. To have served it as well as Lincoln will be immortality."

Lincoln's Gettysburg address is historic, both for the occasion of its delivery, and for the reach of its impact. Inscribed on the wall inside the Lincoln Memorial in Washington, D.C., it reminds us that our job is to ensure those before us have not died in vain but that "that government of the people, by the people, for the people, shall not perish from the earth."

—JGC

〰 〰 〰

Four score and seven years ago our fathers brought forth on this continent, a new nation, conceived in Liberty, and dedicated to the proposition that all men are created equal.

Now we are engaged in a great civil war, testing whether that nation, or any nation so conceived and so dedicated, can long endure. We are met on a great battle field of that war. We have come to dedicate a portion of that field, as a final resting place for those who here gave their lives that that nation might live. It is altogether fitting and proper that we should do this.

But, in a larger sense, we can not dedicate—we can not consecrate—we can not hallow—this ground. The brave men, living and dead, who struggled here, have consecrated it, far above our poor power to add or detract. The world will little note, nor long remember what we say here, but it can never forget what they did here. It is for us the living, rather, to be dedicated here to the unfinished work which they who fought here have thus far so nobly advanced. It is rather for us to be here dedicated to the great task remaining before us—that from these honored dead we take increased devotion to that cause for which they gave the last full measure of devotion—that we here highly resolve that these dead shall not have died in vain—that this nation, under God, shall have a new birth of freedom—and that government of the people, by the people, for the people, shall not perish from the earth.

XIV

"The will of God prevails"

ABRAHAM LINCOLN'S
SECOND INAUGURAL ADDRESS
(1865)

IN THE FALL OF 1864, LINCOLN WROTE A PERSONAL NOTE REGARDING
November's election and his possible loss. "It will be my duty to so cooperate with the president-elect as to save the Union between the election and the
inauguration; as he will have secured his election on such ground that he cannot possibly save it afterwards."

The Democrats nominated George B. McClellan, who had been one of Lincoln's top generals early in the war. While McClellan ran on the platform of
peace, Lincoln's slogan was "No Peace without Victory." As McClellan was
promoting peace, General William T. Sherman was marching to, and then
through, the South. News that Atlanta had fallen to Union forces on September 3, 1864 gave Lincoln's campaign a boost. These military victories reinforced
the belief that the rebels could be beaten, and the Union saved.

Lincoln had shared that belief during his travels and through speeches and letters printed in newspapers. The public understood that Lincoln cherished the Union, and believed he could once again unite the country. As Ronald White, Jr., wrote in his biography of Lincoln, "They believe in him."

On November 8, 1864, Lincoln won again—this time with 55 percent of the popular vote and 91 percent of the Electoral College. Between his election and the inauguration, Congress passed the 13th Amendment, outlawing slavery. The promise of the emancipation was realized for all people in the union.

Lincoln's first inaugural had been laid out to reflect his rational and lawyerly approach, which was intended to calm the citizenry and provide insight into Lincoln's beliefs and positions.

The second inaugural was different. Lincoln was serving as commander-in-chief in the midst of a Civil War. He had lost his son, Willie, to typhoid fever, while he was president. During his first term, he had become more determined to save the Union, and more faithful to God. He was a different man with a different message than the person elected in a peaceful America four years earlier.

Midway through his first term, in September 1862, Lincoln wrote the following private note:

> The will of God prevails. In great contests each party claims to act in accordance with the will of God. Both may be, and one must be wrong. God cannot be for and against the same thing at the same time. In the present civil war it is quite possible that God's purpose is something different from the purpose of either party—and yet the human instrumentalities, working just as they do, are for the best adaptation to effect his purpose.

This sentiment, that he was an instrument in a larger contest to be determined by God, is echoed throughout his second inaugural address.

Lincoln delivered his speech on March 4, 1865, on the east side of the Capitol. The new iron dome that had been half-complete at the time of the first inaugural, with a crane sticking out of the top, had been finished. The Union army had been victorious in recent battles and the war's final outcome was all but determined. Slaves had been freed, and the Capitol was surrounded by the biggest crowd to date, with half of them reported as "persons of color."

The morning was overcast with light rain. After Lincoln was introduced and welcomed with thunderous applause, the clouds broke and the sun came out as he began to speak.

The speech drew praises from all quarters. Frederick Douglass, a free black man, told Lincoln, "Mr. Lincoln, that was a sacred effort."

A few weeks later, on April 14, 1865, Lincoln was shot. He died the next morning.

Lincoln's second inaugural address, so different from his first, reveals the character every American must maintain. While peace is the highest goal, avoiding war might cost too much when our nation's very ideals and values are under attack. Lincoln stood up for the Union and ultimately paid with his life. He has gone down in history as one of America's most devoted sons.

—JGC

❧ ❧ ❧

Fellow Countrymen.

At this second appearing to take the oath of the presidential office, there is less occasion for an extended address than there was at the first. Then a statement, somewhat in detail, of a course to be pursued, seemed fitting and proper. Now, at the expiration of four years, during which public declarations have been constantly called forth on every point and phase of the great contest which still absorbs the attention, and engrosses the energies of the nation, little that is new could be presented. The progress of our arms, upon which all else chiefly depends, is as well known to the public as to myself; and it is, I trust, reasonably satisfactory and encouraging to all. With high hope for the future, no prediction in regard to it is ventured.

On the occasion corresponding to this four years ago, all thoughts were anxiously directed to an impending civil-war. All dreaded it—all sought to avert it.

While the inaugural address was being delivered from this place, devoted alto-gether to *saving* the Union without war, insurgent agents were in the city seeking to *destroy* it without war—seeking to dissolve the Union, and divide effects, by negotiation. Both parties deprecated war; but one of them would *make* war rather than let the nation survive; and the other would *accept* war rather than let it perish. And the war came.

One eighth of the whole population were colored slaves, not distributed generally over the Union, but localized in the Southern part of it. These slaves constituted a peculiar and powerful interest. All knew that this interest was, somehow, the cause of the war. To strengthen, perpetuate, and extend this inter-est was the object for which the insurgents would rend the Union, even by war; while the government claimed no right to do more than to restrict the territo-rial enlargement of it. Neither party expected for the war, the magnitude, or the duration, which it has already attained. Neither anticipated that the *cause* of the conflict might cease with, or even before, the conflict itself should cease. Each looked for an easier triumph, and a result less fundamental and astound-ing. Both read the same Bible, and pray to the same God; and each invokes His aid against the other. It may seem strange that any men should dare to ask a just God's assistance in wringing their bread from the sweat of other men's faces; but let us judge not that we be not judged. The prayers of both could not be answered; that of neither has been answered fully. The Almighty has His own purposes. "Woe unto the world because of offences! for it must needs be that offences come; but woe to that man by whom the offence cometh!" If we shall suppose that American Slavery is one of those offences which, in the prov-idence of God, must needs come, but which, having continued through His appointed time, He now wills to remove, and that He gives to both North and South, this terrible war, as the woe due to those by whom the offence came, shall we discern therein any departure from those divine attributes which the believers in a Living God always ascribe to Him? Fondly do we hope—fer-vently do we pray—that this mighty scourge of war may speedily pass away. Yet, if God wills that it continue, until all the wealth piled by the bond-man's two hundred and fifty years of unrequited toil shall be sunk, and until every drop of blood drawn with the lash, shall be paid by another drawn with the sword, as was said three thousand years ago, so still it must be said "the judgments of the Lord, are true and righteous altogether."

With malice toward none; with charity for all; with firmness in the right, as God gives us to see the right, let us strive on to finish the work we are in; to bind up the nation's wounds; to care for him who shall have borne the battle, and for his widow, and his orphan—to do all which may achieve and cherish a just, and a lasting peace, among ourselves, and with all nations.

XV

"Happy is the nation that has a glorious history"

THEODORE ROOSEVELT'S
THE STRENUOUS LIFE
(1899)

ORN IN NEW YORK ON THE EVE OF THE CIVIL WAR IN 1858, ROOSEVELT grew up in an era of profound change. When he was six, after Lincoln was assassinated, he watched the funeral procession from a window on the second floor of his home in New York.

During his childhood, the Union emerged victorious from the Civil War. Slavery was outlawed. The South began to rebuild and rejoin the Union.

Roosevelt's mother, Mittie Bulloch Roosevelt, was diagnosed with neurasthenia, a then-common condition that included irritability, inability to focus, anxiety, and listlessness. She spent much of her time traveling to spas where she convalesced. Raised in the South, she told her children stories about their great-grandfather, General Daniel Stewart, who served in the Revolutionary War, and their grandfather Major James Bulloch, who fought in the Texas War of Independence.

Roosevelt's father, Thee, was a prosperous businessman and committed philanthropist. He helped found the American Museum of Natural History on New York's Central Park West and established the Metropolitan Museum of Art across the park on Fifth Avenue. Thee believed in muscular Christianity, a philosophy developed during the Victorian era, holding that physical strength and courage is part of being a good Christian. Despite this, Thee did not serve in the military during the Civil War, though he was often gone for long periods of time working on behalf of soldiers.

Roosevelt suffered from severe asthma and was often quite sick as a child. His father would take him out for rides in the family carriage during the nights when the attacks were the worst. When Roosevelt was about thirteen years old, his father told him, "You have the mind but you have not the body. You must make your body." His father had a gymnasium built in their home for the children to use. Though frail, Roosevelt lifted weights and exercised to build strength and stamina.

Roosevelt married twice. His first wife, Alice, died when he was twenty-five years old. Consumed with grief, he left his infant daughter Alice in the care of his sister and departed for the Dakota Territory. There, he lived the rugged outdoor life, learning to rope, ride, and survive in the wilderness. Roosevelt came to believe that the strong individualism of Americans was due in part to the western frontier. He also believed that, without this western wilderness experience, he would never have become president.

In the heat of the Spanish-American War, Roosevelt and his mounted "Rough Riders" led a charge against Spanish troops on San Juan and Kettle Hills in Cuba. The July 1, 1898 battle proved to be a decisive boost for the American cause, and led, after a few days, to the U.S. victory over Spain.

Less than a year later, Roosevelt gave a historic speech at the Hamilton Club in Chicago, Illinois, in the spring of 1899 entitled, "The Strenuous Life."

This speech encapsulated his belief in working hard and overcoming adversity. He correlated a healthy individual to a healthy nation. "In the last analysis a healthy state can exist only when the men and women who make it up can lead clean, vigorous, healthy lives; when the children are so trained that they shall endeavor not to shirk difficulties, but to overcome them."

Roosevelt challenged individuals to exist "not for the life of ease but for the life of strenuous endeavor." He lived this idea out in his own life. While he was sickly as a child, his diligence in exercise allowed him to overcome his physical weaknesses. As an adult he was often hunting and riding, spending a large portion of his time in the outdoors.

Just a few years prior to Roosevelt's "The Strenuous Life" speech, Booker T. Washington, a leading black educator, speaker and political figure, spoke to the same club, noting, "The greatest injury that slavery did my people was to deprive them of that great executive power, that sense of self-dependence which are the glory and the distinction of the Anglo-Saxon race. For 250 years we were taught to depend on someone else for food, clothing, shelter and for every move in life."

Theodore Roosevelt, who came to believe that a full life was one of tests, challenges, and growth, was elected vice president on the Republican ticket under William McKinley in 1900. He became president when McKinley was assassinated in 1901.

More than a century later, his quest for a strenuous life appears to be on the wane in America. Rather than embracing the strenuous life, we appear to be on a quest for the easy life.

Today, we might argue that the injustice Washington noted regarding blacks has spread to children of all races. We have moved from an interested to a self-involved society. Instead of failure, learning the lessons of life, and living the strenuous life, we are becoming ever more dependent on someone else.

In reading the words of Theodore Roosevelt, who grew from a frail, sickly child by challenging himself, remaking his body and mind, we should challenge ourselves to live out the doctrine of the strenuous life.

—JGC

❧ ❧ ❧

In speaking to you, men of the greatest city of the West, men of the State which gave to the country Lincoln and Grant, men who preeminently and distinctly embody all that is most American in the American character, I wish to preach, not the doctrine of ignoble ease, but the doctrine of the strenuous life, the life of toil and effort, of labor and strife; to preach that highest form of success which comes, not to the man who desires mere easy peace, but to the man who does not shrink from danger, from hardship, or from bitter toil, and who out of these wins the splendid ultimate triumph.

A life of slothful ease, a life of that peace which springs merely from lack either of desire or of power to strive after great things, is as little worthy of a nation as of an individual. I ask only that what every self-respecting American demands from himself and from his sons shall be demanded of the American nation as a whole. Who among you would teach your boys that ease, that peace, is to be the first consideration in their eyes—to be the ultimate goal after which they strive? You men of Chicago have made this city great, you men of Illinois have done your share, and more than your share, in making America great, because you neither preach nor practice such a doctrine. You work yourselves, and you bring up your sons to work. If you are rich and are worth your salt, you will teach your sons that though they may have leisure, it is not to be spent in idleness; for wisely used leisure merely means that those who possess it, being free from the necessity of working for their livelihood, are all the more bound to carry on some kind of non-remunerative work in science, in letters, in art, in exploration, in historical research—work of the type we most need in this country, the successful carrying out of which reflects most honor upon the nation. We do not admire the man of timid peace. We admire the man who embodies victorious effort; the man who never wrongs his neighbor, who is prompt to help a friend, but who has those virile qualities necessary to win in the stern strife of actual life. It is hard to fail, but it is worse never to have tried to succeed. In this life we get nothing save by effort. Freedom from effort in the present merely means that there has been some stored up effort in the past. A man can be freed from the necessity of work only by the fact that he or his fathers before him have worked to good purpose. If the freedom thus purchased is used aright, and the man still does actual work, though of a different kind, whether as a writer or a general, whether in the field of politics or in the field of exploration and adventure, he shows he deserves his good fortune. But if he treats this period of freedom from the need of actual labor as a period, not of preparation, but of mere enjoyment, even though perhaps not of vicious enjoyment, he shows that he is simply a cumberer of the earth's surface, and he surely unfits himself to hold his own with his fellows if the need to do so should again arise. A mere life of ease is not in the end a very satisfactory life, and, above all, it is a life which ultimately unfits those who follow it for serious work in the world.

In the last analysis a healthy state can exist only when the men and women who make it up lead clean, vigorous, healthy lives; when the children are so trained that they shall endeavor, not to shirk difficulties, but to overcome them; not to seek ease, but to know how to rest triumph from toil and risk. The man must be glad to do a man's work, to dare and endure and to labor; to keep himself, and to keep those dependent upon him. The woman must be the housewife, the helpmeet of the homemaker, the wise and fearless mother of many healthy children. In one of Daudet's powerful and melancholy books he speaks of "the fear of maternity, the haunting terror of the young wife of the present day." When such words can be truthfully written of a nation, that nation is rotten to the heart's core. When men fear work or fear righteous war, when women fear motherhood, they tremble on the brink of doom; and well it is that they should vanish from the earth, where they are fit subjects for the scorn of all men and women who are themselves strong and brave and high-minded.

As it is with the individual, so it is with the nation. It is a base untruth to say that happy is the nation that has no history. Thrice happy is the nation that has a glorious history. Far better it is to dare mighty things, to win glorious triumphs, even though checkered by failure, than to take rank with those poor spirits who neither enjoy much nor suffer much, because they live in the gray twilight that knows not victory nor defeat. If in 1861 the men who loved the Union had believed that peace was the end of all things, and war and strife the worst of all things, and had acted up to their belief, we would have saved hundreds of thousands of lives, we would have saved hundreds of millions of dollars. Moreover, besides saving all the blood and treasure we then lavished, we would have prevented the heartbreak of many women, the dissolution of many homes, and we would have spared the country those months of gloom and shame when it seemed as if our armies marched only to defeat. We could have avoided all this suffering simply by shrinking from strife. And if we had thus avoided it, we would have shown that we were weaklings, and that we were unfit to stand among the great nations of the earth. Thank God for the iron in the blood of our fathers, the men who upheld the wisdom of Lincoln, and bore sword or rifle in the armies of Grant! Let us, the children of the men who proved themselves equal to the mighty days, let us, the children of the men who carried the great Civil War to a triumphant conclusion, praise the God of our fathers that the ignoble counsels of peace were rejected; that the suffering and loss, the blackness of sorrow and despair, were unflinchingly faced, and the years of strife endured; for in the end the slave was freed, the Union restored, and the mighty American republic placed once more as a helmeted queen among nations.

We of this generation do not have to face a task such as that our fathers faced, but we have our tasks, and woe to us if we fail to perform them! We cannot, if we would, play the part of China, and be content to rot by inches in ignoble ease within our borders, taking no interest in what goes on beyond them, sunk in a scrambling commercialism; heedless of the higher life, the life of aspiration, of toil and risk, busying ourselves only with the wants of our bodies for the day, until suddenly we should find, beyond a shadow of question, what China has already found, that in this world the nation that has trained itself into a career of unwarlike and isolated ease is bound, in the end, to go down before other nations which have not lost the manly and adventurous qualities. If we are to be a really great people, we must strive in good faith to play a great part in the world. We cannot avoid meeting great issues. All that we can determine for ourselves is whether we shall meet them well or ill. In 1898 we could not help being brought face to face with the problem of war with Spain. All we could decide was whether we should shrink like cowards from the contest, or enter into it as beseemed a brave and high-spirited people; and, once in, whether failure or success should crown our banners. So it is now. We cannot avoid the responsibilities that confront us in Hawaii, Cuba, Porto Rico,

[sic] and the Philippines. All we can decide is whether we shall meet them in a way that will redound to the national credit, or whether we shall make of our dealings with these new problems a dark and shameful page in our history. To refuse to deal with them at all merely amounts to dealing with them badly. We have a given problem to solve. If we undertake the solution, there is, of course, always danger that we may not solve it aright; but to refuse to undertake the solution simply renders it certain that we cannot possibly solve it aright. The timid man, the lazy man, the man who distrusts his country, the over-civilized man, who has lost the great fighting, masterful virtues, the ignorant man, and the man of dull mind, whose soul is incapable of feeling the mighty lift that thrills "stern men with empires in their brains"—all these, of course, shrink from seeing the nation undertake its new duties; shrink from seeing us build a navy and an army adequate to our needs; shrink from seeing us do our share of the world's work, by bringing order out of chaos in the great, fair tropic islands from which the valor of our soldiers and sailors has driven the Spanish flag. These are the men who fear the strenuous life, who fear the only national life which is really worth leading. They believe in that cloistered life which saps the hardy virtues in a nation, as it saps them in the individual; or else they are wedded to that base spirit of gain and greed which recognizes in commercialism the be-all and end-all of national life, instead of realizing that, though an indispensable element, it is, after all, but one of the many elements that go to make up true national greatness. No country can long endure if its foundations are not laid deep in the material prosperity which comes from thrift, from business energy and enterprise, from hard, unsparing effort in the fields of industrial activity; but neither was any nation ever yet truly great if it relied upon material prosperity alone. All honor must be paid to the architects of our material prosperity, to the great captains of industry who have built our factories and our railroads, to the strong men who toil for wealth with brain or hand; for great is the debt of the nation to these and their kind. But our debt is yet greater to the men whose highest type is to be found in a statesman like Lincoln, a soldier like Grant. They showed by their lives that they recognized the law of work, the law of strife; they toiled to win a competence for themselves and those

dependent upon them; but they recognized that there were yet other and even loftier duties—duties to the nation and duties to the race.

We cannot sit huddled within our own borders and avow ourselves merely an assemblage of well-to-do hucksters who care nothing for what happens beyond. Such a policy would defeat even its own end; for as the nations grow to have ever wider and wider interests, and are brought into closer and closer contact, if we are to hold our own in the struggle for naval and commercial supremacy, we must build up our power without our own borders. We must build the isthmian canal, and we must grasp the points of vantage which will enable us to have our say in deciding the destiny of the oceans of the East and the West.

So much for the commercial side. From the standpoint of international honor the argument is even stronger. The guns that thundered off Manila and Santiago left us echoes of glory, but they also left us a legacy of duty. If we drove out a medieval tyranny only to make room for savage anarchy, we had better not have begun the task at all. It is worse than idle to say that we have no duty to perform, and can leave to their fates the islands we have conquered. Such a course would be a course of infamy. It would be followed at once by utter chaos in the wretched islands themselves. Some stronger, manlier power would have to step in and do the work, and we would have shown ourselves weaklings, unable to carry to successful completion the labors that great and high-spirited nations are eager to undertake.

The work must be done; we cannot escape our responsibility; and if we are worth our salt, we shall be glad of the chance to do the work—glad of the chance to show ourselves equal to one of the great tasks set modern civilization. But let us not deceive ourselves as to the importance of the task. Let us not be misled by vainglory into underestimating the strain it will put on our powers. Above all, let us, as we value our own self-respect, face the responsibilities with proper seriousness, courage and high resolve. We must demand the highest order of integrity and ability in our public men who are to grapple with these new problems. We must hold to a rigid accountability those public servants who show unfaithfulness to the interests of the nation or inability to rise to the high level of the new demands upon our strength and our resources.

Of course we must remember not to judge any public servant by any one act, and especially should we beware of attacking the men who are merely the occasions and not the causes of disaster. Let me illustrate what I mean by the army and the navy. If twenty years ago we had gone to war, we should have found the navy as absolutely unprepared as the army. At that time our ships could not have encountered with success the fleets of Spain any more than nowadays we can put untrained soldiers, no matter how brave, who are armed with archaic black-powder weapons, against well-drilled regulars armed with the highest type of modern repeating rifle. But in the early eighties the attention of the nation became directed to our naval needs. Congress most wisely made a series of appropriations to build up a new navy, and under a succession of able and patriotic secretaries, of both political parties, the navy was gradually built up, until its material became equal to its splendid personnel, with the result that in the summer of 1898 it leaped to its proper place as one of the most brilliant and formidable fighting navies in the entire world. We rightly pay all honor to the men controlling the navy at the time it won these great deeds, honor to Secretary Long and Admiral Dewey, to the captains who handled the ships in action, to the daring lieutenants who braved death in the smaller craft, and to the heads of bureaus at Washington who saw that the ships were so commanded, so armed, so equipped, so well engined [sic], as to insure the best results. But let us also keep ever in mind that all of this would not have availed if it had not been for the wisdom of the men who during the preceding fifteen years had built up the navy. Keep in mind the secretaries of the navy during those years; keep in mind the senators and congressmen who by their votes gave the money necessary to build and to armor the ships, to construct the great guns, and to train the crews; remember also those who actually did build the ships, the armor, and the guns; and remember the admirals and captains who handled battle-ship, cruiser, and torpedo-boat on the high seas, alone and in squadrons, developing the seamanship, the gunnery, and the power of acting together, which their successors utilized so gloriously at Manila and off Santiago. And, gentlemen, remember the converse, too. Remember that justice has two sides. Be just to those who built up the navy, and, for the sake of the future of the country, keep in mind those who opposed its building up. Read the

Congressional Record. Find out the senators and congressmen who opposed the grants for building the new ships; who opposed the purchase of armor, without which the ships were worthless; who opposed any adequate maintenance for the Navy Department, and strove to cut down the number of men necessary to man our fleets. The men who did these things were one and all working to bring disaster on the country. They have no share in the glory of Manila, in the honor of Santiago. They have no cause to feel proud of the valor of our sea-captains, of the renown of our flag. Their motives may or may not have been good, but their acts were heavily fraught with evil. They did ill for the national honor, and we won in spite of their sinister opposition.

Now, apply all this to our public men of to-day. Our army has never been built up as it should be built up. I shall not discuss with an audience like this the puerile suggestion that a nation of seventy millions of freemen is in danger of losing its liberties from the existence of an army of one hundred thousand men, three fourths of whom will be employed in certain foreign islands, in certain coast fortresses, and on Indian reservations. No man of good sense and stout heart can take such a proposition seriously. If we are such weaklings as the proposition implies, then we are unworthy of freedom in any event. To no body of men in the United States is the country so much indebted as to the splendid officers and enlisted men of the regular army and navy. There is no body from which the country has less to fear, and none of which it should be prouder, none which it should be more anxious to upbuild.

Our army needs complete reorganization—not merely enlarging—and the reorganization can only come as the result of legislation. A proper general staff should be established, and the positions of ordnance, commissary, and quartermaster officers should be filled by detail from the line. Above all, the army must be given the chance to exercise in large bodies. Never again should we see, as we saw in the Spanish war, major-generals in command of divisions who had never before commanded three companies together in the field. Yet, incredible to relate, Congress has shown a queer inability to learn some of the lessons of the war. There were large bodies of men in both branches who opposed the declaration of war, who opposed the ratification of peace, who opposed the upbuilding of the army, and who even opposed the purchase of armor at a reasonable price for the battle-ships and cruisers, thereby putting an absolute stop to the building of any new fighting-ships for the navy. If, during the years to come, any disaster should befall our arms, afloat or ashore, and thereby any shame come to the United States, remember that the blame will lie upon the men whose names appear upon the roll-calls of Congress on the wrong side of these great questions. On them will lie the burden of any loss of our soldiers and sailors, of any dishonor to the flag; and upon you and the people of this country will lie the blame if you do not repudiate, in no unmistakable way, what these men have done. The blame will not rest upon the untrained commander of untried troops, upon the civil officers of a department the organization of which has been left utterly inadequate, or upon the admiral with an insufficient number of ships; but upon the public men who have so lamentably failed in forethought as to refuse to remedy these evils long in advance, and upon the nation that stands behind those public men.

So, at the present hour, no small share of the responsibility for the blood shed in the Philippines, the blood of our brothers, and the blood of their wild and ignorant foes, lies at the thresholds of those who so long delayed the adoption of the treaty of peace, and of those who by their worse than foolish words deliberately invited a savage people to plunge into a war fraught with sure disaster for them—a war, too, in which our own brave men who follow the flag must pay with their blood for the silly, mock humanitarianism of the prattlers who sit at home in peace.

The army and the navy are the sword and the shield which this nation must carry if she is to do her duty among the nations of the earth—if she is not to stand merely as the China of the western hemisphere. Our proper conduct toward the tropic islands we have wrested from Spain is merely the form which our duty has taken at the moment. Of course we are bound to handle the affairs of our own household well. We must see that there is civic honesty, civic cleanliness, civic good sense in our home administration of city, State, and nation. We must strive for honesty in office, for honesty towards the creditors of the nation and of the individual; for the widest freedom of individual initiative where possible, and for the wisest control of individual initiative where it is hostile to the welfare of the many. But because we set our own household in order we are not thereby excused from playing our part in the great affairs of the world. A man's first duty is to his own home, but he is not thereby excused from doing his duty to the State; for if he fails in this second duty it is under the penalty of ceasing to be a freeman. In the same way, while a nation's first duty is within its own borders, it is not thereby absolved from facing its duties in the world as a whole; and if it refuses to do so, it merely forfeits its right to struggle for a place among the peoples that shape the destiny of mankind.

In the West Indies and the Philippines alike we are confronted by most difficult problems. It is cowardly to shrink from solving them in the proper way; for solved they must be, if not by us, then by some stronger and more manful race. If we are too weak, too selfish, or too foolish to solve them, some bolder and abler people must undertake the solution. Personally, I am far too firm a believer in the greatness of my country and the power of my countrymen to admit for one moment that we shall ever be driven to the ignoble alternative.

The problems are different for the different islands. Porto Rico is not large enough to stand alone. We must govern it wisely and well, primarily in the interest of its own people. Cuba is, in my judgment, entitled ultimately to settle for itself whether it shall be an independent state or an integral portion of the mightiest of republics. But until order and stable liberty are secured, we must remain in the island to insure them, and infinite tact, judgment, moderation, and courage must be shown by our military and civil representatives in keeping the island pacified, in relentlessly stamping out brigandage, in protecting all alike, and yet in showing proper recognition to the men who have fought for Cuban liberty. The Philippines offer a yet graver problem. Their population includes half-caste and native Christians, warlike Moslems, and wild pagans. Many of their people are utterly unfit for self-government, and show no signs of becoming fit. Others may in time become fit but at present can only take part in self-government under a wise supervision, at once firm and beneficent. We have driven Spanish tyranny from the islands. If we now let it be replaced by savage anarchy, our work has been for harm and not for good. I have scant patience with those who fear to undertake the task of governing the Philippines, and who openly avow that they do fear to undertake it, or that they shrink from it because of the expense and trouble; but I have even scanter patience with those who make a pretense of humanitarianism to hide and cover their timidity, and who cant about "liberty" and the "consent of the governed," in order to excuse themselves for their unwillingness to play the part of men. Their doctrines, if carried out, would make it incumbent upon us to leave the Apaches of Arizona to work out their own salvation, and to decline to interfere in a single Indian reservation. Their doctrines condemn your forefathers and mine for ever having settled in these United States.

England's rule in India and Egypt has been of great benefit to England, for it has trained up generations of men accustomed to look at the larger and loftier side of public life. It has been of even greater benefit to India and Egypt. And finally, and most of all, it has advanced the cause of civilization. So, if we do our duty aright in the Philippines, we will add to that national renown which is the highest and finest part of national life, will greatly benefit the people of the Philippine Islands, and, above all, we will play our part well in the great work of uplifting mankind. But to do this work, keep ever in mind that we must show in a very high degree the qualities of courage, of honesty, and of good judgment. Resistance must be stamped out. The first and all-important work to be done is to establish the supremacy of our flag. We must put down armed resistance before we can accomplish anything else, and there should be no parleying, no faltering, in dealing with our foe. As for those in our own country who encourage the foe, we can afford contemptuously to disregard them; but it must be remembered that their utterances are not saved from being treasonable merely by the fact that they are despicable.

When once we have put down armed resistance, when once our rule is acknowledged, then an even more difficult task will begin, for then we must see to it that the islands are administered with absolute honesty and with good judgment. If we let the public service of the islands be turned into the prey of the spoils politician, we shall have begun to tread the path which Spain trod to her own destruction. We must send out there only good and able men, chosen for their fitness, and not because of their partisan service, and these men must not only administer impartial justice to the natives and serve their own government with honesty and fidelity, but must show the utmost tact and firmness, remembering that, with such people as those with whom we are to deal, weakness is the greatest of crimes, and that next to weakness comes lack of consideration for their principles and prejudices.

I preach to you, then, my countrymen, that our country calls not for the life of ease but for the life of strenuous endeavor. The twentieth century looms before us big with the fate of many nations. If we stand idly by, if we seek merely swollen, slothful ease and ignoble peace, if we shrink from the hard contests where men must win at hazard of their lives and at the risk of all they hold dear, then the bolder and stronger peoples will pass us by, and will win for themselves the domination of the world. Let us therefore boldly face the life of strife, resolute to do our duty well and manfully; resolute to uphold righteousness by deed and by word, resolute to be both honest and brave, to serve high ideals, yet to use practical methods. Above all, let us shrink from no strife, moral or physical, within or without the nation, provided we are certain that the strife is justified, for it is only through strife, through hard and dangerous endeavor, that we shall ultimately win the goal of true national greatness.

XVI

"The fatherhood of God and the brotherhood of man"

CALVIN COOLIDGE'S
THE INSPIRATION OF THE
DECLARATION OF INDEPENDENCE
(1925)

CALVIN COOLIDGE, AN OFTEN-OVERLOOKED PRESIDENT, DID NOT SERVE during a time of conflict. Historic events did not force him into the American spotlight, nor did he make waves to garner attention. Instead, he provided a steady, stable foundation of American principles, allowing the American People to succeed.

Often referred to as Silent Cal, he was known for quiet strength and minimal fuss. In today's media-frenzied, reality TV show world, he is quickly passed over for someone with more pizzazz, more charisma, more "bling." In a world too focused on celebrity, we would be wise to turn back to fundamentals and reacquaint ourselves with Coolidge and the values that he represents.

Calvin Coolidge was a champion of freedom, liberty, hard work, thrift, economy, and perseverance. He believed that the people, not the government, are the basis for our success as a nation. His belief in people was grounded in his faith in God.

Coolidge became president on August 3, 1923 after President Warren Harding died from a heart attack. Staying at his family's farm in Vermont, Coolidge was awakened a little after midnight and sworn into office at 2:47 a.m. by his father, John Coolidge, a notary public. Immediately afterward, the story goes, Coolidge prayed on his knees and went back to bed.

Calvin Coolidge was born in the small town of Plymouth Notch, Vermont, on July 4, 1872. He graduated from Amherst College in Massachusetts, located 100 miles south of his home, and then became a lawyer in the nearby town of Northampton, Massachusetts in 1897. First serving in the Northampton City Council in 1899, Coolidge steadily worked his way up in politics, successively becoming mayor of Northampton, state representative, state senator, lieutenant governor, and then governor of Massachusetts.

Coolidge first entered into the national spotlight in 1919 when, as governor of Massachusetts, he had to confront a police strike in the city of Boston. Concerned with public safety and not willing to back down, he responded to a message from Samuel Gompers, a leader in the labor movement, asking for restoration of striking police officers' jobs, with "there is not a right to strike against the public safety by anybody, anywhere, any time." Coolidge upheld Boston Police Commissioner Edwin Upton Curtis' decision to fire the striking policemen.

As governor, he slashed the number of departments in state government from 118 to 18. He believed every penny the government spent must be justified. His performance as governor made him a good candidate to become Warren Harding's running mate in 1920. After President Harding's sudden death in 1923, Vice President Coolidge was unexpectedly left in charge of the country.

As president, Coolidge saw big government as a burden for people to bear rather than a means to help those in need. Government was to be the last resort—not the first resort—for solving problems.

"I favor the policy of economy," he said in his inaugural address, March 4, 1925. "Not because I wish to save money, but because I wish to save people. The men and women of this country who toil are the ones who bear the cost of the government. Every dollar we carelessly waste means that their life will be so much the more meager. Every dollar that we prudently save means that their life will be so much the more abundant. Economy is idealism in its most practical form."

While in office, Coolidge ran a budget surplus every year (the last president to do so), the average unemployment figure was about 3.3 percent, and the inflation rate was 1 percent. He accomplished this while cutting top tax rates from 73 percent when Harding took office, to 25 percent. The national debt was one third less at the end of Coolidge's term than it had been prior to his presidency. As he put it simply, "I want taxes to be less so that the people may have more."

What an incredible record of performance.

Coolidge was uninterested in rescuing Americans from themselves, believing that the people, not the president, determined the course of the country. The government could help by providing stable, unobtrusive policies; by encouraging, not encroaching and by clearing a path rather than dictating a process. His vision of government was very different than the incredible activist administrations of today.

"The pressing need of the present day is not to change our constitutional rights, but to observe our constitutional rights," Coolidge said during his first presidential annual address to Congress, which was also the first to be nationally broadcast via radio. He wrote his own speeches, relentlessly revising and rewriting as he worked to secure the perfect words and phrases. He often dictated the first draft to his secretary. The speech would be typed and triple-spaced, and he would then edit in his own hand.

What Coolidge provided was consistency, a value particularly important for businesses, which need predictability in order to plan, invest, and expand. Not surprisingly, healthy businesses led to jobs and economic activity under President Coolidge.

Champions of women's rights, Harding and Coolidge were elected in the first presidential election since women had been given the right to vote. When Coolidge was nominated during the 1924 Republican Convention, twenty-five women served on convention committees.

Coolidge reached out to women in his 1924 acceptance speech, "I know the influence of womanhood will guard the home, which is the citadel of the nation. I know it will be a protector of childhood, I know it will be on the side of humanity. I welcome it as a great instrument of mercy and a mighty agency of peace. I want every woman to vote."

And vote they did.

Coolidge was also a proponent of civil rights. During a 1924 presidential campaign speech at Howard University in Atlanta, Coolidge denounced "the propaganda of prejudice and hatred," criticizing the Ku Klux Klan. Coolidge was the last incumbent Republican president to receive a majority of the African American vote. Coolidge won the 1924 election with 54 percent of the popular vote and 72 percent of the electoral vote.

Coolidge's speech in honor of the 150th anniversary of the signing of the Declaration of Independence delved deep into the significance of that document and what it revealed about the character of our nation. "[T]he Declaration was the result of the religious teachings of the preceding period . . . the texts, the sermons, and the writings of the early colonial clergy who were earnestly undertaking to instruct their congregations in the great mystery of how to live. They preached equality because they believed in the fatherhood of God and the brotherhood of man. They justified freedom by the text that we are all created in the divine image, all partakers of the divine spirit."

It also revealed his own viewpoint. Coolidge believed that the birth of our nation would not have happened without the help of God, and often referred to the Founding Fathers as "ambassadors of Providence." This gave Coolidge a different perspective—that our nation was born from the spirit, not the man. Thus, the spirit is what sustains the nation.

> In its main features, the Declaration is a great spiritual document. It is a declaration not of material but of spiritual conceptions. Equality, liberty, popular sovereignty, the rights of man these are not elements which we can see and touch. They are ideals. They have their source and their roots in the religious convictions. They belong to the unseen

world. Unless the faith of the American people in these religious convictions is to endure, the principles of our Declaration will perish. We cannot continue to enjoy the result if we neglect and abandon the cause.

When President Ronald Reagan moved in to the White House, he requested that President Calvin Coolidge's portrait be transferred to the Cabinet Room. Coolidge cut taxes and government spending—the same goals Reagan had as president. In today's environment, when there are those who would like to replace our nation's historical belief in God and democracy with secularism and socialism, it is important that we refresh our memories, our understanding, and our resolve to stand for the same principles our Founding Fathers understood and promoted: faith in God, liberty, democracy, and the pursuit of happiness.

Today, just as Reagan did in 1981, we would benefit from placing Coolidge in a place of prominence.

—JGC

✖ ✖ ✖

We meet to celebrate the birthday of America. The coming of a new life always excites our interest. Although we know in the case of the individual that it has been an infinite repetition reaching back beyond our vision, that only makes it the more wonderful. But how our interest and wonder increase when we behold the miracle of the birth of a new nation. It is to pay our tribute of reverence and respect to those who participated in such a mighty event that we annually observe the fourth day of July. Whatever may have been the impression created by the news which went out from this city on that summer day in 1776, there can be no doubt as to the estimate which is now placed upon it. At the end of 150 years the four corners of the earth unite in coming to Philadelphia as to a holy shrine in grateful acknowledgement of a service so great, which a few inspired men here rendered to humanity, that it is still the preeminent support of free government throughout the world.

Although a century and a half measured in comparison with the length of human experience is but a short time, yet measured in the life of governments and nations it ranks as a very respectable period. Certainly enough time has elapsed to demonstrate with a great deal of thoroughness the value of our institutions and their dependability as rules for the regulation of human conduct and the advancement of civilization. They have been in existence long enough to become very well seasoned. They have met, and met successfully, the test of experience.

It is not so much then for the purpose of undertaking to proclaim new theories and principles that this annual celebration is maintained, but rather to reaffirm and reestablish those old theories and principles which time and the unerring logic of events have demonstrated to be sound. Amid all the clash of conflicting interests, amid all the welter of partisan politics, every American can turn for solace and consolation to the Declaration of independence and the Constitution of the United States with the assurance and confidence that those two great charters of freedom and justice remain firm and unshaken. Whatever perils appear, whatever dangers threaten, the Nation remains secure in the knowledge that the ultimate application of the law of the land will provide an adequate defense and protection.

It is little wonder that people at home and abroad consider Independence Hall as hallowed ground and revere the Liberty Bell as a sacred relic. That pile of bricks and mortar, that mass of metal, might appear to the uninstructed as only the outgrown meeting place and the shattered bell of a former time, useless now because of more modern conveniences, but to those who know they have become consecrated by the use which men have made of them. They have long been identified with a great cause. They are the framework of a spiritual event. The world looks upon them, because of their associations of one hundred and fifty years ago, as it looks upon the Holy Land because of what took place there nineteen hundred years ago. Through use for a righteous purpose they have become sanctified.

It is not here necessary to examine in detail the causes which led to the American Revolution. In their immediate occasion they were largely economic.

The colonists objected to the navigation laws which interfered with their trade, they denied the power of Parliament to impose taxes which they were obliged to pay, and they therefore resisted the royal governors and the royal forces which were sent to secure obedience to these laws. But the conviction is inescapable that a new civilization had come, a new spirit had arisen on this side of the Atlantic more advanced and more developed in its regard for the rights of the individual than that which characterized the Old World. Life in a new and open country had aspirations which could not be realized in any subordinate position. A separate establishment was ultimately inevitable. It had been decreed by the very laws of human nature. Man everywhere has an unconquerable desire to be the master of his own destiny.

We are obliged to conclude that the Declaration of Independence represented the movement of a people. It was not, of course, a movement from the top. Revolutions do not come from that direction. It was not without the support of many of the most respectable people in the Colonies, who were entitled to all the consideration that is given to breeding, education, and possessions. It had the support of another element of great significance and importance to which I shall later refer. But the preponderance of all those who occupied a position which took on the aspect of aristocracy did not approve of the Revolution and held toward it an attitude either of neutrality or open hostility. It was in no sense a rising of the oppressed and downtrodden. It brought no scum to the surface, for the reason that colonial society had developed no scum. The great body of the people were accustomed to privations, but they were free from depravity. If they had poverty, it was not of the hopeless kind that afflicts great cities, but the inspiring kind that marks the spirit of the pioneer. The American Revolution represented the informed and mature convictions of a great mass of independent, liberty-loving, God-fearing people who knew their rights, and possessed the courage to dare to maintain them.

The Continental Congress was not only composed of great men, but it represented a great people. While its members did not fail to exercise a remarkable leadership, they were equally observant of their representative capacity. They were industrious in encouraging their constituents to instruct them to support independence. But until such instructions were given they were inclined to withhold action.

While North Carolina has the honor of first authorizing its delegates to concur with other Colonies in declaring independence, it was quickly followed by South Carolina and Georgia, which also gave general instructions broad enough to include such action. But the first instructions which unconditionally directed its delegates to declare for independence came from the great Commonwealth of Virginia. These were immediately followed by Rhode Island and Massachusetts, while the other Colonies, with the exception of New York, soon adopted a like course.

This obedience of the delegates to the wishes of their constituents, which in some cases caused them to modify their previous positions, is a matter of great significance. It reveals an orderly process of government in the first place; but more than that, it demonstrates that the Declaration of Independence was the result of the seasoned and deliberate thought of the dominant portion of the people of the Colonies. Adopted after long discussion and as the result of the duly authorized expression of the preponderance of public opinion, it did not partake of dark intrigue or hidden conspiracy. It was well advised. It had about it nothing of the lawless and disordered nature of a riotous insurrection. It was maintained on a plane which rises above the ordinary conception of rebellion. It was in no sense a radical movement but took on the dignity of a resistance to illegal usurpations. It was conservative and represented the action of the colonists to maintain their constitutional rights which from time immemorial had been guaranteed to them under the law of the land.

When we come to examine the action of the Continental Congress in adopting the Declaration of Independence in the light of what was set out in that great document and in the light of succeeding events, we can not escape the conclusion that it had a much broader and deeper significance than a mere secession of territory and the establishment of a new nation. Events of that nature have been taking place since the dawn of history. One empire after another has arisen, only to crumble away as its constituent parts separated from each other and set up independent governments of their own. Such actions long ago became commonplace. They have occurred too often to hold the attention of the world and command the admiration and reverence of humanity. There is something beyond the establishment of a new nation, great as that event would be, in the Declaration of Independence which has ever since caused it to be regarded as one of the great charters that not only was to liberate America but was everywhere to ennoble humanity.

It was not because it was proposed to establish a new nation, but because it was proposed to establish a nation on new principles, that July 4, 1776, has come to be regarded as one of the greatest days in history. Great ideas do not burst upon the world unannounced. They are reached by a gradual development over a length of time usually proportionate to their importance. This is especially true of the principles laid down in the Declaration of Independence. Three very definite propositions were set out in its preamble regarding the nature of mankind and therefore of government. These were the doctrine that all men are created equal, that they are endowed with certain inalienable rights, and that therefore the source of the just powers of government must be derived from the consent of the governed.

If no one is to be accounted as born into a superior station, if there is to be no ruling class, and if all possess rights which can neither be bartered away nor taken from them by any earthly power, it follows as a matter of course that the practical authority of the Government has to rest on the consent of the governed. While these principles were not altogether new in political action, and were very far from new in political speculation, they had never been assembled before and declared in such a combination. But remarkable as this may be, it is not the chief distinction of the Declaration of Independence. The importance of political speculation is not to be under-estimated, as I shall presently disclose. Until the idea is developed and the plan made there can be no action.

It was the fact that our Declaration of Independence containing these immortal truths was the political action of a duly authorized and constituted representative public body in its sovereign capacity, supported by the force of general opinion and by the armies of Washington already in the field, which makes it the most important civil document in the world. It was not only the principles declared, but the fact that therewith a new nation was born which was to be founded upon those principles and which from that time forth in its development has actually maintained those principles, that makes this pronouncement an incomparable event in the history of government. It was an assertion that a people had arisen determined to make every necessary sacrifice for the support of these truths and by their practical application bring the War of Independence to a successful conclusion and adopt the Constitution of the United States with all that it has meant to civilization.

The idea that the people have a right to choose their own rulers was not new in political history. It was the foundation of every popular attempt to depose an undesirable king. This right was set out with a good deal of detail by the Dutch when as early as July 26, 1581, they declared their independence of Philip of Spain. In their long struggle with the Stuarts the British people asserted the same principles, which finally culminated in the Bill of Rights deposing the last of that house and placing William and Mary on the throne. In each of these cases sovereignty through divine right was displaced by sovereignty through the consent of the people. Running through the same documents, though expressed in different terms, is the clear inference of inalienable rights. But we should search these charters in vain for an assertion of the doctrine of equality. This principle had not before appeared as an official political declaration of any nation. It was profoundly revolutionary. It is one of the corner stones of American institutions.

But if these truths to which the declaration refers have not before been adopted in their combined entirety by national authority, it is a fact that they had been long pondered and often expressed in political speculation. It is generally assumed that French thought had some effect upon our public mind during Revolutionary days. This may have been true. But the principles of our declaration had been under discussion in the Colonies for nearly two generations before the advent of the French political philosophy that characterized the middle of the eighteenth century. In fact, they come from an earlier date. A very positive echo of what the Dutch had done in 1581, and what the English were preparing to do, appears in the assertion of the Rev. Thomas Hooker of

Connecticut as early as 1638, when he said in a sermon before the General Court that—

"The foundation of authority is laid in the free consent of the people."

"The choice of public magistrates belongs unto the people by God's own allowance."

This doctrine found wide acceptance among the nonconformist clergy who later made up the Congregational Church. The great apostle of this movement was the Rev. John Wise, of Massachusetts. He was one of the leaders of the revolt against the royal governor Andros in 1687, for which he suffered imprisonment. He was a liberal in ecclesiastical controversies. He appears to have been familiar with the writings of the political scientist, Samuel Pufendorf, who was born in Saxony in 1632. Wise published a treatise, entitled "The Church's Quarrel Espoused," in 1710, which was amplified in another publication in 1717. In it he dealt with the principles of civil government. His works were reprinted in 1772 and have been declared to have been nothing less than a text-book of liberty for our Revolutionary fathers.

While the written word was the foundation, it is apparent that the spoken word was the vehicle for convincing the people. This came with great force and wide range from the successors of Hooker and Wise, It was carried on with a missionary spirit which did not fail to reach the Scotch-Irish of North Carolina, showing its influence by significantly making that Colony the first to give instructions to its delegates looking to independence. This preaching reached the neighborhood of Thomas Jefferson, who acknowledged that his "best ideas of democracy" had been secured at church meetings.

That these ideas were prevalent in Virginia is further revealed by the Declaration of Rights, which was prepared by George Mason and presented to the general assembly on May 27, 1776. This document asserted popular sovereignty and inherent natural rights, but confined the doctrine of equality to the assertion that "All men are created equally free and independent." It can scarcely be imagined that Jefferson was unacquainted with what had been done in his own Commonwealth of Virginia when he took up the task of drafting the Declaration of Independence. But these thoughts can very largely be traced back to

what John Wise was writing in 1710. He said, "Every man must be acknowledged equal to every man." Again, "The end of all good government is to
cultivate humanity and promote the happiness of all and the good of every man
in all his rights, his life, liberty, estate, honor, and so forth. . . ." And again, "For
as they have a power every man in his natural state, so upon combination they
can and do bequeath this power to others and settle it according as their united
discretion shall determine." And still again, "Democracy is Christ's government
in church and state." Here was the doctrine of equality, popular sovereignty, and
the substance of the theory of inalienable rights clearly asserted by Wise at the
opening of the eighteenth century, just as we have the principle of the consent
of the governed stated by Hooker as early as 1638.

When we take all these circumstances into consideration, it is but natural
that the first paragraph of the Declaration of Independence should open with
a reference to Nature's God and should close in the final paragraphs with an
appeal to the Supreme Judge of the world and an assertion of a firm reliance
on Divine Providence. Coming from these sources, having as it did this background, it is no wonder that Samuel Adams could say "The people seem to
recognize this resolution as though it were a decree promulgated from heaven."

No one can examine this record and escape the conclusion that in the great
outline of its principles the Declaration was the result of the religious teachings of the preceding period. The profound philosophy which Jonathan
Edwards applied to theology, the popular preaching of George Whitefield, had
aroused the thought and stirred the people of the Colonies in preparation for
this great event. No doubt the speculations which had been going on in England, and especially on the Continent, lent their influence to the general
sentiment of the times. Of course, the world is always influenced by all the
experience and all the thought of the past. But when we come to a contemplation of the immediate conception of the principles of human relationship which
went into the Declaration of Independence we are not required to extend our
search beyond our own shores. They are found in the texts, the sermons, and
the writings of the early colonial clergy who were earnestly undertaking to
instruct their congregations in the great mystery of how to live. They preached

equality because they believed in the fatherhood of God and the brotherhood of man. They justified freedom by the text that we are all created in the divine image, all partakers of the divine spirit.

Placing every man on a plane where he acknowledged no superiors, where no one possessed any right to rule over him, he must inevitably choose his own rulers through a system of self-government. This was their theory of democracy. In those days such doctrines would scarcely have been permitted to flourish and spread in any other country. This was the purpose which the fathers cherished. In order that they might have freedom to express these thoughts and opportunity to put them into action, whole congregations with their pastors had migrated to the colonies. These great truths were in the air that our people breathed. Whatever else we may say of it, the Declaration of Independence was profoundly American.

If this apprehension of the facts be correct, and the documentary evidence would appear to verify it, then certain conclusions are bound to follow. A spring will cease to flow if its source be dried up; a tree will wither if its roots be destroyed. In its main features the Declaration of Independence is a great spiritual document. It is a declaration not of material but of spiritual conceptions. Equality, liberty, popular sovereignty, the rights of man these are not elements which we can see and touch. They are ideals. They have their source and their roots in the religious convictions. They belong to the unseen world. Unless the faith of the American people in these religious convictions is to endure, the principles of our Declaration will perish. We can not continue to enjoy the result if we neglect and abandon the cause.

We are too prone to overlook another conclusion. Governments do not make ideals, but ideals make governments. This is both historically and logically true. Of course the government can help to sustain ideals and can create institutions through which they can be the better observed, but their source by their very nature is in the people. The people have to bear their own responsibilities. There is no method by which that burden can be shifted to the government. It is not the enactment, but the observance of laws, that creates the character of a nation.

About the Declaration there is a finality that is exceedingly restful. It is often asserted that the world has made a great deal of progress since 1776, that we have had new thoughts and new experiences which have given us a great advance over the people of that day, and that we may therefore very well discard their conclusions for something more modern. But that reasoning can not be applied to this great charter. If all men are created equal, that is final. If they are endowed with inalienable rights, that is final. If governments derive their just powers from the consent of the governed, that is final. No advance, no progress can be made beyond these propositions. If anyone wishes to deny their truth or their soundness, the only direction in which he can proceed historically is not forward, but backward toward the time when there was no equality, no rights of the individual, no rule of the people. Those who wish to proceed in that direction can not lay claim to progress. They are reactionary. Their ideas are not more modern, but more ancient, than those of the Revolutionary fathers.

In the development of its institutions America can fairly claim that it has remained true to the principles which were declared 150 years ago. In all the essentials we have achieved an equality which was never possessed by any other people. Even in the less important matter of material possessions we have secured a wider and wider distribution of wealth. The rights of the individual are held sacred and protected by constitutional guaranties, which even the Government itself is bound not to violate. If there is any one thing among us that is established beyond question, it is self-government—the right of the people to rule. If there is any failure in respect to any of these principles, it is because there is a failure on the part of individuals to observe them. We hold that the duly authorized expression of the will of the people has a divine sanction. But even in that we come back to the theory of John Wise that "Democracy is Christ's government." The ultimate sanction of law rests on the righteous authority of the Almighty.

On an occasion like this a great temptation exists to present evidence of the practical success of our form of democratic republic at home and the ever-broadening acceptance it is securing abroad. Although these things are well known, their frequent consideration is an encouragement and an inspiration. But it is not results and effects so much as sources and causes that I believe it is even more necessary constantly to contemplate. Ours is a government of the people. It represents their will. Its officers may sometimes go astray, but that is not a reason for criticizing the principles of our institutions. The real heart of the American Government depends upon the heart of the people. It is from that source that we must look for all genuine reform. It is to that cause that we must ascribe all our results.

It was in the contemplation of these truths that the fathers made their declaration and adopted their Constitution. It was to establish a free government, which must not be permitted to degenerate into the unrestrained authority of a mere majority or the unbridled weight of a mere influential few. They undertook the balance these interests against each other and provide the three separate independent branches, the executive, the legislative, and the judicial departments of the Government, with checks against each other in order that neither one might encroach upon the other. These are our guaranties of liberty. As a result of these methods enterprise has been duly protected from confiscation, the people have been free from oppression, and there has been an ever-broadening and deepening of the humanities of life.

Under a system of popular government there will always be those who will seek for political preferment by clamoring for reform. While there is very little of this which is not sincere, there is a large portion that is not well informed. In my opinion very little of just criticism can attach to the theories and principles of our institutions. There is far more danger of harm than there is hope of good in any radical changes. We do need a better understanding and comprehension of them and a better knowledge of the foundations of government in general. Our forefathers came to certain conclusions and decided upon certain courses of action which have been a great blessing to the world. Before we can understand their conclusions we must go back and review the course which they followed. We must think the thoughts which they thought. Their intellectual life centered around the meeting-house. They were intent upon religious worship. While there were always among them men of deep learning, and later those who had comparatively large possessions, the mind of the people was not so much engrossed in how much they knew, or how much they had, as in how they were going to live. While scantily provided with other literature, there was a wide acquaintance with the Scriptures. Over a period as great as that which measures the existence of our independence they were subject to this discipline not only in their religious life and educational training, but also in their political thought. They were a people who came under the influence of a great spiritual development and acquired a great moral power.

No other theory is adequate to explain or comprehend the Declaration of Independence. It is the product of the spiritual insight of the people. We live in an age of science and of abounding accumulation of material things. These did not create our Declaration. Our Declaration created them. The things of the spirit come first. Unless we cling to that, all our material prosperity, overwhelming though it may appear, will turn to a barren sceptre in our grasp. If we are to maintain the great heritage which has been bequeathed to us, we must be like-minded as the fathers who created it. We must not sink into a pagan materialism. We must cultivate the reverence which they had for the things that are holy. We must follow the spiritual and moral leadership which they showed. We must keep replenished, that they may glow with a more compelling flame, the altar fires before which they worshiped.

XVII

"A date which will live in infamy"

FRANKLIN D. ROOSEVELT'S JOINT ADDRESS TO CONGRESS LEADING TO A DECLARATION OF WAR AGAINST JAPAN (1941)

FRANKLIN ROOSEVELT WAS SERVING AN UNPRECEDENTED THIRD TERM AS President of the United States when the Japanese launched a sneak attack on Pearl Harbor on December 7, 1941. Prior to the attack, most of the attention of the press and the public had been focused on the war being waged in Europe between the Axis powers (Nazi Germany and Fascist Italy) and the Allies (Britain, France, and eventually the Soviet Union). America had remained technically neutral even though we were selling weapons to Britain.

Roosevelt became involved in politics despite contracting polio in the fall of 1921 at the age of thirty-nine. His legs would never regain their strength. He learned to walk again by putting heavy braces on his legs, swinging his hips and holding onto someone's arm and a cane. His mother had assumed he would take over the country estate and live out his life as an invalid, but Roosevelt had other ideas.

When Roosevelt nominated Al Smith for president at the 1928 Democratic convention, he described Smith as "the 'Happy Warrior' of the political battlefield." He might have been describing himself.

The stock market crashed in 1929. Roosevelt, who promised a "New Deal," defeated incumbent Herbert Hoover in 1932 with 57 percent of the popular vote and 89 percent of the Electoral College. When Roosevelt took the oath of office, unemployment was 25 percent.

In his first inaugural address, Roosevelt took on what he determined to be America's enemy at that time. "The only thing we have to fear is fear itself," he stated.

His presidency began during the Great Depression. Banks were under duress, having closed in many states. Roosevelt ordered a bank holiday and pushed through banking regulation that did not take over the banks as many had feared, but instead allowed them to reopen or reorganize if needed.

On March 12, 1933, Roosevelt held his first of what would become thirty fireside chats during his presidency, broadcast over the radio. In each one, he talked directly to the American people. This allowed him to set the tone and deliver the message he wanted to deliver instead allowing the press to edit it. During the first chat, he explained the rationale behind the bank holiday and the legislation. The nation was understandably nervous, and his words provided comfort and room for movement toward reform to be accepted.

Roosevelt was known for being firm and optimistic. "Demoralization caused by vast unemployment is our greatest extravagance," he said. He refused "to accept as a necessary condition of our future a permanent army of unemployed." Roosevelt won his second election in 1936 with 60 percent of the popular vote and 98 percent of the Electoral College. Believing he had secured a mandate, he soon pushed too far with what he called court reform. It failed.

In the fall of 1938, Roosevelt spoke in Canada, noting that "We in the Americas are no longer in a far-away continent, to which the eddies of controversies beyond the seas could bring no interest or no harm." Though he spoke of the importance of the rest of the world to the United States, he insisted on neutrality until we were forced into the war.

In 1940, Roosevelt told the delegates at the Democratic National Convention that they could vote for whomever they wanted; they wanted him. He won an unprecedented third term with 55 percent of the popular vote and 85 percent of the Electoral College. In May 1941, in another fireside chat, Roosevelt prepared the nation for war, declaring a state of "unlimited national emergency." And he communicated the seriousness of the war the nation was about to enter:

> Today the whole world is divided between human slavery and human freedom—between pagan brutality and the Christian ideal. We choose human freedom—which is the Christian ideal.... We will accept only a world consecrated to freedom of speech and expression—freedom of every person to worship God in his own way—freedom from want—and freedom from terror.

In September 1941, Roosevelt put the nation on notice about the Nazi threat during a fireside chat, stating, "The danger is here now." He did not mention Japan. While Roosevelt and the nation were focused on the threat of Nazi Germany, Japan was planning an attack on Pearl Harbor.

The attack began about 8:00 on a Sunday morning and ended less than two hours later with more than 2,000 Americans dead; eight battleships and ten other ships were lost. We were caught unaware. The nation was in shock.

That day, Roosevelt dictated the main portion of the speech he would deliver to Congress the next day. The speech provided the background for what he was requesting—a declaration of war. The motion passed with only one vote against.

We were at war, determined to fulfill the promise in Roosevelt's speech, which said, "No matter how long it may take us to overcome this premeditated invasion, the American people, in their righteous might, will win through to absolute victory.... With confidence in our armed forces, with the un-bounding determination of our people, we will gain the inevitable triumph. So help us God."

—JGC

❧ ❧ ❧

Mr. Vice President, and Mr. Speaker, and Members of the Senate and House of Representatives:

Yesterday, December 7, 1941—a date which will live in infamy—the United States of America was suddenly and deliberately attacked by naval and air forces of the Empire of Japan.

The United States was at peace with that Nation and, at the solicitation of Japan, was still in conversation with its Government and its Emperor looking toward the maintenance of peace in the Pacific. Indeed, one hour after Japanese air squadrons had commenced bombing in the American Island of Oahu, the Japanese Ambassador to the United States and his colleague delivered to our Secretary of State a formal reply to a recent American message. And while this reply stated that it seemed useless to continue the existing diplomatic negotiations, it contained no threat or hint of war or of armed attack.

It will be recorded that the distance of Hawaii from Japan makes it obvious that the attack was deliberately planned many days or even weeks ago. During the intervening time, the Japanese Government has deliberately sought to deceive the United States by false statements and expressions of hope for continued peace.

The attack yesterday on the Hawaiian Islands has caused severe damage to American naval and military forces. I regret to tell you that very many American lives have been lost. In addition, American ships have been reported torpedoed on the high seas between San Francisco and Honolulu.

Yesterday the Japanese Government also launched an attack against Malaya.

Last night Japanese forces attacked Hong Kong.

Last night Japanese forces attacked Guam.

Last night Japanese forces attacked the Philippine Islands.

Last night the Japanese attacked Wake Island. And this morning the Japanese attacked Midway Island.

Japan has, therefore, undertaken a surprise offensive extending throughout the Pacific area. The facts of yesterday and today speak for themselves. The people of the United States have already formed their opinions and well understand the implications to the very life and safety of our Nation.

As Commander in Chief of the Army and Navy, I have directed that all measures be taken for our defense.

But always will our whole Nation remember the character of the onslaught against us.

No matter how long it may take us to overcome this premeditated invasion, the American people in their righteous might will win through to absolute victory. I believe that I interpret the will of the Congress and of the people when I assert that we will not only defend ourselves to the uttermost, but will make it very certain that this form of treachery shall never again endanger us.

Hostilities exist. There is no blinking at the fact that our people, our territory, and our interests are in grave danger.

With confidence in our armed forces—with the un-bounding determination of our people—we will gain the inevitable triumph—so help us God.

I ask that the Congress declare that since the unprovoked and dastardly attack by Japan on Sunday, December 7, 1941, a state of war has existed between the United States and the Japanese Empire.

XVIII

"Nothing less than full victory"

GENERAL DWIGHT D. EISENHOWER'S ORDER OF THE DAY (1944)

WHEN THE UNITED STATES ENTERED WORLD WAR II IN DECEMBER 1941, the Allies—France, Great Britain, and later, the Soviet Union—had been fighting the Axis—Germany, Japan, and Italy—since the invasion and fall of Poland in 1939. France had fallen to Germany in June 1940.

In 1942, Soviet leader Joseph Stalin repeatedly asked British Prime Minister Winston Churchill and American President Franklin Delano Roosevelt to open a second front on the Atlantic Coast of Europe. At this point, a vast majority of the fighting in the European Theater was taking place on the eastern front, on the border between Nazi Germany and the Soviet Union. Stalin's Red Army had sustained devastating casualties, and a second front would provide the Russian troops with relief by dividing the German forces. However, as they were fighting Hitler's armies in North Africa while preparing to invade Italy from the south, the British and Americans were not ready for a full-scale invasion of western Europe. They bided their time to gather enough troops, supplies, ships, munitions, and planes in the immediate area.

In December of 1943, President Roosevelt chose General Dwight D. Eisenhower to be the Supreme Allied Commander in Europe. Eisenhower would plan and carry out the liberation of western Europe and invasion of Germany, code-named Operation Overlord.

David Dwight Eisenhower was the third of seven sons born to Ida and David Eisenhower in Denison, Texas. When he was a child, he moved with his family to Abilene, Kansas, where he grew up. He entered West Point, where, as he went by "Dwight," he switched his first and middle names, and graduated in 1915. He served as chief of staff to Brigadier General Fox Conner in Panama in 1922 during which, in addition to drafting orders and reviewing tactics, Eisenhower pursued reading and further education assigned to him by Conner.

Conner believed that 1919's Treaty of Versailles had created the potential for another world war within thirty years. This influenced Eisenhower to begin thinking through the potential ramifications of a world war as early as the mid 1920s.

Eisenhower subsequently worked for General Douglas MacArthur in 1933, and General George C. Marshall, starting in December 1941 in the War Plans Division, where he was charged with crafting the plan to defeat the Axis powers in Europe. He focused on Germany, designing an invasion to be launched from Britain which would sweep through northern France. Eisenhower's work caught the eye of Army Chief of Staff George Marshall, who, at that point, was President Roosevelt's chief adviser on the conduct of the war.

Under Marshall's guidance, Eisenhower's rise through the ranks continued, and he was promoted from major general to commander-in-chief of the Allied forces in North Africa preparing for and leading the U.S. and British invasion there in November 1942. As the Americans and the British battled the German army through the deserts of Morocco, Tunisia, Libya, and Egypt, Ike gained valuable field experience as a commander and learned that political and diplomatic skills were also important.

In November of 1943, Stalin, Churchill, and Roosevelt met in Tehran, Iran to discuss opening a western european front against Germany. On the way back from the meeting, Roosevelt informed Eisenhower that he would be leading the invasion. The planning for Operation Overlord required hundreds of thousands of troops to be assembled and trained for amphibious landing. The plans had to account for beach attacks, and required information on the terrain, and weather tracking.

On Christmas Eve, Roosevelt updated Americans on his meeting in Tehran with a fireside chat that previewed events of the following year. "We agreed on every point concerned with the launching of the gigantic attack upon Germany...we shall all have to look forward to long casualty lists—dead, wounded, and missing," he said. "War entails all that. There is no easy road to victory. And the end is not yet in sight."

Back at home, both Churchill and Roosevelt were coming under increased political pressure. Roosevelt, in particular, was facing a presidential election in the fall of 1944, and was in poor health. Both were impatient for the next phase of the war: the invasion.

The assault was initially planned for June 5, 1944, but a large storm over the English Channel delayed it a day. Before the invasion began, Eisenhower sent a message of encouragement and support to the troops. He compared the invasion with a "crusade" and noted that their goal was nothing less than "security for ourselves in a free world." He relayed "confidence in your courage and devotion to duty and skill in battle," while noting, "we will accept nothing less than full victory."

He ended with a request for assistance from "God Almighty upon this great and noble undertaking."

The invasion began on June 6. It included nearly 3 million soldiers, sailors, airmen and marines, some 11,000 planes and nearly 7,000 vessels carrying close to 200,000 tanks and other vehicles.

After months of extensive preparation, Eisenhower knew that he had to step back and allow the event to unfold. As a precaution, if the invasion was not successful, he had a message prepared for release.

That night, Roosevelt broadcast his D-Day prayer. Biographer Jon Meacham noted, "the White House had distributed the text beforehand so that the audience—an estimated 100 million Americans—could recite the words with Roosevelt."

While there were more than 10,000 casualties among the U.S., British and Canadian troops, the invasion was a success and changed the direction of the war.

Less than a year later, on May 7, 1945, the Germans surrendered unconditionally to the Allies.

The resolution of the war depended upon the execution of the invasion. General Eisenhower's message in a time of crisis focused his soldiers by bringing home the importance of their mission—saving the world as they knew it—while motivating them to succeed. And succeed they did.

—JGC

❥ ❥ ❥

SUPREME HEADQUARTERS ALLIED EXPEDITIONARY FORCE

Soldiers, Sailors, and Airmen of the Allied Expeditionary Force!

You are about to embark upon the Great Crusade, toward which we have striven these many months. The eyes of the world are upon you. The hope and prayers of liberty-loving people everywhere march with you. In company with our brave Allies and brothers-in-arms on other Fronts, you will bring about the destruction of the German war machine, the elimination of Nazi tyranny over the oppressed peoples of Europe, and security for ourselves in a free world.

Your task will not be an easy one. Your enemy is well trained, well equipped and battle-hardened. He will fight savagely.

But this is the year 1944! Much has happened since the Nazi triumphs of 1940–41. The United Nations have inflicted upon the Germans great defeats, in open battle, man-to-man. Our air offensive has seriously reduced their strength in the air and their capacity to wage war on the ground. Our Home

Fronts have given us an overwhelming superiority in weapons and munitions of war, and placed at our disposal great reserves of trained fighting men. The tide has turned! The free men of the world are marching together to Victory!

I have full confidence in your courage, devotion to duty and skill in battle. We will accept nothing less than full Victory!

Good luck! And let us beseech the blessing of Almighty God upon this great and noble undertaking.

—Gen. Dwight D. Eisenhower

XIX

"Ask not what your country can do for you ..."

JOHN F. KENNEDY'S INAUGURAL ADDRESS (1961)

O N JANUARY 20, 1961, JOHN F. KENNEDY STRODE TO THE PLATFORM on the east side of the Capitol to deliver his inaugural address. The election, held on November 8, 1960, had been close. Kennedy won with 56 percent of the electoral votes but only a little more than 110,000 votes—about two-tenths of a percent of the votes cast. His Republican challenger, then-Vice President Richard M. Nixon, had campaigned on Kennedy's lack of experience. Kennedy's inaugural address was his opportunity to let the public get to know him; Americans had merely been introduced to him on the campaign trail, but were not sure who he really was.

Kennedy had campaigned on rebuilding America's strength, both militarily and economically. The campaign included the first televised debate between presidential candidates. Those who heard it on the radio tended to think that Nixon came out ahead, while those who watched it on TV tended to give it to Kennedy. Kennedy was the first American politician to master the fledgling medium of television. On camera, he appeared younger, more energetic, and more appealing than Nixon, who was battling flu and looked pale and morose.

Kennedy, then forty-three, was the youngest president elected, with a 3-year-old daughter and an infant son who was born between Election Day and inauguration. The new president symbolized a young, vibrant America. "Above all, Kennedy held out such promise of hope," noted historian Arthur Schlesinger, Jr., who served as Kennedy's special assistant. "Euphoria reigned; we thought for a moment that the world was plastic and the future unlimited."

The president was born May 29, 1917, the second son to Joe Kennedy and Rose Fitzgerald Kennedy. Joe, who had made a fortune in business, was ambitious, not only for himself, but also for his family. Joe's plan was for his eldest son, Joe, Jr., to go into politics, and become president one day.

When he was thirteen, John F. Kennedy began suffering from physical issues that would plague him all his life: severe colitis, back pain, and Addison's disease. After graduating from Harvard, Kennedy joined the Navy, serving during World War II as captain of a PT boat. When his boat was cut in two by a Japanese destroyer during a skirmish in 1943, he and the crew had to swim to shore. Kennedy towed one of his crewmembers three miles to safety by putting the strap of his life jacket in his teeth. He was awarded the Navy and Marine Corps Medal and the Purple Heart for his actions and injuries sustained.

A little more than a year later, his older brother Joe, a Navy bomber, was lost during a mission over England. His body was never recovered. The son who was supposed to go into politics and become president was gone.

Not long after, Kennedy's father began to talk to his second son, Jack, about entering politics. "I told him Joe was dead and that it was his responsibility to run for Congress," Joe Kennedy said to a reporter years later. After working as a journalist for a while, Kennedy ran for Congress in Massachusetts in 1946. He went door to door, shaking hands and listening to people's concerns. "The effect he has on women voters was almost naughty," wrote James Reston, a *New York Times* columnist, "Every woman either wants to mother him or marry him."

Kennedy won his race handily in an overwhelmingly Democratic Boston district, though the Democrats were swept from power in the House in a historic Republican landslide. That same year, his future foe, Richard Nixon was elected to his first term representing a Southern California district.

At the time, President Harry Truman's approval rating was 32 percent, which was reflected in his party's dismal showing in the midterm congressional elections. With the defeat of their common enemy, Nazi Germany, tension between the United States and the Soviet Union increased. We had the atomic bomb, but did not want to use it again, though it was only a matter of time before Moscow had the nuclear option as well. Concern grew about Communists and subversion of the U.S. political system.

After serving three terms in Congress, Kennedy was elected to the U.S. Senate. "Tip" O'Neill, who would later become speaker of the House, succeeded Kennedy in his congressional district. Kennedy and Jacqueline Bouvier married in 1953. While recovering from back surgery, he collaborated with his young (27-year-old) speechwriter Ted Sorensen, to write *Profiles in Courage* (1956), for which Kennedy was awarded the Pulitzer Prize in 1957.

Kennedy's 1960 presidential campaign was run on the themes of going toward new frontiers, exploration, and opportunity. At the 1960 Democratic National Convention in Los Angeles, Kennedy laid out his plan, "For the problems are not all solved and the battles are not all won—and we stand today on the edge of a new frontier... But the new frontier of which I speak is not a set of promises—it is a set of challenges. It sums up not what I intend to offer the American people, but what I intend to ask of them." Initial concerns that Kennedy's Catholicism might adversely affect the campaign were brushed aside after his primary win in overwhelmingly Protestant West Virginia.

When Kennedy took the stage a little after noon on the day of his inauguration, the audience was not only those in attendance, but also the millions of Americans who were watching on television. Additionally, due to the strained relationship between the Soviet Union and the United States, leaders throughout the world were listening for signs of what was to come from the new, young, American leader.

Kennedy inspired through his presence—young and energetic—and through his words. He knew that his inaugural address would set the tone for his administration, and worked on it with Ted Sorensen from the time of the election until delivery.

He began by celebrating freedom; he referred to God three times, saying, "the rights of man come . . . from the hand of God."

He invoked the revolution, spoke of a "new generation of Americans—proud of our ancient heritage" and said that we would "pay any price. . . . in order to assure the survival and the success of liberty."

While he mentioned a quest for peace, it was tempered with the promise of military might. "We dare not tempt them with weakness. For only when our arms are sufficient beyond doubt can we be certain beyond doubt that they will never be employed."

Kennedy, who supported government programs to help those in need, was clear about overall expectations, declaring, "Ask not what your country can do for you—ask what you can do for your country."

Upon closing, he acknowledged that we are a nation, under God: "Let us go forth to lead the land we love, asking His blessing and His help, but knowing that here on Earth, God's work must truly be our own."

On rereading this inaugural speech, we are reminded that the Democratic Party of the 1960s, which supported a strong national defense and, until President Lyndon B. Johnson, only a limited welfare state, is different from the party we know today. As Ronald Reagan so famously said, "I didn't leave the Democratic Party, the Democratic Party left me." As it has pushed an agenda that would erode the very foundation of American life, the Democratic Party today has become something John F. Kennedy may not have recognized.

—JGC

❧ ❧ ❧

Washington, D.C.

January 20, 1961

Vice President Johnson, Mr. Speaker, Mr. Chief Justice, President Eisenhower, Vice President Nixon, President Truman, Reverend Clergy, fellow citizens:

We observe today not a victory of party but a celebration of freedom—symbolizing an end as well as a beginning—signifying renewal as well as change. For I have sworn before you and Almighty God the same solemn oath our forebears prescribed nearly a century and three-quarters ago.

The world is very different now. For man holds in his mortal hands the power to abolish all forms of human poverty and all forms of human life. And yet the same revolutionary beliefs for which our forebears fought are still at issue around the globe—the belief that the rights of man come not from the generosity of the state but from the hand of God.

We dare not forget today that we are the heirs of that first revolution. Let the word go forth from this time and place, to friend and foe alike, that the torch has been passed to a new generation of Americans—born in this century, tempered by war, disciplined by a hard and bitter peace, proud of our ancient heritage—and unwilling to witness or permit the slow undoing of those human rights to which this nation has always been committed, and to which we are committed today at home and around the world.

Let every nation know, whether it wishes us well or ill, that we shall pay any price, bear any burden, meet any hardship, support any friend, oppose any foe to assure the survival and the success of liberty.

This much we pledge—and more.

To those old allies whose cultural and spiritual origins we share, we pledge the loyalty of faithful friends. United there is little we cannot do in a host of cooperative ventures. Divided there is little we can do—for we dare not meet a powerful challenge at odds and split asunder.

To those new states whom we welcome to the ranks of the free, we pledge our word that one form of colonial control shall not have passed away merely to be replaced by a far more iron tyranny. We shall not always expect to find them supporting our view. But we shall always hope to find them strongly supporting their own freedom—and to remember that, in the past, those who foolishly sought power by riding the back of the tiger ended up inside.

To those people in the huts and villages of half the globe struggling to break the bonds of mass misery, we pledge our best efforts to help them help themselves, for whatever period is required—not because the communists may be doing it, not because we seek their votes, but because it is right. If a free society cannot help the many who are poor, it cannot save the few who are rich.

To our sister republics south of our border, we offer a special pledge—to convert our good words into good deeds—in a new alliance for progress—to assist free men and free governments in casting off the chains of poverty. But this peaceful revolution of hope cannot become the prey of hostile powers. Let all our neighbors know that we shall join with them to oppose aggression or subversion anywhere in the Americas. And let every other power know that this Hemisphere intends to remain the master of its own house.

To that world assembly of sovereign states, the United Nations, our last best hope in an age where the instruments of war have far outpaced the instruments of peace, we renew our pledge of support—to prevent it from becoming merely a forum for invective—to strengthen its shield of the new and the weak—and to enlarge the area in which its writ may run.

Finally, to those nations who would make themselves our adversary, we offer not a pledge but a request: that both sides begin anew the quest for peace, before the dark powers of destruction unleashed by science engulf all humanity in planned or accidental self-destruction.

We dare not tempt them with weakness. For only when our arms are sufficient beyond doubt can we be certain beyond doubt that they will never be employed.

But neither can two great and powerful groups of nations take comfort from our present course—both sides overburdened by the cost of modern weapons, both rightly alarmed by the steady spread of the deadly atom, yet both racing to alter that uncertain balance of terror that stays the hand of mankind's final war.

So let us begin anew—remembering on both sides that civility is not a sign of weakness, and sincerity is always subject to proof. Let us never negotiate out of fear. But let us never fear to negotiate.

Let both sides explore what problems unite us instead of belaboring those problems which divide us.

Let both sides, for the first time, formulate serious and precise proposals for the inspection and control of arms—and bring the absolute power to destroy other nations under the absolute control of all nations.

Let both sides seek to invoke the wonders of science instead of its terrors. Together let us explore the stars, conquer the deserts, eradicate disease, tap the ocean depths, and encourage the arts and commerce.

Let both sides unite to heed in all corners of the earth the command of Isaiah—to "undo the heavy burdens . . . (and) let the oppressed go free."

And if a beachhead of cooperation may push back the jungle of suspicion, let both sides join in creating a new endeavor, not a new balance of power, but a new world of law, where the strong are just and the weak secure and the peace preserved.

All this will not be finished in the first one hundred days. Nor will it be finished in the first one thousand days, nor in the life of this Administration, nor even perhaps in our lifetime on this planet. But let us begin.

In your hands, my fellow citizens, more than mine, will rest the final success or failure of our course. Since this country was founded, each generation of Americans has been summoned to give testimony to its national loyalty. The graves of young Americans who answered the call to service surround the globe.

Now the trumpet summons us again—not as a call to bear arms, though arms we need—not as a call to battle, though embattled we are—but a call to bear the burden of a long twilight struggle, year in and year out, "rejoicing in hope, patient in tribulation"—a struggle against the common enemies of man: tyranny, poverty, disease, and war itself.

Can we forge against these enemies a grand and global alliance, North and South, East and West, that can assure a more fruitful life for all mankind? Will you join in that historic effort?

In the long history of the world, only a few generations have been granted the role of defending freedom in its hour of maximum danger. I do not shrink from this responsibility—I welcome it. I do not believe that any of us would exchange places with any other people or any other generation. The energy, the faith, the devotion which we bring to this endeavor will light our country and all who serve it—and the glow from that fire can truly light the world.

And so, my fellow Americans: ask not what your country can do for you—ask what you can do for your country.

My fellow citizens of the world: ask not what America will do for you, but what together we can do for the freedom of man.

Finally, whether you are citizens of America or citizens of the world, ask of us here the same high standards of strength and sacrifice which we ask of you. With a good conscience our only sure reward, with history the final judge of our deeds, let us go forth to lead the land we love, asking His blessing and His help, but knowing that here on earth, God's work must truly be our own.

XX

"Duty, Honor, Country"

GENERAL DOUGLAS MACARTHUR'S SYLVANUS THAYER AWARD ACCEPTANCE ADDRESS (1962)

O N MAY 12, 1962, RETIRED GENERAL DOUGLAS MACARTHUR DELIVERED an acceptance speech for the Sylvanus Thayer Award presented by the West Point Association of Graduates. "Throughout more than a half-century of active Army duty," the citation for the award notes, "Douglas MacArthur advanced his country's welfare by his outstanding military leadership, both in war and in peace."

MacArthur was eighty-two years old at the time of the speech and had been retired for almost eleven years. He was the grandson of a judge and the son of a soldier—his father fought in the Civil War and in the Spanish-American War in the Philippines, where Douglas would also serve.

MacArthur attended West Point and graduated first in his class in 1903. After supervising construction in the Philippines, and as chief engineer in the Division of the Pacific, MacArthur became an aide to President Theodore Roosevelt.

During World War I, MacArthur was promoted to brigadier general and commanded the 84th Infantry Brigade. He held a variety of jobs in the 1920s, including superintendent at West Point and head of the United States Olympic Committee for the 1928 Olympics; he returned to the Philippines in 1928. The youngest major general in the U.S. Army at age fifty, MacArthur became Army chief of staff in November 1930.

As chief of staff, he had to do more with less, modernizing the Army in the face of budget cuts brought on by the Great Depression. Following the Democrats' victory in the 1932 elections, he supported President Franklin Roosevelt's various New Deal infrastructure programs, assisting with the Civilian Conservation Corps that provided jobs for millions of out-of-work American men. In 1935, he went back to the Philippines once again, this time to oversee the creation of a national army there.

He retired from active duty in 1937, but was recalled in July 1941 to serve as commander, United States Army Forces in the Far East. He was forced to move his headquarters from the Philippines to Australia following Japanese advances in 1942. In a railway station in South Australia, MacArthur provided his view of this temporary setback:

> The president of the United States ordered me to break through the Japanese lines and proceed from Corregidor to Australia for the purpose, as I understand it, of organizing an American offensive against Japan, the primary purpose of which is the relief of the Philippines. I came through and I will return.

Return he did, on October 20, 1944. American forces swept across the Philippines, and MacArthur was elevated to the new wartime rank of five-star "General of the Army" in December. His leadership in driving back Axis forces in Papua New Guinea, Indonesia, and the Philippines was critical to the eventual Japanese defeat, and fittingly, as commander-in-chief of U.S. Army Forces, Pacific, he formally accepted the Japanese Terms of Surrender in September 1945.

After the surrender of the Japanese at the end of World War II, MacArthur served as the head of the Allied occupation of Japan, where he helped Japan transition to a democracy and rebuild after the war.

Six decades later, the "MacArthur Constitution" is still the law of the land in Japan and has provided the backbone for a country that has become the most prosperous and stable democracy in Asia.

In 1950, MacArthur was named commander of the United Nations' troops in Korea. Public disagreement with the Truman administration led to his being relieved of his command in April 1951, effectively ending fifty-two years of military service. Despite the controversial end to MacArthur's career, (he had violated the time-honored tradition and legal requirement of subordination of the military to civilian power by publicly disparaging the commander-in-chief and the official policies of the U.S. government), it illustrated his unbending will to say and do what he believed was right for his country. Many people regard MacArthur as a hero for challenging Truman.

When MacArthur stepped up to the microphone on that spring day in 1962, he was living in a world that had changed dramatically from when he was born in 1880. He had seen the invention of airplanes, telephones, nuclear weapons, communism, and space travel. What had not changed is what never changes: Duty, Honor, Country—the motto of West Point and the words that MacArthur lived by. MacArthur's speech was the culmination of a life lived by his convictions, and it perfectly expressed the ideals that every American strives to live up to: Duty, Honor, Country.

Today, as we ponder the almost unfathomable changes that have occurred in our lifetimes and the overwhelming rate of that change, we would be wise to remember that our values and essential character, immortally expressed in MacArthur's simple words—Duty, Honor, Country—will never change.

—JGC

⊗ ⊗ ⊗

General Westmoreland, General Grove, distinguished guests, and gentlemen of the Corps!

As I was leaving the hotel this morning, a doorman asked me, "Where are you bound for, General?" And when I replied, "West Point," he remarked, "Beautiful place. Have you ever been there before?"

No human being could fail to be deeply moved by such a tribute as this [Thayer Award]. Coming from a profession I have served so long, and a people I have loved so well, it fills me with an emotion I cannot express. But this award is not intended primarily to honor a personality, but to symbolize a great moral code—the code of conduct and chivalry of those who guard this beloved land of culture and ancient descent. That is the animation of this medallion. For all eyes and for all time, it is an expression of the ethics of the American soldier. That I should be integrated in this way with so noble an ideal arouses a sense of pride and yet of humility which will be with me always.

Duty, Honor, Country: Those three hallowed words reverently dictate what you ought to be, what you can be, what you will be. They are your rallying points: to build courage when courage seems to fail; to regain faith when there seems to be little cause for faith; to create hope when hope becomes forlorn.

Unhappily, I possess neither that eloquence of diction, that poetry of imagination, nor that brilliance of metaphor to tell you all that they mean.

The unbelievers will say they are but words, but a slogan, but a flamboyant phrase. Every pedant, every demagogue, every cynic, every hypocrite, every troublemaker, and I am sorry to say, some others of an entirely different character, will try to downgrade them even to the extent of mockery and ridicule.

But these are some of the things they do. They build your basic character. They mold you for your future roles as the custodians of the nation's defense. They make you strong enough to know when you are weak, and brave enough to face yourself when you are afraid. They teach you to be proud and unbending in honest failure, but humble and gentle in success; not to substitute words for actions, not to seek the path of comfort, but to face the stress and spur of difficulty and challenge; to learn to stand up in the storm but to have compassion on those who fall; to master yourself before you seek to master others; to have a heart that is clean, a goal that is high; to learn to laugh, yet never forget how to weep; to reach into the future yet never neglect the past; to be serious yet never to take yourself too seriously; to be modest so that you will remember the simplicity of true greatness, the open mind of true wisdom, the meekness of true strength. They give you a temper of the will, a quality of the imagination, a vigor of the emotions, a freshness of the deep springs of life, a temperamental predominance of courage over timidity, of an appetite for adventure over love of ease. They create in your heart the sense of wonder, the unfailing hope of what next, and the joy and inspiration of life. They teach you in this way to be an officer and a gentleman.

And what sort of soldiers are those you are to lead? Are they reliable? Are they brave? Are they capable of victory? Their story is known to all of you. It is the story of the American man-at-arms. My estimate of him was formed on the battlefield many, many years ago, and has never changed. I regarded him then as I regard him now—as one of the world's noblest figures, not only as one of the finest military characters, but also as one of the most stainless. His name and fame are the birthright of every American citizen. In his youth and strength, his love and loyalty, he gave all that mortality can give.

He needs no eulogy from me or from any other man. He has written his own history and written it in red on his enemy's breast. But when I think of his patience under adversity, of his courage under fire, and of his modesty in victory, I am filled with an emotion of admiration I cannot put into words. He belongs to history as furnishing one of the greatest examples of successful patriotism. He belongs to posterity as the instructor of future generations in the principles of liberty and freedom. He belongs to the present, to us, by his virtues and by his achievements. In 20 campaigns, on a hundred battlefields, around a thousand campfires, I have witnessed that enduring fortitude, that patriotic self-abnegation, and that invincible determination which have carved his statue in the hearts of his people. From one end of the world to the other he has drained deep the chalice of courage.

As I listened to those songs [of the glee club], in memory's eye I could see those staggering columns of the First World War, bending under soggy packs, on many a weary march from dripping dusk to drizzling dawn, slogging ankle-deep through the mire of shell-shocked roads, to form grimly for the attack, blue-lipped, covered with sludge and mud, chilled by the wind and rain, driving home to their objective, and for many, to the judgment seat of God.

I do not know the dignity of their birth, but I do know the glory of their death. They died unquestioning, uncomplaining, with faith in their hearts, and on their lips the hope that we would go on to victory. Always, for them: Duty, Honor, Country; always their blood and sweat and tears, as we sought the way and the light and the truth.

And 20 years after, on the other side of the globe, again the filth of murky foxholes, the stench of ghostly trenches, the slime of dripping dugouts; those boiling suns of relentless heat, those torrential rains of devastating storms; the loneliness and utter desolation of jungle trails; the bitterness of long separation from those they loved and cherished; the deadly pestilence of tropical disease; the horror of stricken areas of war; their resolute and determined defense, their swift and sure attack, their indomitable purpose, their complete and decisive victory—always victory. Always through the bloody haze of their last reverberating shot, the vision of gaunt, ghastly men reverently following your password of: Duty, Honor, Country.

The code which those words perpetuate embraces the highest moral laws and will stand the test of any ethics or philosophies ever promulgated for the uplift of mankind. Its requirements are for the things that are right, and its restraints are from the things that are wrong.

The soldier, above all other men, is required to practice the greatest act of religious training—sacrifice.

In battle and in the face of danger and death, he discloses those divine attributes which his Maker gave when he created man in his own image. No physical courage and no brute instinct can take the place of the Divine help which alone can sustain him.

However horrible the incidents of war may be, the soldier who is called upon to offer and to give his life for his country is the noblest development of mankind.

You now face a new world—a world of change. The thrust into outer space of the satellite, spheres, and missiles mark the beginning of another epoch in the long story of mankind. In the five or more billions of years the scientists tell us it has taken to form the earth, in the three or more billion years of development of the human race, there has never been a more abrupt or staggering evolution. We deal now not with things of this world alone, but with the illimitable distances and as yet unfathomed mysteries of the universe. We are reaching out for a new and boundless frontier.

We speak in strange terms: of harnessing the cosmic energy; of making winds and tides work for us; of creating unheard synthetic materials to supplement or even replace our old standard basics; to purify sea water for our drink; of mining ocean floors for new fields of wealth and food; of disease preventatives to expand life into the hundreds of years; of controlling the weather for a more equitable distribution of heat and cold, of rain and shine; of space ships to the moon; of the primary target in war, no longer limited to the armed forces of an enemy, but instead to include his civil populations; of ultimate conflict between a united human race and the sinister forces of some other planetary galaxy; of such dreams and fantasies as to make life the most exciting of all time.

And through all this welter of change and development, your mission remains fixed, determined, inviolable: it is to win our wars.

Everything else in your professional career is but corollary to this vital dedication. All other public purposes, all other public projects, all other public needs, great or small, will find others for their accomplishment. But you are the ones who are trained to fight. Yours is the profession of arms, the will to win, the sure knowledge that in war there is no substitute for victory; that if you lose, the nation will be destroyed; that the very obsession of your public service must be: Duty, Honor, Country.

Others will debate the controversial issues, national and international, which divide men's minds; but serene, calm, aloof, you stand as the Nation's warguardian, as its lifeguard from the raging tides of international conflict, as its gladiator in the arena of battle. For a century and a half you have defended, guarded, and protected its hallowed traditions of liberty and freedom, of right and justice.

Let civilian voices argue the merits or demerits of our processes of government; whether our strength is being sapped by deficit financing, indulged in too long, by federal paternalism grown too mighty, by power groups grown too arrogant, by politics grown too corrupt, by crime grown too rampant, by morals grown too low, by taxes grown too high, by extremists grown too violent; whether our personal liberties are as thorough and complete as they should be. These great national problems are not for your professional participation or military solution. Your guidepost stands out like a ten-fold beacon in the night: Duty, Honor, Country.

You are the leaven which binds together the entire fabric of our national system of defense. From your ranks come the great captains who hold the nation's destiny in their hands the moment the war tocsin sounds. The Long Gray Line has never failed us. Were you to do so, a million ghosts in olive drab, in brown khaki, in blue and gray, would rise from their white crosses thundering those magic words: Duty, Honor, Country.

This does not mean that you are war mongers.

On the contrary, the soldier, above all other people, prays for peace, for he must suffer and bear the deepest wounds and scars of war.

But always in our ears ring the ominous words of Plato, that wisest of all philosophers: "Only the dead have seen the end of war."

The shadows are lengthening for me. The twilight is here. My days of old have vanished, tone and tint. They have gone glimmering through the dreams of things that were. Their memory is one of wondrous beauty, watered by tears, and coaxed and caressed by the smiles of yesterday. I listen vainly, but with thirsty ears, for the witching melody of faint bugles blowing reveille, of far drums beating the long roll. In my dreams I hear again the crash of guns, the rattle of musketry, the strange, mournful mutter of the battlefield.

But in the evening of my memory, always I come back to West Point.

Always there echoes and re-echoes: Duty, Honor, Country.

Today marks my final roll call with you, but I want you to know that when I cross the river my last conscious thoughts will be of The Corps, and The Corps, and The Corps.

I bid you farewell.

Reprinted with the permission of the General Douglas MacArthur Foundation, Norfolk, Virginia.

XXI

"Judged . . . by the content of their character"

MARTIN LUTHER KING'S
I HAVE A DREAM
(1963)

M ARTIN LUTHER KING, JR., SPEAKING FROM THE STEPS OF THE LIN-
coln Memorial, delivered his "I Have a Dream" speech on August 28,
1963. Various civil rights groups including the National Association for the
Advancement of Colored People, the Congress of Racial Equality, the Southern Christian Leadership Council, and the Student Non-Violent Coordinating
Center had organized the crowd of over 250,000 Americans. The crowd was
black and white, came from the north and the south, and included students
and adults.

Born in Atlanta in January 1929—the eve of the Great Depression—to
Alberta Williams King and Michael King, the pastor of Ebenezer Baptist
Church, Martin Luther King, Jr. attended a segregated school as a youngster.
He went on to attend Morehouse College (a historically all-male and pre-
dominantly black college), then left the south to attend seminary at Crozer

Theological Seminary in Pennsylvania. From there he moved to Boston for graduate studies, earning a doctorate of Philosophy from Boston University in 1955.

After school, King and his wife Coretta Scott, whom he met in Boston, moved to Montgomery, Alabama, where King served as pastor at the Dexter Avenue Baptist Church. On December 1, 1955 in Montgomery, Rosa Parks refused to give up her seat on a segregated bus, leading to her arrest. As a result, a boycott of the city-owned buses was organized, with King participating as the president of a new group, the Montgomery Improvement Association (MIA). On January 26th of the following year, while the boycott was still in effect, King was arrested for the first time. Four days later his home was bombed, and nearly two months later he was once again arrested, tried, and convicted. The 381-day boycott ended when the Supreme Court decided that the segregation laws were illegal. These events were the basis for King being awarded the 1964 Nobel Peace Prize.

King helped establish the Southern Christian Leadership Council (SCLC) and served as its president. He patterned SCLC's participation in the civil rights movement after Mahatma Gandhi's non-violent resistance, speaking more than 2,500 times and traveling six million miles between 1957 and 1968.

It was an era of turmoil for America. As the civil rights movement demanding equal treatment under the law grew, Cuba was taken over in 1959 by dictator Fidel Castro, President John F. Kennedy was elected to the White House in 1960, and America's unsuccessful attempt to overthrow Castro during the Bay of Pigs fiasco occurred in 1961. The next year, tension in foreign affairs increased during the Cuban missile crisis, and America's school children were warned to "duck and cover" under desks in the event of a missile attack.

As affairs overseas heated up, so did the civil rights struggle here at home. President Kennedy addressed the country over radio and television on June 11, 1963, saying, "This afternoon, following a series of threats and defiant statements, the presence of Alabama National Guardsmen was required on the University of Alabama to carry out the final and unequivocal order of the United States District Court of the Northern District of Alabama. That order called for the admission of two clearly qualified young Alabama residents who happened to have been born Negro."

"Next week," stated Kennedy, "I shall ask the Congress of the United States to act, to make a commitment it has not fully made in this century to the proposition that race has no place in American life or law."

The same day that Kennedy spoke of civil rights legislation, the SCLC announced plans to organize a "Jobs and Freedom" march on Washington, D.C. Other groups soon joined in to organize the yet unscheduled march.

The Kennedy administration attempted to facilitate a cancellation of the march, but unable to deter the organizers, it instead focused on efforts to simply manage it. Organizers agreed to a one-day event that would prevent the marchers from remaining in Washington overnight.

The march was to be dedicated to jobs and freedom. On the day of the event, August 28, 1963, more than 2,000 buses arrived in our nation's capital. Many shops closed down, and alcohol sales were banned for the day. The National Guard was called in to assist, additional police were on hand, and the army ordered 17,000 troops to be stationed near Washington. The event included singing, music, and speakers from 10 organizations. King was the final speaker.

Martin Luther King, Jr.'s wealth of experience as a preacher and speaker provided him with the cadence, rhythm, and emotion to connect with the audience. His speech did not simply address the problems of the time, but provided an expanded view—a higher goal—to which our country should reach. Rather than focusing on condemnation of the administration and complaints of unfair treatment, King focused his speech on aiming higher and making progress together, delivering an optimistic message of what could be if Americans worked together.

Let us not wallow in the valley of despair, I say to you today, my friends. And so even though we face the difficulties of today and tomorrow, I still have a dream. It is a dream deeply rooted in the American dream. I have a dream that one day this nation will rise up and live out the true meaning of its creed: "We hold these truths to be self-evident, that all men are created equal." . . . I have a dream that my four little children will one day live in a nation where they will not be judged by the color of their skin but by the content of their character. . . . Looking forward to "that day when *all* of God's children, black men and white men, Jews and Gentiles, Protestants and Catholics, will be able to join hands and sing in the words of the old Negro spiritual: *Free at last! Free at last! Thank God Almighty, we are free at last!*

The peaceful march has left a lasting impression on our nation. Today, when Americans visit the Lincoln Memorial, they see a plaque that marks the location where King delivered his historic remarks. It was donated by the National Park Service and installed August 28, 2003, on the 40th anniversary of his speech.

Three months after King's momentous remarks on November 22 in Dallas, Texas, President John. F. Kennedy was assassinated. The Civil Rights Act of 1964 was signed into law on July 2, 1964, and President Lyndon B. Johnson signed the Voting Rights Act on August 6, 1965. Yet the passage of those acts did not make Dr. King safe; while standing on the balcony of his motel room in Memphis, Tennessee on April 4, 1968, he was assassinated.

King's work for civil rights and his message of a positive dream for all Americans still echoes among our generations as we continue to work for the fulfillment of his dream: that all people be judged not by the color of their skin but by the content of their character.

—JGC

❧ ❧ ❧

I am happy to join with you today in what will go down in history as the greatest demonstration for freedom in the history of our nation.

Five score years ago, a great American, in whose symbolic shadow we stand today, signed the Emancipation Proclamation. This momentous decree came as a great beacon light of hope to millions of Negro slaves who had been seared in the flames of withering injustice. It came as a joyous daybreak to end the long night of their captivity.

But one hundred years later, the Negro still is not free. One hundred years later, the life of the Negro is still sadly crippled by the manacles of segregation and the chains of discrimination. One hundred years later, the Negro lives on a lonely island of poverty in the midst of a vast ocean of material prosperity. One hundred years later, the Negro is still languished in the corners of American society and finds himself an exile in his own land. And so we've come here today to dramatize a shameful condition.

In a sense we've come to our nation's capital to cash a check. When the architects of our republic wrote the magnificent words of the Constitution and the Declaration of Independence, they were signing a promissory note to which every American was to fall heir. This note was a promise that all men, yes, black men as well as white men, would be guaranteed the "unalienable Rights" of "Life, Liberty and the pursuit of Happiness." It is obvious today that America has defaulted on this promissory note, insofar as her citizens of color are concerned. Instead of honoring this sacred obligation, America has given the Negro people a bad check, a check which has come back marked "insufficient funds."

But we refuse to believe that the bank of justice is bankrupt. We refuse to believe that there are insufficient funds in the great vaults of opportunity of this nation. And so, we've come to cash this check, a check that will give us upon demand the riches of freedom and the security of justice.

We have also come to this hallowed spot to remind America of the fierce urgency of Now. This is no time to engage in the luxury of cooling off or to take the tranquilizing drug of gradualism. Now is the time to make real the promises of democracy. Now is the time to rise from the dark and desolate valley of segregation to the sunlit path of racial justice. Now is the time to lift our nation from the quicksands of racial injustice to the solid rock of brotherhood. Now is the time to make justice a reality for all of God's children.

It would be fatal for the nation to overlook the urgency of the moment. This sweltering summer of the Negro's legitimate discontent will not pass until there is an invigorating autumn of freedom and equality. Nineteen sixty-three is not an end, but a beginning. And those who hope that the Negro needed to blow off steam and will now be content will have a rude awakening if the nation returns to business as usual. And there will be neither rest nor tranquility in America until the Negro is granted his citizenship rights. The whirlwinds of revolt will continue to shake the foundations of our nation until the bright day of justice emerges.

But there is something that I must say to my people, who stand on the warm threshold which leads into the palace of justice: In the process of gaining our rightful place, we must not be guilty of wrongful deeds. Let us not seek to satisfy our thirst for freedom by drinking from the cup of bitterness and hatred. We must forever conduct our struggle on the high plane of dignity and discipline. We must not allow our creative protest to degenerate into physical violence. Again and again, we must rise to the majestic heights of meeting physical force with soul force.

The marvelous new militancy which has engulfed the Negro community must not lead us to a distrust of all white people, for many of our white brothers, as evidenced by their presence here today, have come to realize that their destiny is tied up with our destiny. And they have come to realize that their freedom is inextricably bound to our freedom.

We cannot walk alone.

And as we walk, we must make the pledge that we shall always march ahead. We cannot turn back.

There are those who are asking the devotees of civil rights, "When will you be satisfied?" We can never be satisfied as long as the Negro is the victim of the unspeakable horrors of police brutality. We can never be satisfied as long as our bodies, heavy with the fatigue of travel, cannot gain lodging in the motels of the highways and the hotels of the cities. We cannot be satisfied as long as the negro's basic mobility is from a smaller ghetto to a larger one. We can never be satisfied as long as our children are stripped of their self-hood and robbed of their dignity by signs stating: "For Whites Only." We cannot be satisfied as long as a Negro in Mississippi cannot vote and a Negro in New York believes he has nothing for which to vote. No, no, we are not satisfied, and we will not be satisfied until "justice rolls down like waters, and righteousness like a mighty stream."

I am not unmindful that some of you have come here out of great trials and tribulations. Some of you have come fresh from narrow jail cells. And some of you have come from areas where your quest—quest for freedom left you battered by the storms of persecution and staggered by the winds of police brutality. You have been the veterans of creative suffering. Continue to work with the faith that unearned suffering is redemptive. Go back to Mississippi, go back to Alabama, go back to South Carolina, go back to Georgia, go back to Louisiana, go back to the slums and ghettos of our northern cities, knowing that somehow this situation can and will be changed.

Let us not wallow in the valley of despair, I say to you today, my friends.

And so even though we face the difficulties of today and tomorrow, I still have a dream. It is a dream deeply rooted in the American dream.

I have a dream that one day this nation will rise up and live out the true meaning of its creed: "We hold these truths to be self-evident, that all men are created equal."

I have a dream that one day on the red hills of Georgia, the sons of former slaves and the sons of former slave owners will be able to sit down together at the table of brotherhood.

I have a dream that one day even the state of Mississippi, a state sweltering with the heat of injustice, sweltering with the heat of oppression, will be transformed into an oasis of freedom and justice.

I have a dream that my four little children will one day live in a nation where they will not be judged by the color of their skin but by the content of their character.

I have a *dream* today!

I have a dream that one day, down in Alabama, with its vicious racists, with its governor having his lips dripping with the words of "interposition" and "nullification"—one day right there in Alabama little black boys and black girls will be able to join hands with little white boys and white girls as sisters and brothers.

I have a *dream* today!

I have a dream that one day every valley shall be exalted, and every hill and mountain shall be made low, the rough places will be made plain, and the crooked places will be made straight; "and the glory of the Lord shall be revealed and all flesh shall see it together."

This is our hope, and this is the faith that I go back to the South with.

With this faith, we will be able to hew out of the mountain of despair a stone of hope. With this faith, we will be able to transform the jangling discords of our nation into a beautiful symphony of brotherhood. With this faith, we will be able to work together, to pray together, to struggle together, to go to jail together, to stand up for freedom together, knowing that we will be free one day.

And this will be the day—this will be the day when all of God's children will be able to sing with new meaning:

> My country 'tis of thee, sweet land of liberty, of thee I sing.
> Land where my fathers died, land of the Pilgrim's pride,
> From every mountainside, let freedom ring!

And if America is to be a great nation, this must become true.

And so let freedom ring from the prodigious hilltops of New Hampshire.

Let freedom ring from the mighty mountains of New York.

Let freedom ring from the heightening Alleghenies of Pennsylvania.

Let freedom ring from the snow-capped Rockies of Colorado.

Let freedom ring from the curvaceous slopes of California.

But not only that:

Let freedom ring from Stone Mountain of Georgia.

Let freedom ring from Lookout Mountain of Tennessee.

Let freedom ring from every hill and molehill of Mississippi.

From every mountainside, let freedom ring.

And when this happens, when we allow freedom ring, when we let it ring from every village and every hamlet, from every state and every city, we will be able to speed up that day when *all* of God's children, black men and white men, Jews and Gentiles, Protestants and Catholics, will be able to join hands and sing in the words of the old Negro spiritual:

> *Free at last! Free at last!*
> *Thank God Almighty, we are free at last!*

XXII

"A rendezvous with destiny"

Ronald Reagan's
A Time for Choosing
(1964)

"THE SPEECH," AS IT BECAME KNOWN, WAS DELIVERED BY RONALD Reagan in support of then-Republican presidential candidate Barry Goldwater, and televised nationwide on October 27, 1964. It was a half-hour political program, which was paid for by Goldwater and a contribution from Brothers for Goldwater, chaired by actor John Wayne. This was the nation's first view of Reagan, the politician, who would promote American values and conservatism for the rest of his life.

The foundation for "the Speech" had formed over the previous decade while Reagan was a spokesman for a General Electric (GE) initiative to promote citizenship among employees by touting education and what everyday men and women could accomplish. It had been created by GE Vice President Lemuel Boulware, who was also behind the hiring of Reagan. Boulware believed that "the average citizen cannot afford to leave politics to the politicians." Reagan was the perfect man for the message.

From 1954 to 1962, Reagan crisscrossed the country numerous times, visiting all 130 GE plants and meeting more than 250,000 employees. He gave various versions of this speech, honing and sharpening his core message, by adding to and subtracting from the index cards he used while delivering his talk.

While Reagan promoted conservatism in the speech, he also continually talked about the strength and resilience of the American people, and common issues every American faced.

"I believe that the issues confronting us cross party lines," he said.

"There is no such thing as a Left or Right. There's only an up or down—[up,] man's [age-old] dream, the ultimate in individual freedom consistent with law and order, or down to the ant heap of totalitarianism."

Reagan, at heart, was a uniter. He believed that conservatism, the belief that individuals rather than government should be in charge, was the way to solve all our national ills, saying, "You can't control the economy without controlling the people. . . . We either take responsibility for our own destiny, or we abandon the American Revolution and confess that an intellectual belief in a far-distant capital can plan our lives for us better than we can plan them ourselves."

Reagan also understood that the freedom enjoyed by the American people, and our method of government, make the United States an extraordinary place to live. He noted that America's method of self-government is what makes it exceptional, "If we lose freedom here, there's no place to escape to. This is the last stand on Earth."

While Goldwater's presidential bid ended in defeat to incumbent President Lyndon Johnson, "The Speech" had started a nationwide focus on conservative values and beliefs that resounded with voters. Reagan served as the governor of California from 1967 to 1975. And in 1980, sixteen years after delivering "The Speech," Reagan was elected president.

Today we find ourselves at a similar crossroads. Abandon the American Revolution or take control of our destiny. Once again, the American people are called to action. Every generation must decide if it wants to leave politics to the politicians—or whether we, like Reagan, are ready for our rendezvous with destiny.

—JGC

❧ ❧ ❧

Thank you. Thank you very much. Thank you and good evening. The sponsor has been identified, but unlike most television programs, the performer hasn't been provided with a script. As a matter of fact, I have been permitted to choose my own words and discuss my own ideas regarding the choice that we face in the next few weeks.

I have spent most of my life as a Democrat. I recently have seen fit to follow another course. I believe that the issues confronting us cross party lines. Now, one side in this campaign has been telling us that the issues of this election are the maintenance of peace and prosperity. The line has been used, "We've never had it so good."

But I have an uncomfortable feeling that this prosperity isn't something on which we can base our hopes for the future. No nation in history has ever survived a tax burden that reached a third of its national income. Today, 37 cents out of every dollar earned in this country is the tax collector's share, and yet our government continues to spend 17 million dollars a day more than the government takes in. We haven't balanced our budget twenty-eight out of the last thirty-four years. We've raised our debt limit three times in the last twelve months, and now our national debt is one and a half times bigger than all the combined debts of all the nations of the world. We have 15 billion dollars in gold in our treasury; we don't own an ounce. Foreign dollar claims are 27.3 billion dollars. And we've just had announced that the dollar of 1939 will now purchase 45 cents in its total value.

As for the peace that we would preserve, I wonder who among us would like to approach the wife or mother whose husband or son has died in South Vietnam and ask them if they think this is a peace that should be maintained indefinitely. Do they mean peace, or do they mean we just want to be left in peace? There can be no real peace while one American is dying some place in the world for the rest of us. We're at war with the most dangerous enemy that has ever faced mankind in his long climb from the swamp to the stars, and it's been said if we lose that war, and in so doing lose this way of freedom of ours, history will record with the greatest astonishment that those who had the most to lose did the least to prevent its happening. Well I think it's time we ask ourselves if we still know the freedoms that were intended for us by the Founding Fathers.

Not too long ago, two friends of mine were talking to a Cuban refugee, a businessman who had escaped from Castro, and in the midst of his story one of my friends turned to the other and said, "We don't know how lucky we are." And the Cuban stopped and said, "How lucky you are? I had someplace to escape to." And in that sentence he told us the entire story. If we lose freedom here, there's no place to escape to. This is the last stand on earth.

And this idea that government is beholden to the people, that it has no other source of power except the sovereign people, is still the newest and the most unique idea in all the long history of man's relation to man.

This is the issue of this election: whether we believe in our capacity for self-government or whether we abandon the American revolution and confess that a little intellectual elite in a far-distant capitol can plan our lives for us better than we can plan them ourselves.

You and I are told increasingly we have to choose between a Left or Right. Well I'd like to suggest there is no such thing as a Left or Right. There's only an up or down—[up,] man's [age-old] dream, the ultimate in individual freedom consistent with law and order, or down to the ant heap of totalitarianism. And regardless of their sincerity, their humanitarian motives, those who would trade our freedom for security have embarked on this downward course.

In this vote-harvesting time, they use terms like the "Great Society," or as we were told a few days ago by the president, we must accept a greater government activity in the affairs of the people. But they've been a little more explicit in the past and among themselves; and all of the things I now will quote have appeared in print. These are not Republican accusations. For example, they have voices that say, "The cold war will end through our acceptance of a not undemocratic socialism." Another voice says, "The profit motive has become outmoded. It must be replaced by the incentives of the welfare state." Or, "Our traditional system of individual freedom is incapable of solving the complex problems of the 20th century." Senator Fullbright has said at Stanford University that the Constitution is outmoded. He referred to the president as "our moral teacher and our leader," and he says he is "hobbled in his task by the restrictions of power imposed on him by this antiquated document." He must "be freed," so that he "can do for us" what he knows "is best." And Senator Clark of Pennsylvania, another articulate spokesman, defines liberalism as "meeting the material needs of the masses through the full power of centralized government."

Well, I, for one, resent it when a representative of the people refers to you and me, the free men and women of this country, as "the masses." This is a term we haven't applied to ourselves in America. But beyond that, "the full power of centralized government"—this was the very thing the Founding Fathers sought to minimize. They knew that governments don't control things. A government can't control the economy without controlling people. And they know when a government sets out to do that, it must use force and coercion to achieve its purpose. They also knew, those Founding Fathers, that outside of its legitimate functions, government does nothing as well or as economically as the private sector of the economy.

Now, we have no better example of this than government's involvement in the farm economy over the last 30 years. Since 1955, the cost of this program has nearly doubled. One-fourth of farming in America is responsible for 85 percent of the farm surplus. Three-fourths of farming is out on the free market and has known a 21 percent increase in the per capita consumption of all its produce. You see, that one-fourth of farming—that's regulated and controlled by the federal government. In the last three years we've spent 43 dollars in the feed grain program for every dollar bushel of corn we don't grow.

Senator Humphrey last week charged that Barry Goldwater, as president, would seek to eliminate farmers. He should do his homework a little better, because he'll find out that we've had a decline of 5 million in the farm population under these government programs. He'll also find that the Democratic administration has sought to get from Congress [an] extension of the farm program to include that three-fourths that is now free. He'll find that they've also asked for the right to imprison farmers who wouldn't keep books as prescribed by the federal government. The secretary of Agriculture asked for the right to seize farms through condemnation and resell them to other individuals. And contained in that same program was a provision that would have allowed the federal government to remove 2 million farmers from the soil.

At the same time, there's been an increase in the Department of Agriculture employees. There's now one for every 30 farms in the United States, and still they can't tell us how sixty-six shiploads of grain headed for Austria disappeared without a trace and Billie Sol Estes never left shore.

Every responsible farmer and farm organization has repeatedly asked the government to free the farm economy, but how—who are farmers to know what's best for them? The wheat farmers voted against a wheat program. The government passed it anyway. Now the price of bread goes up; the price of wheat to the farmer goes down.

Meanwhile, back in the city, under urban renewal the assault on freedom carries on. Private property rights [are] so diluted that public interest is almost anything a few government planners decide it should be. In a program that takes from the needy and gives to the greedy, we see such spectacles as in Cleveland, Ohio, a million-and-a-half-dollar building completed only three years ago must be destroyed to make way for what government officials call a "more compatible use of the land." The president tells us he's now going to start building public housing units in the thousands, where heretofore we've only built them in the hundreds. But FHA [Federal Housing Authority] and the Veterans Administration tell us they have 120,000 housing units they've taken back through mortgage foreclosure. For three decades, we've sought to solve the problems of unemployment through government planning, and the more the plans fail, the more the planners plan. The latest is the Area Redevelopment Agency.

They've just declared Rice County, Kansas, a depressed area. Rice County, Kansas, has two hundred oil wells, and the 14,000 people there have over 30 million dollars on deposit in personal savings in their banks. And when the government tells you you're depressed, lie down and be depressed.

We have so many people who can't see a fat man standing beside a thin one without coming to the conclusion the fat man got that way by taking advantage of the thin one. So they're going to solve all the problems of human misery through government and government planning. Well, now, if government planning and welfare had the answer—and they've had almost thirty years of it—shouldn't we expect government to read the score to us once in a while? Shouldn't they be telling us about the decline each year in the number of people needing help? The reduction in the need for public housing?

But the reverse is true. Each year the need grows greater; the program grows greater. We were told four years ago that 17 million people went to bed hungry each night. Well that was probably true. They were all on a diet. But now we're told that 9.3 million families in this country are poverty-stricken on the basis of earning less than 3,000 dollars a year. Welfare spending [is] 10 times greater than in the dark depths of the Depression. We're spending 45 billion dollars on welfare. Now do a little arithmetic, and you'll find that if we divided the 45 billion dollars up equally among those 9 million poor families, we'd be able to give each family 4,600 dollars a year. And this added to their present income should eliminate poverty. Direct aid to the poor, however, is only running only about 600 dollars per family. It would seem that someplace there must be some overhead.

Now—so now we declare "war on poverty," or "You, too, can be a Bobby Baker." Now do they honestly expect us to believe that if we add 1 billion dollars to the 45 billion we're spending, one more program to the 30-odd we have—and remember, this new program doesn't replace any, it just duplicates existing programs—do they believe that poverty is suddenly going to disappear by magic? Well, in all fairness I should explain there is one part of the new program that isn't duplicated. This is the youth feature. We're now going to solve the dropout problem, juvenile delinquency, by reinstituting something like the old CCC camps [Civilian Conservation Corps], and we're going to put our young people in these camps. But again we do some arithmetic, and we find that we're going to spend each year just on room and board for each young person we help 4,700 dollars a year. We can send them to Harvard for 2,700! 'Course, don't get me wrong. I'm not suggesting Harvard is the answer to juvenile delinquency.

But seriously, what are we doing to those we seek to help? Not too long ago, a judge called me here in Los Angeles. He told me of a young woman who'd come before him for a divorce. She had six children, was pregnant with her seventh. Under his questioning, she revealed her husband was a laborer earning 250 dollars a month. She wanted a divorce to get an 80 dollar raise. She's eligible for 330 dollars a month in the Aid to Dependent Children Program. She got the idea from two women in her neighborhood who'd already done that very thing.

Yet anytime you and I question the schemes of the do-gooders, we're denounced as being against their humanitarian goals. They say we're always "against" things—we're never "for" anything.

Well, the trouble with our liberal friends is not that they're ignorant; it's just that they know so much that isn't so.

Now—we're for a provision that destitution should not follow unemployment by reason of old age, and to that end we've accepted Social Security as a step toward meeting the problem.

But we're against those entrusted with this program when they practice deception regarding its fiscal shortcomings, when they charge that any criticism of the program means that we want to end payments to those people who depend on them for a livelihood. They've called it "insurance" to us in a hundred million pieces of literature. But then they appeared before the Supreme Court and they testified it was a welfare program. They only use the term "insurance" to sell it to the people. And they said Social Security dues are a tax for the general use of the government, and the government has used that tax. There is no fund, because Robert Byers, the actuarial head, appeared before a congressional committee and admitted that Social Security as of this moment is 298 billion dollars in the hole. But he said there should be no cause for worry, because as long as they have the power to tax, they could always take away from the people whatever they needed to bail them out of trouble. And they're doing just that.

A young man, twenty-one years of age, working at an average salary—his Social Security contribution would, in the open market, buy him an insurance policy that would guarantee 220 dollars a month at age 65. The government promises 127. He could live it up until he's 31 and then take out a policy that would pay more than Social Security. Now are we so lacking in business sense that we can't put this program on a sound basis, so that people who do require those payments will find they can get them when they're due—that the cupboard isn't bare?

Barry Goldwater thinks we can.

At the same time, can't we introduce voluntary features that would permit a citizen who can do better on his own to be excused upon presentation of evidence that he had made provision for the non-earning years? Should we not allow a widow with children to work, and not lose the benefits supposedly paid for by her deceased husband? Shouldn't you and I be allowed to declare who our beneficiaries will be under this program, which we cannot do? I think we're for telling our senior citizens that no one in this country should be denied medical care because of a lack of funds. But I think we're against forcing all citizens, regardless of need, into a compulsory government program, especially when we have such examples, as was announced last week, when France admitted that their Medicare program is now bankrupt. They've come to the end of the road.

In addition, was Barry Goldwater so irresponsible when he suggested that our government give up its program of deliberate, planned inflation, so that when you do get your Social Security pension, a dollar will buy a dollar's worth, and not 45 cents worth?

I think we're for an international organization, where the nations of the world can seek peace. But I think we're against subordinating American interests to an organization that has become so structurally unsound that today you can muster a two-thirds vote on the floor of the General Assembly among nations that represent less than 10 percent of the world's population. I think we're against the hypocrisy of assailing our allies because here and there they cling to a colony, while we engage in a conspiracy of silence and never open our mouths about the millions of people enslaved in the Soviet colonies in the satellite nations.

I think we're for aiding our allies by sharing of our material blessings with those nations which share in our fundamental beliefs, but we're against doling out money government to government, creating bureaucracy, if not socialism, all over the world. We set out to help 19 countries. We're helping 107. We've spent 146 billion dollars. With that money, we bought a 2 million dollar yacht for Haile Selassie. We bought dress suits for Greek undertakers, extra wives for Kenya[n] government officials. We bought a thousand TV sets for a place where they have no electricity. In the last six years, fifty-two nations have bought 7 billion dollars worth of our gold, and all fifty-two are receiving foreign aid from this country.

No government ever voluntarily reduces itself in size. So governments' programs, once launched, never disappear.

Actually, a government bureau is the nearest thing to eternal life we'll ever see on this earth.

Federal employees—federal employees number two and a half million; and federal, state, and local, one out of six of the nation's work force employed by government. These proliferating bureaus with their thousands of regulations have cost us many of our constitutional safeguards. How many of us realize that today federal agents can invade a man's property without a warrant? They can impose a fine without a formal hearing, let alone a trial by jury? And they can seize and sell his property at auction to enforce the payment of that fine. In Chico County, Arkansas, James Wier over-planted his rice allotment. The government obtained a 17,000 dollar judgment. And a U.S. marshal sold his 960-acre farm at auction. The government said it was necessary as a warning to others to make the system work.

Last February 19th at the University of Minnesota, Norman Thomas, six-times candidate for president on the Socialist Party ticket, said, "If Barry

Goldwater became president, he would stop the advance of socialism in the United States." I think that's exactly what he will do.

But as a former Democrat, I can tell you Norman Thomas isn't the only man who has drawn this parallel to socialism with the present administration, because back in 1936, Mr. Democrat himself, Al Smith, the great American, came before the American people and charged that the leadership of his Party was taking the Party of Jefferson, Jackson, and Cleveland down the road under the banners of Marx, Lenin, and Stalin. And he walked away from his Party, and he never returned 'til the day he died—because to this day, the leadership of that Party has been taking that Party, that honorable Party, down the road in the image of the labor Socialist Party of England.

Now it doesn't require expropriation or confiscation of private property or business to impose socialism on a people. What does it mean whether you hold the deed to the—or the title to your business or property if the government holds the power of life and death over that business or property? And such machinery already exists. The government can find some charge to bring against any concern it chooses to prosecute. Every businessman has his own tale of harassment. Somewhere a perversion has taken place. Our natural, unalienable rights are now considered to be a dispensation of government, and freedom has never been so fragile, so close to slipping from our grasp as it is at this moment.

Our Democratic opponents seem unwilling to debate these issues. They want to make you and I believe that this is a contest between two men—that we're to choose just between two personalities.

Well what of this man that they would destroy—and in destroying, they would destroy that which he represents, the ideas that you and I hold dear? Is he the brash and shallow and trigger-happy man they say he is? Well I've been privileged to know him "when." I knew him long before he ever dreamed of trying for high office, and I can tell you personally I've never known a man in my life I believed so incapable of doing a dishonest or dishonorable thing.

This is a man who, in his own business before he entered politics, instituted a profit-sharing plan before unions had ever thought of it. He put in health and medical insurance for all his employees. He took 50 percent of the profits before taxes and set up a retirement program, a pension plan for all his employees. He sent monthly checks for life to an employee who was ill and couldn't work. He provides nursing care for the children of mothers who work in the stores. When Mexico was ravaged by the floods in the Rio Grande, he climbed in his airplane and flew medicine and supplies down there.

An ex-GI told me how he met him. It was the week before Christmas during the Korean War, and he was at the Los Angeles airport trying to get a ride home to Arizona for Christmas. And he said that [there were] a lot of servicemen there and no seats available on the planes. And then a voice came over the loudspeaker and said, "Any men in uniform wanting a ride to Arizona, go to runway such-and-such," and they went down there, and there was a fellow named Barry Goldwater sitting in his plane. Every day in those weeks before Christmas, all day long, he'd load up the plane, fly it to Arizona, fly them to their homes, fly back over to get another load.

During the hectic split-second timing of a campaign, this is a man who took time out to sit beside an old friend who was dying of cancer. His campaign managers were understandably impatient, but he said, "There aren't many left who care what happens to her. I'd like her to know I care." This is a man who said to his 19-year-old son, "There is no foundation like the rock of honesty and fairness, and when you begin to build your life on that rock, with the cement of the faith in God that you have, then you have a real start." This is not a man who could carelessly send other people's sons to war. And that is the issue of this campaign that makes all the other problems I've discussed academic, unless we realize we're in a war that must be won.

Those who would trade our freedom for the soup kitchen of the welfare state have told us they have a utopian solution of peace without victory. They call their policy "accommodation." And they say if we'll only avoid any direct confrontation with the enemy, he'll forget his evil ways and learn to love us. All who oppose them are indicted as warmongers. They say we offer simple answers to complex problems. Well, perhaps there is a simple answer—not an easy answer—but simple: If you and I have the courage to tell our elected officials that we want our national policy based on what we know in our hearts is morally right.

We cannot buy our security, our freedom from the threat of the bomb by committing an immorality so great as saying to a billion human beings now enslaved behind the Iron Curtain, "Give up your dreams of freedom because to save our own skins, we're willing to make a deal with your slave masters." Alexander Hamilton said, "A nation which can prefer disgrace to danger is prepared for a master, and deserves one." Now let's set the record straight. There's no argument over the choice between peace and war, but there's only one guaranteed way you can have peace—and you can have it in the next second—surrender.

Admittedly, there's a risk in any course we follow other than this, but every lesson of history tells us that the greater risk lies in appeasement, and this is the specter our well-meaning liberal friends refuse to face—that their policy of accommodation is appeasement, and it gives no choice between peace and war, only between fight or surrender. If we continue to accommodate, continue to back and retreat, eventually we have to face the final demand—the ultimatum. And what then—when Nikita Khrushchev has told his people he knows what our answer will be? He has told them that we're retreating under the pressure of the Cold War, and someday, when the time comes to deliver the final ultimatum, our surrender will be voluntary, because by that time we will have been weakened from within spiritually, morally, and economically. He believes this because from our side he's heard voices pleading for "peace at any price" or "better Red than dead," or as one commentator put it, he'd rather "live on his knees than die on his feet." And therein lies the road to war, because those voices don't speak for the rest of us.

You and I know and do not believe that life is so dear and peace so sweet as to be purchased at the price of chains and slavery. If nothing in life is worth dying for, when did this begin—just in the face of this enemy? Or should Moses have told the children of Israel to live in slavery under the pharaohs? Should Christ have refused the cross? Should the patriots at Concord Bridge have thrown down their guns and refused to fire the shot heard 'round the world? The martyrs of history were not fools, and our honored dead who gave their lives to stop the advance of the Nazis didn't die in vain. Where, then, is the road to peace? Well it's a simple answer after all.

You and I have the courage to say to our enemies, "There is a price we will not pay." "There is a point beyond which they must not advance." And this— this is the meaning in the phrase of Barry Goldwater's "peace through strength." Winston Churchill said, "The destiny of man is not measured by material computations. When great forces are on the move in the world, we learn we're spirits—not animals." And he said, "There's something going on in time and space, and beyond time and space, which, whether we like it or not, spells duty."

You and I have a rendezvous with destiny.

We'll preserve for our children this, the last best hope of man on earth, or we'll sentence them to take the last step into a thousand years of darkness.

We will keep in mind and remember that Barry Goldwater has faith in us. He has faith that you and I have the ability and the dignity and the right to make our own decisions and determine our own destiny.

Thank you very much.

XXIII

"Blame America first crowd"

JEANE KIRKPATRICK'S SPEECH TO THE REPUBLICAN NATIONAL CONVENTION (1984)

J EANE KIRKPATRICK GAVE THE NOW FAMOUS "BLAME AMERICA FIRST"
speech at the 1984 Republican National Convention in Dallas, Texas. At
the time, Kirkpatrick was the United States representative to the United
Nations and—unique amongst President Reagan's inner circle—a Democrat.

However, by the time Kirkpatrick took the stage at Reunion Arena on that
August night, she had become quite a critic of the foreign policy elite in her
party. As a student and young academic, she had been drawn to the Democratic Party of Truman and Kennedy: in favor of a sizable welfare state at home,
but with a robust national security policy that was unequivocal about American exceptionalism and the superiority of a capitalist, democratic society. But
the Democrats had taken a new course since then, nominating such presidential candidates as George McGovern and Jimmy Carter, neither of whom
shared Truman and Kennedy's more aggressive stance on foreign policy.

A Midwesterner, Kirkpatrick was born in Duncan, Oklahoma, on November 19, 1926 to Leona and Welcher Jordan. The family moved to Illinois when she was twelve. She earned a B.A. from Barnard College, and M.A. and Ph.D. degrees from Columbia University. Kirkpatrick was a faculty member at Georgetown University in the political science department beginning in the late 1960s. She was named the Thomas and Dorothy Leavey University Professor at Georgetown University in 1978.

Active in the Democratic Party, she served as vice chairman of the Coalition for a Democratic Majority and as a member of the Democratic National Convention's National Commission on Party Structure and Presidential Nomination.

However, in the mid-1970s, she joined a group of prominent Democrats who began to raise doubts about the party's approach to the Cold War. A number of intellectuals, foreign policy experts, and politicians who had been associated with the party since the New Deal Era began to question the scaling down of American presence overseas and the policy of détente towards the Soviet Union. Détente produced a temporary thawing of relations between Washington and Moscow, but it came at the cost of the United States scaling down both its conventional and nuclear forces and fighting the spread of communism overseas less aggressively. She became friendly with Washington Democratic Senator Henry "Scoop" Jackson, who believed that both Democrats and Republicans were underestimating the extent of the Soviet threat.

In November 1979, her essay, "Dictatorships & Double Standards," published in *Commentary* magazine, caught presidential candidate Ronald Reagan's eye.

Her criticism of President Carter was scathing. She contended that his policy of loosening ties with our non-democratic, anti-communist allies would create a vacuum—one that the Soviets would be all too willing to fill:

> In the thirty-odd months since the inauguration of Jimmy Carter as President there has occurred a dramatic Soviet military buildup, matched by the stagnation of American armed forces, and a dramatic extension of Soviet influence in the Horn of Africa, Afghanistan,

Southern Africa, and the Caribbean, matched by a declining American position in all these areas. The U.S. has never tried so hard and failed so utterly to make and keep friends in the Third World.

Kirkpatrick had never worked closely with Republicans before, but agreed to meet with Reagan. He came away impressed with the Georgetown professor. Though she still characterized herself as an "AFL-CIO Democrat," she signed on as national security adviser to Reagan's 1980 presidential campaign. After his election, Reagan appointed her to serve as the United States Ambassador to the United Nations.

The Reagan administration's forceful and unequivocal stance contrasted with Carter's internationalist and dovish position. Reagan was convinced that communism could and must be defeated.

Reagan's policy reflected Kirkpatrick's view that it was sometimes necessary to befriend authoritarian regimes overseas because the alternative—leftwing, communist, insurgent governments—was much worse. Although an authoritarian government was not ideal, it was certainly superior to the brand of totalitarian communism endorsed by the Soviets.

As Kirkpatrick noted in a 1979 essay,

> Authority in traditional autocracies is transmitted through personal relations: from the ruler to his close associates (relatives, household members, personal friends) and from them to people to whom the associates are related by personal ties resembling their own relation to the ruler. The fabric of authority unravels quickly when the power and status of the man at the top are undermined or eliminated.... Without him, the organized life of the society will collapse, like an arch from which the keystone has been removed.... The speed with which armies collapse, bureaucracies abdicate, and social structures dissolve once the autocrat is removed frequently surprises American policymakers and journalists accustomed to public institutions based on universalistic norms rather than particularistic relations.

The ability of nations to transition to a democracy is much more complex than simply removing the autocratic government. She explained, "Hurried efforts to force complex and unfamiliar political practices on societies lacking the requisite political culture, tradition, and social structures not only fail to produce desired outcomes; if they are undertaken at a time when the traditional regime is under attack, they actually facilitate the job of the insurgents."

The Democratic Party, although defeated in the 1980 presidential election, continued to endorse a foreign policy that questioned American exceptionalism and was willing to sit idly by as Soviet communism encroached. Kirkpatrick's 1984 speech was direct, forceful, and laid out the clear differences between Reagan's approach and that of his opponent, Walter Mondale.

While the Carter administration had a hands-off policy toward national security, "The inauguration of President Reagan signaled a reaffirmation of historic American ideals," she stated in her speech. Noting that the prior administration and Democrats in general had a policy to "blame America first," she reminded Americans that there was no moral equivalency between Soviet totalitarianism and us.

But the American people "understand just as the distinguished French writer, Jean Francois Revel, understands the dangers of endless self-criticism and self-denigration," stated Kirkpatrick during her speech. "Clearly, a civilization that feels guilty for everything it is and does will lack the energy and conviction to defend itself."

May the truth of her words never be proved by leaders who are quicker to apologize than they are to defend our great nation.

—JGC

❧ ❧ ❧

Thank you very much for that warm welcome.
Thank you for inviting me.
This is the first Republican Convention I have ever attended.

I am grateful that you should invite me, a lifelong Democrat. On the other hand, I realize that you are inviting many lifelong Democrats to join this common cause.

I want to begin tonight by quoting the speech of the president whom I very greatly admire, Harry Truman, who once said to the Congress:

"The United States has become great because we, as a people, have been able to work together for great objectives even while differing about details."

He continued:

"The elements of our strength are many. They include our democratic government, our economic system, our great natural resources. But, the basic source of our strength is spiritual. We believe in the dignity of man."

That's the way Democratic presidents and presidential candidates used to talk about America.

These were the men who developed NATO, who developed the Marshall Plan, who devised the Alliance for Progress.

They were not afraid to be resolute nor ashamed to speak of America as a great nation. They didn't doubt that we must be strong enough to protect ourselves and to help others.

They didn't imagine that America should depend for its very survival on the promises of its adversaries.

They happily assumed the responsibilities of freedom.

I am not alone in noticing that the San Francisco Democrats took a very different approach.

A recent article in The New York Times noted that "the foreign policy line that emerged from the Democratic National Convention in San Francisco is a distinct shift from the policies of such [Democratic] presidents as Harry S Truman, John F. Kennedy and Lyndon B. Johnson."

I agree.

I shall speak tonight of foreign affairs even though the other party's convention barely touched the subject.

When the San Francisco Democrats treat foreign affairs as an afterthought, as they did, they behaved less like a dove or a hawk than like an ostrich—convinced it would shut out the world by hiding its head in the sand.

Today, foreign policy is central to the security, to the freedom, to the prosperity, even to the survival of the United States.

And our strength, for which we make many sacrifices, is essential to the independence and freedom of our allies and our friends.

Ask yourself:

What would become of Europe if the United States withdrew?

What would become of Africa if Europe fell under Soviet domination?

What would become of Europe if the Middle East came under Soviet control?

What would become of Israel, if surrounded by Soviet client states?

What would become of Asia if the Philippines or Japan fell under Soviet domination?

What would become of Mexico if Central America became a Soviet satellite?

What then could the United States do?

These are questions the San Francisco Democrats have not answered. These are questions they haven't even asked.

The United States cannot remain an open, democratic society if we are left alone—a garrison state in a hostile world.

We need independent nations with whom to trade, to consult and cooperate.

We need friends and allies with whom to share the pleasures and the protection of our civilization.

We cannot, therefore, be indifferent to the subversion of others' independence or to the development of new weapons by our adversaries or of new vulnerabilities by our friends.

The last Democratic administration did not seem to notice much, or care much or do much about these matters.

And at home and abroad, our country slid into real deep trouble.

North and South, East and West, our relations deteriorated.

The Carter administration's motives were good, but their policies were inadequate, uninformed and mistaken.

They made things worse, not better.

Those who had least, suffered most.

Poor countries grew poorer.

Rich countries grew poorer, too.

The United States grew weaker.

Meanwhile, the Soviet Union grew stronger.

The Carter administration's unilateral "restraint" in developing and deploying weapon systems was accompanied by an unprecedented Soviet buildup, military and political.

The Soviets, working on the margins and through the loopholes of SALT I, developed missiles of stunning speed and accuracy and targeted the cities of our friends in Europe.

They produced weapons capable of wiping out our land-based missiles.

And then, feeling strong, the Soviet leaders moved with boldness and skill to exploit their new advantages.

Facilities were completed in Cuba during those years that permit Soviet nuclear submarines to roam our coasts, that permit planes to fly reconnaissance missions over the eastern United States, and that permit Soviet electronic surveillance to monitor our telephone calls and our telegrams.

Those were the years the Ayatollah Khomeini came to power in Iran, while in Nicaragua and Sandanista developed a one-party dictatorship based on the Cuban model.

From the fall of Saigon in 1975 'til January 1981, Soviet influence expanded dramatically into Laos, Cambodia, Afghanistan, Angola, Ethiopia, Mozambique, South Yemen, Libya, Syria, Aden, Congo, Madagascar, Seychelles, Nicaragua, and Grenada.

Soviet block forces and advisers sought to guarantee what they called the "irreversibility" of their newfound influence and to stimulate insurgencies in a dozen other places.

During this period, the Soviet Union invaded Afghanistan, murdered its president and began a ghastly war against the Afghan people.

The American people were shocked by these events.

We were greatly surprised to learn of our diminished economic and military strength.

We were demoralized by the treatment of our hostages in Iran.

And we were outraged by harsh attacks on the United States in the United Nations.

As a result, we lost confidence in ourselves and in our government.

Jimmy Carter looked for an explanation for all these problems and thought he found it in the American people.

But the people knew better.

It wasn't malaise we suffered from; it was Jimmy Carter—and Walter Mondale.

And so, in 1980, the American people elected a very different president.

The election of Ronald Reagan marked an end to the dismal period of retreat and decline.

His inauguration, blessed by the simultaneous release of our hostages, signaled an end to the most humiliating episode in our national history.

The inauguration of President Reagan signaled a reaffirmation of historic American ideals.

Ronald Reagan brought to the presidency confidence in the American experience.

Confidence in the legitimacy and success of American institutions.

Confidence in the decency of the American people.

And confidence in the relevance of our experience to the rest of the world.

That confidence has proved contagious.

Our nation's subsequent recovery in domestic and foreign affairs, the restoration of military and economic strength has silenced the talk of inevitable American decline and reminded the world of the advantages of freedom.

President Reagan faced a stunning challenge and he met it.

In the 3 and $1/2$ years since his inauguration, the United States has grown stronger, safer, more confident, and we are at peace.

The Reagan administration has restored the American economy.

It is restoring our military strength.

It has liberated the people of Grenada from terror and tyranny.

With NATO, it has installed missiles to defend the cities of Europe.

The Reagan administration has prevented the expulsion of Israel from the United Nations.

It has developed flexible new forms of international cooperation with which to deal with new threats to world order.

The Reagan administration has given more economic assistance to developing countries than any other administration or any other government, and has encouraged the economic freedom needed to promote self-sustaining economic growth.

The Reagan administration has helped to sustain democracy and encourage its development elsewhere.

And at each step of the way, the same people who were responsible for America's decline have insisted that the president's policies would fail.

They said we could never deploy missiles to protect Europe's cities.

But today Europe's cities enjoy that protection.

They said it would never be possible to hold an election in El Salvador because the people were too frightened and the country too disorganized.

But the people of El Salvador proved them wrong, and today President Napoleon Duarte has impressed the democratic world with his skillful, principled leadership.

They said we could not use America's strength to help others—Sudan, Chad, Central America, the Gulf states, the Caribbean nations—without being drawn into war.

But we have helped others resist Soviet, Libyan, Cuban subversion, and we are at peace.

They said that saving Grenada from terror and totalitarianism was the wrong thing to do—they didn't blame Cuba or the communists for threatening American students and murdering Grenadians—they blamed the United States instead.

But then, somehow, they always blame America first.

When our Marines, sent to Lebanon on a multinational peacekeeping mission with the consent of the United States Congress, were murdered in their sleep, the "blame America first crowd" didn't blame the terrorists who murdered the Marines, they blamed the United States.

But then, they always blame America first.

When the Soviet Union walked out of arms control negotiations, and refused even to discuss the issues, the San Francisco Democrats didn't blame Soviet intransigence. They blamed the United States.

But then, they always blame America first.

When Marxist dictators shoot their way to power in Central America, the San Francisco Democrats don't blame the guerrillas and their Soviet allies, they blame United States policies of 100 years ago.

But then, they always blame America first.

The American people know better.

They know that Ronald Reagan and the United States didn't cause Marxist dictatorship in Nicaragua, or the repression in Poland, or the brutal new offensives in Afghanistan, or the destruction of the Korean airliner, or the new attacks on religious and ethnic groups in the Soviet Union, or the jamming of western broadcasts, or the denial of Jewish emigration, or the brutal imprisonment of Anatoly Shcharansky and Ida Nudel, or the obscene treatment of Andrei Sakharov and Yelena Bonner, or the re-Stalinization of the Soviet Union.

The American people know that it's dangerous to blame ourselves for terrible problems that we did not cause.

They understand just as the distinguished French writer, Jean Francois Revel, understands the dangers of endless self- criticism and self-denigration.

He wrote: "Clearly, a civilization that feels guilty for everything it is and does will lack the energy and conviction to defend itself."

With the election of Ronald Reagan, the American people declared to the world that we have the necessary energy and conviction to defend ourselves, and that we have as well a deep commitment to peace.

And now, the American people, proud of our country, proud of our freedom, proud of ourselves, will reject the San Francisco Democrats and send Ronald Reagan back to the White House.

Thank you very much.

XXIV

"Mr. Gorbachev, tear down this wall!"

RONALD REAGAN'S REMARKS ON EAST-WEST RELATIONS AT THE BRANDENBURG GATE (1987)

KING FREDERICK WILLIAM II OF PRUSSIA COMMISSIONED THE BRAN-denburg Gate in 1788, as a symbol of peace. In 1961, the Soviet-backed East German government constructed the Berlin Wall adjacent to the gate, shutting off communist East Berlin from democratic West Berlin. After the Berlin Wall fell in 1989, the Brandenburg Gate became a symbol of defiance to tyranny.

When President John F. Kennedy visited the Brandenburg Gate in 1963, East Germany hung large banners across the gate so he could not see into the East German side. In a city split between Soviet-administered East Germany and U.S.-supported West Germany, it was a physical symbol of the divide between the freedom of democracy and the oppression of communism. Kennedy, who spoke to a crowd of 150,000, said, "All free men, wherever they may live, are citizens of Berlin, and, therefore, as a free man, I take pride in the words *'Ich bin ein Berliner.'*" (I am a Berliner).

After Kennedy was assassinated five months later, U.S. foreign policy transitioned into a détente maintained by the next four presidents. In the late 1970s, the Soviet Union began to adopt a more militaristic stance, invading Afghanistan in December 1979 and engaging in a swift nuclear buildup, shattering the tenuous peace of détente. At the same time, in the wake of the American defeat in Vietnam in 1975, the Carter administration pursued a policy of reducing America's military presence overseas and tempering defense spending.

This was the atmosphere when Ronald Reagan entered the scene. Like Kennedy, and unlike the political elites in the United States and Britain in the 1970s, Reagan and his British counterpart, Prime Minister Margaret Thatcher, believed that Soviet communism could and must be defeated.

On March 8, 1983, Reagan delivered a speech in Orlando, Florida, to the annual convention of the National Association of Evangelicals. He laid out the moral argument against the Soviet Union. "Freedom prospers when religion is vibrant and the rule of law under God is acknowledged," said Reagan. He raised the crisis from one of military might to one of spiritual and moral faith. "The real crisis we face today is a spiritual one; at root, it is a test of moral will and faith," he said.

Not content to define only what we were for, Reagan also defined our enemy, saying, "Let us be aware that while they preach the supremacy of the state, declare its omnipotence over individual man, and predict its eventual domination of all peoples on the earth, they are the focus of evil in the modern world."

Two weeks later, Reagan announced the Strategic Defense Initiative, a program to build a space-based, anti-missile system. While many did not believe that this system would ever become operational, the idea put the Soviets on notice that Reagan was serious and would not back down easily.

In the fall of 1983, the Soviets deliberately shot down Korean Airlines Flight 007, killing 269 passengers; 63 were Americans, one of them a congressman. Reagan made an impassioned speech noting the "savagery of their crime" and described the tragedy as "an act of barbarism, born of a society which wantonly disregards individual rights and the value of human life and seeks constantly to expand and dominate other nations."

Tensions continued to mount in the fall of 1983. NATO powers conducted a now infamous massive joint exercise simulating a nuclear launch, called Able Archer, which almost fooled the Russians into thinking it was the real thing. "On September 26, Lieutenant Colonel Stanislav Yevgrafovich Petrov sat watch in the Serpukhov-15 bunker," wrote Claire Berlinski in *There is no Alternative: Why Margaret Thatcher Matters*. When the warning system in the bunker signaled nuclear missile launches, Petrov "decided this simply couldn't be happening... He broke his orders outright and refused to press the button" to launch the Soviet missiles. We came very close to confrontation, but few Americans or Europeans realized it at the time.

In 1984, Russia walked out of the Geneva talks on intermediate-range missiles and then the Strategic Arms Reduction Treaty.

Mikhail Gorbachev became general secretary of the Communist Party of the Soviet Union in 1985. Gorbachev was very different from the sickly, crusty predecessors who had occupied the Kremlin before him. He was young (only fifty-four in 1985), educated, and had given some indication that he would be open to political and economic reforms.

In the fall of 1984, Thatcher had met Gorbachev in England and pronounced after the meeting, "I like Mr. Gorbachev. We can do business with him." Lady Thatcher's message certainly resonated with Reagan. He had not met with a Soviet leader during his first four years in office, but was ready to sit down with Gorbachev in Geneva in November 1985. Later, Reagan told his advisers, "Maggie was right. We can do business with this man."

In 1986, Gorbachev offered to eliminate nuclear weapons if Reagan would abandon the Strategic Defense Initiative. Reagan refused. The Soviets had been spending massive amounts of money on the military and Gorbachev needed to focus on domestic issues. But Reagan's stance forced the Soviet Union to continue military spending, hastening the eventual economic and then political collapse of the Soviet Union.

In June 1987, Reagan traveled to Berlin to give a speech at the Brandenburg Gate. Tensions were high. Reagan upped the ante. Instead of trying to placate the communists, he provided clear language regarding who he felt had "won the war" and what must come next.

Confronting the Soviets as no president had ever done, he stated that there was "one great and inescapable conclusion: freedom leads to prosperity. Freedom replaces the ancient hatreds among the nations with comity and peace. Freedom is the victor."

"General Secretary Gorbachev, if you seek peace, if you seek prosperity for the Soviet Union and Eastern Europe, if you seek liberalization: Come here to this gate! Mr. Gorbachev, open this gate! Mr. Gorbachev, tear down this wall!"

The Berlin Wall was torn down on November 9, 1989, hastened by Reagan's unflinching position that "rhetorical confrontation causes geopolitical conciliation," as chief speechwriter Anthony Dolan recalled. The Soviet Union wouldn't last much longer, ceasing to exist on Christmas Day 1991.

Reagan proved that words have incredible power. We must be unafraid to speak out against evil, using our words to support and encourage freedom and liberty.

—JGC

✢ ✢ ✢

Thank you very much. Chancellor Kohl, Governing Mayor Diepgen, ladies and gentlemen: Twenty-four years ago, President John F. Kennedy visited Berlin, speaking to the people of this city and the world at the city hall. Well, since then two other presidents have come, each in his turn, to Berlin. And today I, myself, make my second visit to your city.

We come to Berlin, we American presidents, because it's our duty to speak, in this place, of freedom. But I must confess, we're drawn here by other things as well: by the feeling of history in this city, more than 500 years older than our own nation; by the beauty of the Grunewald and the Tiergarten; most of all, by your courage and determination. Perhaps the composer, Paul Lincke, understood something about American presidents. You see, like so many presidents before me, I come here today because wherever I go, whatever I do: "Ich hab noch einen koffer in Berlin." [I still have a suitcase in Berlin.]

Our gathering today is being broadcast throughout Western Europe and North America. I understand that it is being seen and heard as well in the East. To those listening throughout Eastern Europe, I extend my warmest greetings and the good will of the American people. To those listening in East Berlin, a special word: Although I cannot be with you, I address my remarks to you just as surely as to those standing here before me. For I join you, as I join your fellow countrymen in the West, in this firm, this unalterable belief: *Es gibt nur ein Berlin.* [There is only one Berlin.]

Behind me stands a wall that encircles the free sectors of this city, part of a vast system of barriers that divides the entire continent of Europe. From the Baltic, south, those barriers cut across Germany in a gash of barbed wire, concrete, dog runs, and guard towers. Farther south, there may be no visible, no obvious wall. But there remain armed guards and checkpoints all the same—still a restriction on the right to travel, still an instrument to impose upon ordinary men and women the will of a totalitarian state. Yet it is here in Berlin where the wall emerges most clearly; here, cutting across your city, where the news photo and the television screen have imprinted this brutal division of a continent upon the mind of the world. Standing before the Brandenburg Gate, every man is a German, separated from his fellow men. Every man is a Berliner, forced to look upon a scar.

President von Weizsacker has said: "The German question is open as long as the Brandenburg Gate is closed." Today I say: As long as this gate is closed, as long as this scar of a wall is permitted to stand, it is not the German question alone that remains open, but the question of freedom for all mankind. Yet I do not come here to lament. For I find in Berlin a message of hope, even in the shadow of this wall, a message of triumph.

In this season of spring in 1945, the people of Berlin emerged from their air raid shelters to find devastation. Thousands of miles away, the people of the United States reached out to help. And in 1947 Secretary of State—as you've been told—George Marshall announced the creation of what would become known as the Marshall plan. Speaking precisely 40 years ago this month, he said: "Our policy is directed not against any country or doctrine, but against hunger, poverty, desperation, and chaos."

In the Reichstag a few moments ago, I saw a display commemorating this 40th anniversary of the Marshall plan. I was struck by the sign on a burnt-out, gutted structure that was being rebuilt. I understand that Berliners of my own generation can remember seeing signs like it dotted throughout the Western sectors of the city. The sign read simply: "The Marshall plan is helping here to strengthen the free world." A strong, free world in the West, that dream became real. Japan rose from ruin to become an economic giant. Italy, France, Belgium—virtually every nation in Western Europe saw political and economic rebirth; the European Community was founded.

In West Germany and here in Berlin, there took place an economic miracle, the Wirtschaftswunder. Adenauer, Erhard, Reuter, and other leaders understood the practical importance of liberty—that just as truth can flourish only when the journalist is given freedom of speech, so prosperity can come about only when the farmer and businessman enjoy economic freedom. The German leaders reduced tariffs, expanded free trade, lowered taxes. From 1950 to 1960 alone, the standard of living in West Germany and Berlin doubled.

Where four decades ago there was rubble, today in West Berlin there is the greatest industrial output of any city in Germany—busy office blocks, fine homes and apartments, proud avenues, and the spreading lawns of park land. Where a city's culture seemed to have been destroyed, today there are two great universities, orchestras and an opera, countless theaters, and museums. Where there was want, today there's abundance—food, clothing, automobiles—the wonderful goods of the Ku'damm. From devastation, from utter ruin, you Berliners have, in freedom, rebuilt a city that once again ranks as one of the greatest on Earth. The Soviets may have had other plans. But, my friends, there were a few things the Soviets didn't count on: *Berliner herz, Berliner humor, ja, und Berliner schnauze.* [Berliner heart, Berliner humor, yes, and a Berliner schnauze.]

In the 1950s, Khrushchev predicted: "We will bury you." But in the West today, we see a free world that has achieved a level of prosperity and well-being unprecedented in all human history. In the Communist world, we see failure, technological backwardness, declining standards of health, even want of the most basic kind-too little food. Even today, the Soviet Union still cannot feed itself. After these four decades, then, there stands before the entire world one great and inescapable conclusion: freedom leads to prosperity. Freedom replaces the ancient hatreds among the nations with comity and peace. Freedom is the victor.

And now the Soviets themselves may, in a limited way, be coming to understand the importance of freedom. We hear much from Moscow about a new policy of reform and openness. Some political prisoners have been released. Certain foreign news broadcasts are no longer being jammed. Some economic enterprises have been permitted to operate with greater freedom from state control. Are these the beginnings of profound changes in the Soviet state? Or are they token gestures, intended to raise false hopes in the West, or to strengthen the Soviet system without changing it? We welcome change and openness; for we believe that freedom and security go together, that the advance of human liberty can only strengthen the cause of world peace.

There is one sign the Soviets can make that would be unmistakable, that would advance dramatically the cause of freedom and peace. General Secretary Gorbachev, if you seek peace, if you seek prosperity for the Soviet Union and Eastern Europe, if you seek liberalization: Come here to this gate! Mr. Gorbachev, open this gate! Mr. Gorbachev, tear down this wall!

I understand the fear of war and the pain of division that afflict this continent—and I pledge to you my country's efforts to help overcome these burdens. To be sure, we in the West must resist Soviet expansion. So we must maintain defenses of unassailable strength. Yet we seek peace; so we must strive to reduce arms on both sides. Beginning ten years ago, the Soviets challenged the Western alliance with a grave new threat, hundreds of new and more deadly SS-20 nuclear missiles, capable of-striking every capital in Europe. The Western alliance responded by committing itself to a counter-deployment unless the Soviets agreed to negotiate a better solution; namely, the elimination of such weapons on both sides. For many months, the Soviets refused to bargain in earnestness. As the alliance, in turn, prepared to go forward with its counter-deployment, there were difficult days—days of protests like those during my 1982 visit to this city—and the Soviets later walked away from the table.

But through it all, the alliance held firm. And I invite those who protested then—I invite those who protest today—to mark this fact: because we remained strong, the Soviets came back to the table. And because we remained strong, today we have within reach the possibility, not merely of limiting the growth of arms, but of eliminating, for the first time, an entire class of nuclear weapons from the face of the Earth. As I speak, NATO ministers are meeting in Iceland to review the progress of our proposals for eliminating these weapons. At the talks in Geneva, we have also proposed deep cuts in strategic offensive weapons. And the Western allies have likewise made far-reaching proposals to reduce the danger of conventional war and to place a total ban on chemical weapons.

While we pursue these arms reductions, I pledge to you that we will maintain the capacity to deter Soviet aggression at any level at which it might occur. And in cooperation with many of our allies, the United States is pursuing the Strategic Defense Initiative-research to base deterrence not on the threat of offensive retaliation, but on defenses that truly defend; on systems, in short, that will not target populations, but shield them. By these means we seek to increase the safety of Europe and all the world. But we must remember a crucial fact: East and West do not mistrust each other because we are armed; we are armed because we mistrust each other. And our differences are not about weapons but about liberty. When President Kennedy spoke at the City Hall those twenty-four years ago, freedom was encircled, Berlin was under siege. And today, despite all the pressures upon this city, Berlin stands secure in its liberty. And freedom itself is transforming the globe.

In the Philippines, in South and Central America, democracy has been given a rebirth. Throughout the Pacific, free markets are working miracle after miracle of economic growth. In the industrialized nations, a technological revolution is taking place—a revolution marked by rapid, dramatic advances in computers and telecommunications.

In Europe, only one nation and those it controls refuse to join the community of freedom. Yet in this age of redoubled economic growth, of information and innovation, the Soviet Union faces a choice: It must make fundamental changes, or it will become obsolete. Today thus represents a moment of hope. We in the West stand ready to cooperate with the East to promote true openness, to break down barriers that separate people, to create a safer, freer world.

And surely there is no better place than Berlin, the meeting place of East and West, to make a start. Free people of Berlin, today, as in the past, the United States stands for the strict observance and full implementation of all parts of the Four Power Agreement of 1971. Let us use this occasion, the 750th anniversary of this city, to usher in a new era, to seek a still fuller, richer life for the Berlin of the future. Together, let us maintain and develop the ties between the Federal Republic and the Western sectors of Berlin, which is permitted by the 1971 agreement.

And I invite Mr. Gorbachev: let us work to bring the Eastern and Western parts of the city closer together, so that all the inhabitants of all Berlin can enjoy the benefits that come with life in one of the great cities of the world. To open Berlin still further to all Europe, East and West, let us expand the vital air access to this city, finding ways of making commercial air service to Berlin more convenient, more comfortable, and more economical. We look to the day when West Berlin can become one of the chief aviation hubs in all central Europe.

With our French and British partners, the United States is prepared to help bring international meetings to Berlin. It would be only fitting for Berlin to serve as the site of United Nations meetings, or world conferences on human rights and arms control or other issues that call for international cooperation. There is no better way to establish hope for the future than to enlighten young minds, and we would be honored to sponsor summer youth exchanges, cultural events, and other programs for young Berliners from the East. Our French and British friends, I'm certain, will do the same. And it's my hope that an authority can be found in East Berlin to sponsor visits from young people of the Western sectors.

One final proposal, one close to my heart: sport represents a source of enjoyment and ennoblement, and you many have noted that the Republic of Korea—South Korea-has offered to permit certain events of the 1988 Olympics to take place in the North. International sports competitions of all kinds could take place in both parts of this city. And what better way to demonstrate to the world the openness of this city than to offer in some future year to hold the Olympic games here in Berlin, East and West?

In these four decades, as I have said, you Berliners have built a great city. You've done so in spite of threats—the Soviet attempts to impose the East-mark, the blockade. Today the city thrives in spite of the challenges implicit in the very presence of this wall. What keeps you here? Certainly there's a great deal to be said for your fortitude, for your defiant courage. But I believe there's something deeper, something that involves Berlin's whole look and feel and way of life—not mere sentiment. No one could live long in Berlin without being completely disabused of illusions. Something instead, that has seen the difficulties of life in Berlin but chose to accept them, that continues to build this good and proud city in contrast to a surrounding totalitarian presence that refuses to release human energies or aspirations. Something that speaks with a powerful voice of affirmation, that says yes to this city, yes to the future, yes to freedom. In a word, I would submit that what keeps you in Berlin is love—love both profound and abiding.

Perhaps this gets to the root of the matter, to the most fundamental distinction of all between East and West. The totalitarian world produces backwardness because it does such violence to the spirit, thwarting the human impulse to create, to enjoy, to worship. The totalitarian world finds even symbols of love and of worship an affront. Years ago, before the East Germans began rebuilding their churches, they erected a secular structure: the television tower at Alexander Platz. Virtually ever since, the authorities have been working to correct what they view as the tower's one major flaw, treating the glass sphere at the top with paints and chemicals of every kind. Yet even today when the Sun strikes that sphere—that sphere that towers over all Berlin—the light makes the sign of the cross. There in Berlin, like the city itself, symbols of love, symbols of worship, cannot be suppressed.

As I looked out a moment ago from the Reichstag, that embodiment of German unity, I noticed words crudely spray-painted upon the wall, perhaps by a young Berliner, "This wall will fall. Beliefs become reality." Yes, across Europe, this wall will fall. For it cannot withstand faith; it cannot withstand truth. The wall cannot withstand freedom.

And I would like, before I close, to say one word. I have read, and I have been questioned since I've been here about certain demonstrations against my coming. And I would like to say just one thing, and to those who demonstrate so. I wonder if they have ever asked themselves that if they should have the kind of government they apparently seek, no one would ever be able to do what they're doing again.

Thank you and God bless you all.

XXV

"Grief has turned to anger, and anger to resolution"

GEORGE W. BUSH'S ADDRESS TO A JOINT SESSION OF CONGRESS AND THE AMERICAN PEOPLE (2001)

THE AL-QAEDA ATTACKS THAT OCCURRED ON SEPTEMBER 11, 2001 shocked the United States and the world. Al-Qaeda operatives hijacked four commercial planes, two of which were deliberately crashed into the World Trade Center's Twin Towers in New York City. The third plane was deliberately flown into the Pentagon. On the fourth airplane, United Airlines Flight 93, passenger Todd Beamer led a group of other passengers to rush the hijackers using the phrase, "Let's Roll," which was overheard on an air-to-ground phone call. Instead of demolishing its target, believed to have been the White House or Capitol building, the fourth plane ended up crashing in a rural area of Pennsylvania.

I became aware of the attacks when I was passing a television playing without sound. The picture showed a plane crashing into a building. Initially, I thought that it was an errant small private plane that had lost control and hit the tower by accident. Half an hour later, I learned that it was a deliberate attack. A mother of a 23-month-old and a 6-week old, I immediately fled home, every protective instinct aroused, to hold my children and watch the terrible story develop on television with the rest of the nation.

As I sat with my children, I wondered how the future—*their* future—would unfold. I was worried. I was nervous. I was troubled.

As a nation, we all were shocked, worried, nervous, and troubled. The attackers had deliberately used commercial airliners as weapons to kill civilians. Our attackers had lived for months and even years in our country, plotting to kill us even as they coexisted with us. Their goal was not only destruction, but terror: to make us afraid. They were determined to destroy us and our way of life.

Recovering from shock, the American people immediately responded with compassion and action. People drove to New York from around the country to assist in rescue operations. Americans held blood drives and collected provisions and did volunteer work. The American people pulled together in solidarity and patriotism.

President George W. Bush was visiting Emma E. Booker Elementary School in Sarasota, Florida when the attacks occurred. Returning to Washington that day, he addressed the American people from the Oval Office; his first speech from the White House. His presidency, like the nation he led, would never be the same.

Fearful of another attack, unsure of what lay ahead, and hearing rumors of possible war, the American people were in need of clear leadership. Three days after the towers collapsed, President Bush impulsively climbed to the top of a heap of rubble at Ground Zero to address the emergency responders and volunteers who had been searching tirelessly for survivors. Speaking into a bullhorn, when those on the edge of the crowd called out that they could not hear him, he shouted in response, "I can hear you!" Interrupted by cheers, he continued, "I can hear you, the rest of the world hears you, and the people who knocked these buildings down will hear all of us soon."

On the night of September 20, Bush addressed Americans from the well of the House of Representatives: the People's House. While identifying the enemy as radical Islamists who want to change the world, Bush carefully distinguished between them and the hundreds of millions of Muslims who practice their faith in peace. Bush put the Taliban, who were ruling Afghanistan, on notice. If they did not cooperate, they would share the same fate as the terrorists.

His speech at such a crucial time—right after America had been attacked, while the rubble at the World Trade Center site still smoldered—reassured the nation when we needed it most.

According to Gallup research, Bush's approval rating moved from 51 percent before the terrorist attacks to 90 percent after he delivered his speech. The American people were able to begin the process of rebuilding.

—JGC

✸ ✸ ✸

Mr. Speaker, Mr. President Pro Tempore, members of Congress, and fellow Americans:

In the normal course of events, Presidents come to this chamber to report on the state of the Union. Tonight, no such report is needed. It has already been delivered by the American people.

We have seen it in the courage of passengers, who rushed terrorists to save others on the ground—passengers like an exceptional man named Todd Beamer. And would you please help me to welcome his wife, Lisa Beamer, here tonight. We have seen the state of our Union in the endurance of rescuers, working past exhaustion. We've seen the unfurling of flags, the lighting of candles, the giving of blood, the saying of prayers—in English, Hebrew, and Arabic. We have seen the decency of a loving and giving people who have made the grief of strangers their own. My fellow citizens, for the last nine days, the entire world has seen for itself the state of our Union—and it is strong.

Tonight we are a country awakened to danger and called to defend freedom. Our grief has turned to anger, and anger to resolution. Whether we bring our enemies to justice, or bring justice to our enemies, justice will be done. I thank the Congress for its leadership at such an important time. All of America was touched on the evening of the tragedy to see Republicans and Democrats joined together on the steps of this Capitol, singing "God Bless America." And you did more than sing; you acted, by delivering 40 billion dollars to rebuild our communities and meet the needs of our military. Speaker Hastert, Minority Leader Gephardt, Majority Leader Daschle, and Senator Lott, I thank you for your friendship, for your leadership, and for your service to our country. And on behalf of the American people, I thank the world for its outpouring of support. America will never forget the sounds of our National Anthem playing at Buckingham Palace, on the streets of Paris, and at Berlin's Brandenburg Gate.

We will not forget South Korean children gathering to pray outside our embassy in Seoul, or the prayers of sympathy offered at a mosque in Cairo. We will not forget moments of silence and days of mourning in Australia and Africa and Latin America. Nor will we forget the citizens of 80 other nations who died with our own: dozens of Pakistanis; more than 130 Israelis; more than 250 citizens of India; men and women from El Salvador, Iran, Mexico, and Japan; and hundreds of British citizens. America has no truer friend than Great Britain. Once again, we are joined together in a great cause—so honored the British Prime Minister has crossed an ocean to show his unity with America. Thank you for coming, friend.

On September the 11th, enemies of freedom committed an act of war against our country. Americans have known wars—but for the past 136 years, they have been wars on foreign soil, except for one Sunday in 1941. Americans have known the casualties of war—but not at the center of a great city on a peaceful morning. Americans have known surprise attacks—but never before on thousands of civilians. All of this was brought upon us in a single day—and night fell on a different world, a world where freedom itself is under attack. Americans have many questions tonight. Americans are asking: Who attacked our country? The evidence we have gathered all points to a collection of loosely affiliated terrorist organizations known as al·Qaeda. They are some of the murderers indicted for bombing American embassies in Tanzania and Kenya, and responsible for bombing the USS Cole. Al Qaeda is to terror what the mafia is to crime. But its goal is not making money; its goal is remaking the world—and imposing its radical beliefs on people everywhere.

The terrorists practice a fringe form of Islamic extremism that has been rejected by Muslim scholars and the vast majority of Muslim clerics, a fringe movement that perverts the peaceful teachings of Islam. The terrorists' directive commands them to kill Christians and Jews, to kill all Americans, and make no distinctions among military and civilians, including women and children. This group and its leader—a person named Osama bin Laden—are linked to many other organizations in different countries, including the Egyptian Islamic Jihad and the Islamic Movement of Uzbekistan. There are thousands of these terrorists in more than sixty countries. They are recruited from their own nations and neighborhoods and brought to camps in places like Afghanistan, where they are trained in the tactics of terror. They are sent back to their homes or sent to hide in countries around the world to plot evil and destruction.

The leadership of al Qaeda has great influence in Afghanistan and supports the Taliban regime in controlling most of that country. In Afghanistan, we see al Qaeda's vision for the world. Afghanistan's people have been brutalized; many are starving and many have fled. Women are not allowed to attend school. You can be jailed for owning a television. Religion can be practiced only as their leaders dictate. A man can be jailed in Afghanistan if his beard is not long enough.

The United States respects the people of Afghanistan. After all, we are currently its largest source of humanitarian aid; but we condemn the Taliban regime. It is not only repressing its own people, it is threatening people everywhere by sponsoring and sheltering and supplying terrorists. By aiding and abetting murder, the Taliban regime is committing murder.

And tonight, the United States of America makes the following demands on the Taliban: Deliver to United States authorities all the leaders of al Qaeda who hide in your land. Release all foreign nationals, including American citizens, you have unjustly imprisoned. Protect foreign journalists, diplomats, and aid workers in your country. Close immediately and permanently every terrorist training camp in Afghanistan, and hand over every terrorist, and every person in their support structure, to appropriate authorities. Give the United States full access to terrorist training camps, so we can make sure they are no longer operating. These demands are not open to negotiation or discussion. The Taliban must act, and act immediately. They will hand over the terrorists, or they will share in their fate.

I also want to speak tonight directly to Muslims throughout the world. We respect your faith. It's practiced freely by many millions of Americans, and by millions more in countries that America counts as friends. Its teachings are good and peaceful, and those who commit evil in the name of Allah blaspheme the name of Allah. The terrorists are traitors to their own faith, trying, in effect, to hijack Islam itself. The enemy of America is not our many Muslim friends; it is not our many Arab friends. Our enemy is a radical network of terrorists, and every government that supports them. Our war on terror begins with al Qaeda, but it does not end there. It will not end until every terrorist group of global reach has been found, stopped, and defeated.

Americans are asking, why do they hate us? They hate what they see right here in this chamber—a democratically elected government. Their leaders are self-appointed. They hate our freedoms—our freedom of religion, our freedom of speech, our freedom to vote and assemble and disagree with each other. They want to overthrow existing governments in many Muslim countries, such as Egypt, Saudi Arabia, and Jordan. They want to drive Israel out of the Middle East. They want to drive Christians and Jews out of vast regions of Asia and Africa. These terrorists kill not merely to end lives, but to disrupt and end a way of life. With every atrocity, they hope that America grows fearful, retreating from the world and forsaking our friends. They stand against us, because we stand in their way.

We are not deceived by their pretenses to piety. We have seen their kind before. They are the heirs of all the murderous ideologies of the 20th century. By sacrificing human life to serve their radical visions—by abandoning every value except the will to power—they follow in the path of fascism, Nazism, and totalitarianism. And they will follow that path all the way, to where it ends:

in history's unmarked grave of discarded lies. Americans are asking: How will we fight and win this war? We will direct every resource at our command—every means of diplomacy, every tool of intelligence, every instrument of law enforcement, every financial influence, and every necessary weapon of war—to the disruption and to the defeat of the global terror network.

Now this war will not be like the war against Iraq a decade ago, with a decisive liberation of territory and a swift conclusion. It will not look like the air war above Kosovo two years ago, where no ground troops were used and not a single American was lost in combat. Our response involves far more than instant retaliation and isolated strikes. Americans should not expect one battle, but a lengthy campaign, unlike any other we have ever seen. It may include dramatic strikes, visible on TV, and covert operations, secret even in success. We will starve terrorists of funding, turn them one against another, drive them from place to place, until there is no refuge or no rest. And we will pursue nations that provide aid or safe haven to terrorism. Every nation, in every region, now has a decision to make. Either you are with us, or you are with the terrorists. From this day forward, any nation that continues to harbor or support terrorism will be regarded by the United States as a hostile regime.

Our nation has been put on notice: We're not immune from attack. We will take defensive measures against terrorism to protect Americans. Today, dozens of federal departments and agencies, as well as state and local governments, have responsibilities affecting homeland security. These efforts must be coordinated at the highest level. So tonight I announce the creation of a Cabinet-level position reporting directly to me—the Office of Homeland Security. And tonight I also announce a distinguished American to lead this effort, to strengthen American security: a military veteran, an effective governor, a true patriot, a trusted friend—Pennsylvania's Tom Ridge. He will lead, oversee, and coordinate a comprehensive national strategy to safeguard our country against terrorism, and respond to any attacks that may come.

These measures are essential. But the only way to defeat terrorism as a threat to our way of life is to stop it, eliminate it, and destroy it where it grows. Many will be involved in this effort, from FBI agents to intelligence operatives to the reservists we have called to active duty. All deserve our thanks, and all have our prayers. And tonight, a few miles from the damaged Pentagon, I have a message for our military: Be ready. I've called the Armed Forces to alert, and there is a reason. The hour is coming when America will act, and you will make us proud. This is not, however, just America's fight. And what is at stake is not just America's freedom. This is the world's fight. This is civilization's fight. This is the fight of all who believe in progress and pluralism, tolerance and freedom.

We ask every nation to join us. We will ask, and we will need, the help of police forces, intelligence services, and banking systems around the world. The United States is grateful that many nations and many international organizations have already responded—with sympathy and with support. Nations from Latin America, to Asia, to Africa, to Europe, to the Islamic world. Perhaps the NATO Charter reflects best the attitude of the world: An attack on one is an attack on all. The civilized world is rallying to America's side. They understand that if this terror goes unpunished, their own cities, their own citizens may be next. Terror, unanswered, can not only bring down buildings, it can threaten the stability of legitimate governments. And you know what? We're not going to allow it.

Americans are asking: What is expected of us? I ask you to live your lives, and hug your children. I know many citizens have fears tonight, and I ask you to be calm and resolute, even in the face of a continuing threat. I ask you to uphold the values of America, and remember why so many have come here. We are in a fight for our principles, and our first responsibility is to live by them. No one should be singled out for unfair treatment or unkind words because of their ethnic background or religious faith. I ask you to continue to support the victims of this tragedy with your contributions. Those who want to give can go to a central source of information, libertyunites.org, to find the names of groups providing direct help in New York, Pennsylvania, and Virginia.

The thousands of FBI agents who are now at work in this investigation may need your cooperation, and I ask you to give it. I ask for your patience, with the delays and inconveniences that may accompany tighter security; and for your patience in what will be a long struggle. I ask your continued participation and confidence in the American economy. Terrorists attacked a symbol of American prosperity. They did not touch its source. America is successful because of the hard work, and creativity, and enterprise of our people. These were the true strengths of our economy before September 11th, and they are our strengths today. And, finally, please continue praying for the victims of terror and their families, for those in uniform, and for our great country. Prayer has comforted us in sorrow, and will help strengthen us for the journey ahead.

Tonight I thank my fellow Americans for what you have already done and for what you will do. And ladies and gentlemen of the Congress, I thank you, their representatives, for what you have already done and for what we will do together. Tonight, we face new and sudden national challenges. We will come together to improve air safety, to dramatically expand the number of air marshals on domestic flights, and take new measures to prevent hijacking. We will come together to promote stability and keep our airlines flying, with direct assistance during this emergency. We will come together to give law enforcement the additional tools it needs to track down terror here at home. We will come together to strengthen our intelligence capabilities to know the plans of terrorists before they act, and to find them before they strike.

We will come together to take active steps that strengthen America's economy, and put our people back to work. Tonight we welcome two leaders who embody the extraordinary spirit of all New Yorkers: Governor George Pataki, and Mayor Rudolph Giuliani. As a symbol of America's resolve, my administration will work with Congress, and these two leaders, to show the world that we will rebuild New York City.

After all that has just passed—all the lives taken, and all the possibilities and hopes that died with them—it is natural to wonder if America's future is one of fear. Some speak of an age of terror. I know there are struggles ahead, and dangers to face. But this country will define our times, not be defined by them. As long as the United States of America is determined and strong, this will not be an age of terror; this will be an age of liberty, here and across the world.

Great harm has been done to us. We have suffered great loss. And in our grief and anger we have found our mission and our moment. Freedom and fear are at war. The advance of human freedom—the great achievement of our time, and the great hope of every time—now depends on us. Our nation, this generation will lift a dark threat of violence from our people and our future. We will rally the world to this cause by our efforts, by our courage. We will not tire, we will not falter, and we will not fail.

It is my hope that in the months and years ahead, life will return almost to normal. We'll go back to our lives and routines, and that is good. Even grief recedes with time and grace. But our resolve must not pass. Each of us will remember what happened that day, and to whom it happened. We'll remember the moment the news came—where we were and what we were doing. Some will remember an image of a fire, or a story of rescue. Some will carry memories of a face and a voice gone forever.

And I will carry this: It is the police shield of a man named George Howard, who died at the World Trade Center trying to save others. It was given to me by his mom, Arlene, as a proud memorial to her son. This is my reminder of lives that ended, and a task that does not end. I will not forget this wound to our country or those who inflicted it. I will not yield; I will not rest; I will not relent in waging this struggle for freedom and security for the American people. The course of this conflict is not known, yet its outcome is certain. Freedom and fear, justice and cruelty, have always been at war, and we know that God is not neutral between them.

Fellow citizens, we'll meet violence with patient justice—assured of the rightness of our cause, and confident of the victories to come. In all that lies before us, may God grant us wisdom, and may He watch over the United States of America. Thank you.

Presidents & First Ladies
of the United States

PRESIDENT & FIRST LADY	TERM
1. George Washington	1789–1797
Martha Dandridge Custis Washington	
2. John Adams	1797–1801
Abigail Smith Adams	
3. Thomas Jefferson	1801–1809
Martha Wayles Skelton Jefferson	
4. James Madison	1809–1817
Dolley Payne Todd Madison	
5. James Monroe	1817–1825
Elizabeth Kortright Monroe	
6. John Quincy Adams	1825–1829
Louisa Catherine Johnson Adams	
7. Andrew Jackson	1829–1837
Rachel Donelson Jackson	
8. Martin Van Buren	1837–1841
Hannah Hoes Van Buren	
9. William Henry Harrison	1841
Anna Tuthill Symmes Harrison	
10. John Tyler	1841–1845
Letitia Christian Tyler (d.1842)	
Julia Gardiner Tyler	

11.	James K. Polk	1845–1849
	Sarah Childress Polk	
12.	Zachary Taylor	1849–1850
	Margaret Mackall Smith Taylor	
13.	Millard Fillmore	1850–1853
	Abigail Powers Fillmore	
14.	Franklin Pierce	1853–1857
	Jane Means Appleton Pierce	
15.	James Buchanan	1857–1861
	Harriet Lane	
16.	Abraham Lincoln	1861–1865
	Mary Todd Lincoln	
17.	Andrew Johnson	1865–1869
	Eliza McCardle Johnson	
18.	Ulysses S. Grant	1869–1877
	Julia Dent Grant	
19.	Rutherford B. Hayes	1877–1881
	Lucy Ware Webb Hayes	
20.	James Garfield	1881
	Lucretia Rudolph Garfield	
21.	Chester A. Arthur	1881–1885
	Ellen Lewis Herndon Arthur	
22.	Grover Cleveland	1885–1889
	Frances Folsom Cleveland	
23.	Benjamin Harrison	1889–1893
	Caroline Lavinia Scott Harrison	
24.	Grover Cleveland	1893–1897
	Frances Folsom Cleveland	
25.	William McKinley	1897–1901
	Ida Saxton McKinley	
26.	Theodore Roosevelt	1901–1909
	Edith Kermit Cardow Roosevelt	

27.	William Howard Taft	1901–1913
	Helen Herron Taft	
28.	Woodrow Wilson	1913–1921
	Ellen Axson Wilson (d.1914)	
	Edith Bolling Galt Wilson	
29.	Warren G. Harding	1921–1923
	Florence Kling Harding	
30.	Calvin Coolidge	1923–1929
	Grace Anna Goodhue Coolidge	
31.	Herbert Hoover	1929–1933
	Lou Henry Hoover	
32.	Franklin D. Roosevelt	1933–1945
	Anna Eleanor Roosevelt	
33.	Harry S. Truman	1945–1953
	Elizabeth Virginia Wallace Truman	
34.	Dwight D. Eisenhower	1953–1961
	Mamie Geneva Doud Eisenhower	
35.	John F. Kennedy	1961–1963
	Jacqueline Lee Bouvier Kennedy	
36.	Lyndon B. Johnson	1963–1969
	Claudia Taylor (Lady Bird) Johnson	
37.	Richard M. Nixon	1969–1974
	Patricia Ryan Nixon	
38.	Gerald R. Ford	1974–1977
	Elizabeth Bloomer Ford	
39.	James Carter	1977–1981
	Rosalynn Smith Carter	
40.	Ronald Reagan	1981–1989
	Nancy Davis Reagan	
41.	George H. W. Bush	1989–1993
	Barbara Pierce Bush	

42.	William J. Clinton	1993–2001
	Hillary Rodham Clinton	
43.	George W. Bush	2001–2008
	Laura Welch Bush	
44.	Barack Obama	2008–
	Michelle Obama	

VICE PRESIDENTS
OF THE UNITED STATES

NAME	PRESIDENCY	TERM
John Adams	George Washington	1789–1797
Thomas Jefferson	John Adams	1797–1801
Aaron Burr	Thomas Jefferson	1801–1805
George Clinton	Thomas Jefferson	1805–1809
George Clinton	James Madison	1809–1812

Died in office April 20, 1812; vice presidency remained vacant until 1813.

Elbridge Gerry	James Madison	1813–1814

Died in office November 23, 1814; vice presidency remained vacant until 1817.

Daniel D. Tompkins	James Monroe	1817–1825
John C. Calhoun	John Quincy Adams	1825–1829
John C. Calhoun	Andrew Jackson	1829–1832

Resigned December 28, 1832; vice presidency remained vacant until 1833.

Martin Van Buren	Andrew Jackson	1833–1837
Richard Mentor Johnson	Martin Van Buren	1837–1841
John Tyler	William H. Harrison	1841

Succeeded to presidency on April 6, 1841; vice presidency remained vacant until 1845.

George Mifflin Dallas	James K. Polk	1845–1849
Millard Fillmore	Zachary Taylor	1849–1850

Succeeded to presidency on July 10, 1850; vice presidency remained vacant until 1853.

William Rufus King	Franklin Pierce	1853

Died in office April 18, 1853; vice presidency remained vacant until 1857.

John C. Breckinridge   James Buchanan   1857–1861
Hannibal Hamlin   Abraham Lincoln   1861–1865
Andrew Johnson   Abraham Lincoln   1865

Succeeded to presidency on April 15, 1865; vice presidency remained vacant until 1869.

Schuyler Colfax   Ulysses S. Grant   1869–1873
Henry Wilson   Ulysses S. Grant   1873–1875

Died in office on November 22, 1875; vice presidency remained vacant until 1877.

William A. Wheeler   Rutherford B. Hayes   1877–1881
Chester A. Arthur   James A. Garfield   1881

Succeeded to presidency on September 20, 1881;
vice presidency remained vacant until 1885.

Thomas A. Hendricks   Grover Cleveland   1885

Died in office on November 25, 1885; vice presidency remained vacant until 1889.

Levi P. Morton   Benjamin Harrison   1889–1893
Adlai E. Stevenson   Grover Cleveland   1893–1897
Garret Augustus Hobart   William McKinley   1897–1899

Died in office on November 21, 1899; vice presidency remained vacant until 1901.

Theodore Roosevelt   William McKinley   1901

Succeeded to presidency on September 14, 1901; vice presidency remained vacant until 1905.

Charles W. Fairbanks   Theodore Roosevelt   1905–1909
James S. Sherman   William H. Taft   1909–1912

Died in office on October 30, 1912; vice presidency remained vacant until 1913.

Thomas R. Marshall   Woodrow Wilson   1913–1921
Calvin Coolidge   Warren G. Harding   1921–1923

Succeeded to presidency on August 3, 1923; vice presidency remained vacant until 1925.

Charles G. Dawes   Calvin Coolidge   1925–1929
Charles Curtis   Herbert C. Hoover   1929–1933
John Nance Garner   Franklin Roosevelt   1933–1941
Henry A. Wallace   Franklin Roosevelt   1941–1945
Harry S. Truman   Franklin Roosevelt   1945

Succeeded to presidency on April 12, 1945; vice presidency remained vacant until 1949.

Alben W. Barkley	Harry Truman	1949–1953
Richard M. Nixon	Dwight D. Eisenhower	1953–1961
Lyndon B. Johnson	John F. Kennedy	1961–1963

Succeeded to presidency on November 22, 1963; vice presidency remained vacant until 1965.

Hubert H. Humphrey	Lyndon B. Johnson	1965–1969
Spiro T. Agnew	Richard Nixon	1969–1973

Resigned on October 10, 1973; vice presidency remained vacant until December 6, 1973.

Gerald R. Ford	Richard Nixon	1973–1974

Succeeded to presidency on August 9, 1974; vice presidency remained vacant until December 19, 1974.

Nelson A. Rockefeller	Gerald Ford	1974–1977
Walter F. Mondale	Jimmy Carter	1977–1981
George H.W. Bush	Ronald Reagan	1981–1989
J. Danforth Quayle	George H.W. Bush	1989–1993
Albert A. Gore, Jr.	William Clinton	1993–2001
Richard B. Cheney	George W. Bush	2001–2009
Joseph R. Biden, Jr.	Barack Obama	2009–2013

Vice Presidents of the United States, 1789–1993 (Washington: U.S. Govt. Printing Office, 1997).

Supreme Court Justices
of the United States

Name	Appointed by President	Judicial Oath Taken	Date Service Terminated
CHIEF JUSTICES			
Jay, John	Washington	(a) October 19, 1789	June 29, 1795
Rutledge, John	Washington	August 12, 1795	December 15, 1795
Ellsworth, Oliver	Washington	March 8, 1796	December 15, 1800
Marshall, John	Adams, John	February 4, 1801	July 6, 1835
Taney, Roger Brooke	Jackson	March 28, 1836	October 12, 1864
Chase, Salmon Portland	Lincoln	December 15, 1864	May 7, 1873
Waite, Morrison Remick	Grant	March 4, 1874	March 23, 1888
Fuller, Melville Weston	Cleveland	October 8, 1888	July 4, 1910
White, Edward Douglass	Taft	December 19, 1910	May 19, 1921
Taft, William Howard	Harding	July 11, 1921	February 3, 1930
Hughes, Charles Evans	Hoover	February 24, 1930	June 30, 1941
Stone, Harlan Fiske	Roosevelt, F.	July 3, 1941	April 22, 1946
Vinson, Fred Moore	Truman	June 24, 1946	September 8, 1953
Warren, Earl	Eisenhower	October 5, 1953	June 23, 1969
Burger, Warren Earl	Nixon	June 23, 1969	September 26, 1986
Rehnquist, William H.	Reagan	September 26, 1986	September 3, 2005
Roberts, John G., Jr.	Bush, G. W.	September 29, 2005	
ASSOCIATE JUSTICES			
Rutledge, John	Washington	(a) February 15, 1790	March 5, 1791
Cushing, William	Washington	(c) February 2, 1790	September 13, 1810
Wilson, James	Washington	(b) October 5, 1789	August 21, 1798
Blair, John	Washington	(c) February 2, 1790	October 25, 1795
Iredell, James	Washington	(b) May 12, 1790	October 20, 1799
Johnson, Thomas	Washington	(a) August 6, 1792	January 16, 1793

Paterson, William	Washington	(a) March 11, 1793	September 9, 1806
Chase, Samuel	Washington	February 4, 1796	June 19, 1811
Washington, Bushrod	Adams, John	(c) February 4, 1799	November 26, 1829
Moore, Alfred	Adams, John	(a) April 21, 1800	January 26, 1804
Johnson, William	Jefferson	May 7, 1804	August 4, 1834
Livingston, Henry Brockholst	Jefferson	January 20, 1807	March 18, 1823
Todd, Thomas	Jefferson	(a) May 4, 1807	February 7, 1826
Duvall, Gabriel	Madison	(a) November 23, 1811	January 14, 1835
Story, Joseph	Madison	(c) February 3, 1812	September 10, 1845
Thompson, Smith	Monroe	(b) September 1, 1823	December 18, 1843
Trimble, Robert	Adams, J. Q.	(a) June 16, 1826	August 25, 1828
McLean, John	Jackson	(c) January 11, 1830	April 4, 1861
Baldwin, Henry	Jackson	January 18, 1830	April 21, 1844
Wayne, James Moore	Jackson	January 14, 1835	July 5, 1867
Barbour, Philip Pendleton	Jackson	May 12, 1836	February 25, 1841
Catron, John	Jackson	May 1, 1837	May 30, 1865
McKinley, John	Van Buren	(c) January 9, 1838	July 19, 1852
Daniel, Peter Vivian	Van Buren	(c) January 10, 1842	May 31, 1860
Nelson, Samuel	Tyler	February 27, 1845	November 28, 1872
Woodbury, Levi	Polk	(b) September 23, 1845	September 4, 1851
Grier, Robert Cooper	Polk	August 10, 1846	January 31, 1870
Curtis, Benjamin Robbins	Fillmore	(b) October 10, 1851	September 30, 1857
Campbell, John Archibald	Pierce	(c) April 11, 1853	April 30, 1861
Clifford, Nathan	Buchanan	January 21, 1858	July 25, 1881
Swayne, Noah Haynes	Lincoln	January 27, 1862	January 24, 1881
Miller, Samuel Freeman	Lincoln	July 21, 1862	October 13, 1890
Davis, David	Lincoln	December 10, 1862	March 4, 1877
Field, Stephen Johnson	Lincoln	May 20, 1863	December 1, 1897
Strong, William	Grant	March 14, 1870	December 14, 1880
Bradley, Joseph P.	Grant	March 23, 1870	January 22, 1892
Hunt, Ward	Grant	January 9, 1873	January 27, 1882
Harlan, John Marshall	Hayes	December 10 1877	October 14, 1911
Woods, William Burnham	Hayes	January 5, 1881	May 14, 1887
Matthews, Stanley	Garfield	May 17, 1881	March 22, 1889
Gray, Horace	Arthur	January 9, 1882	September 15, 1902
Blatchford, Samuel	Arthur	April 3, 1882	July 7, 1893
Lamar, Lucius Quintus C.	Cleveland	January 18, 1888	January 23, 1893
Brewer, David Josiah	Harrison	January 6, 1890	March 28, 1910
Brown, Henry Billings	Harrison	January 5, 1891	May 28, 1906
Shiras, George, Jr.	Harrison	October 10, 1892	February 23, 1903

Jackson, Howell Edmunds	Harrison	March 4, 1893	August 8, 1895
White, Edward Douglass	Cleveland	March 12, 1894	December 18, 1910*
Peckham, Rufus Wheeler	Cleveland	January 6, 1896	October 24, 1909
McKenna, Joseph	McKinley	January 26, 1898	January 5, 1925
Holmes, Oliver Wendell	Roosevelt, T.	December 8, 1902	January 12, 1932
Day, William Rufus	Roosevelt, T.	March 2, 1903	November 13, 1922
Moody, William Henry	Roosevelt, T.	December 17, 1906	November 20, 1910
Lurton, Horace Harmon	Taft	January 3, 1910	July 12, 1914
Hughes, Charles Evans	Taft	October 10, 1910	June 10, 1916
Van Devanter, Willis	Taft	January 3, 1911	June 2, 1937
Lamar, Joseph Rucker	Taft	January 3, 1911	January 2, 1916
Pitney, Mahlon	Taft	March 18, 1912	December 31, 1922
McReynolds, James Clark	Wilson	October 12, 1914	January 31, 1941
Brandeis, Louis Dembitz	Wilson	June 5, 1916	February 13, 1939
Clarke, John Hessin	Wilson	October 9, 1916	September 18, 1922
Sutherland, George	Harding	October 2, 1922	January 17, 1938
Butler, Pierce	Harding	January 2, 1923	November 16, 1939
Sanford, Edward Terry	Harding	February 19, 1923	March 8, 1930
Stone, Harlan Fiske	Coolidge	March 2, 1925	July 2, 1941*
Roberts, Owen Josephus	Hoover	June 2, 1930	July 31, 1945
Cardozo, Benjamin Nathan	Hoover	March 14, 1932	July 9, 1938
Black, Hugo Lafayette	Roosevelt, F.	August 19, 1937	September 17, 1971
Reed, Stanley Forman	Roosevelt, F.	January 31, 1938	February 25, 1957
Frankfurter, Felix	Roosevelt, F.	January 30, 1939	August 28, 1962
Douglas, William Orville	Roosevelt, F.	April 17, 1939	November 12, 1975
Murphy, Frank	Roosevelt, F.	February 5, 1940	July 19, 1949
Byrnes, James Francis	Roosevelt, F.	July 8, 1941	October 3, 1942
Jackson, Robert Houghwout	Roosevelt, F.	July 11, 1941	October 9, 1954
Rutledge, Wiley Blount	Roosevelt, F.	February 15, 1943	September 10, 1949
Burton, Harold Hitz	Truman	October 1, 1945	October 13, 1958
Clark, Tom Campbell	Truman	August 24, 1949	June 12, 1967
Minton, Sherman	Truman	October 12, 1949	October 15, 1956
Harlan, John Marshall	Eisenhower	March 28, 1955	September 23, 1971
Brennan, William J., Jr.	Eisenhower	October 16, 1956	July 20, 1990
Whittaker, Charles Evans	Eisenhower	March 25, 1957	March 31, 1962
Stewart, Potter	Eisenhower	October 14, 1958	July 3, 1981
White, Byron Raymond	Kennedy	April 16, 1962	June 28, 1993
Goldberg, Arthur Joseph	Kennedy	October 1, 1962	July 25, 1965
Fortas, Abe	Johnson, L.	October 4, 1965	May 14, 1969
Marshall, Thurgood	Johnson, L.	October 2, 1967	October 1, 1991

Blackmun, Harry A.	Nixon	June 9, 1970	August 3, 1994
Powell, Lewis F., Jr.	Nixon	January 7, 1972	June 26, 1987
Rehnquist, William H.	Nixon	January 7, 1972	September 26, 1986*
Stevens, John Paul	Ford	December 19, 1975	June 29, 2010
O'Connor, Sandra Day	Reagan	September 25, 1981	January 31, 2006
Scalia, Antonin	Reagan	September 26, 1986	
Kennedy, Anthony M.	Reagan	February 18, 1988	
Souter, David H.	Bush, G. H. W.	October 9, 1990	June 29, 2009
Thomas, Clarence	Bush, G. H. W.	October 23, 1991	
Ginsburg, Ruth Bader	Clinton	August 10, 1993	
Breyer, Stephen G.	Clinton	August 3, 1994	
Alito, Samuel A., Jr.	Bush, G. W.	January 31, 2006	
Sotomayor, Sonia	Obama	August 8, 2009	
Kagan, Elena	Obama	August 7, 2010	

*Elevated.

Notes: The acceptance of the appointment and commission by the appointee, as evidenced by the taking of the prescribed oaths, is here implied; otherwise the individual is not carried on this list of the Members of the Court. Examples: Robert Hanson Harrison is not carried, as a letter from President Washington of February 9, 1790 states Harrison declined to serve. Neither is Edwin M. Stanton who died before he could take the necessary steps toward becoming a Member of the Court. Chief Justice Rutledge is included because he took his oaths, presided over the August Term of 1795, and his name appears on two opinions of the Court for that Term.

The date a Member of the Court took his/her Judicial oath (the Judiciary Act provided "That the Justices of the Supreme Court, and the district judges, before they proceed to execute the duties of their respective offices, shall take the following oath …") is here used as the date of the beginning of his/her service, for until that oath is taken he/she is not vested with the prerogatives of the office. The dates given in this column are for the oaths taken following the receipt of the commissions. Dates without small-letter references are taken from the Minutes of the Court or from the original oath which are in the Curator's collection. The small letter (a) denotes the date is from the Minutes of some other court; (b) from some other unquestionable authority; (c) from authority that is questionable.

TIMELINE OF SIGNIFICANT EVENTS IN AMERICAN HISTORY

August 3, 1492	Christopher Columbus sets sail to find a westward route to the east
October 12, 1492	Christopher Columbus reportedly the first European to set foot on the New World (in what is now the Bahamas)
September 1565	Spanish settle St. Augustine in present-day Florida; it is the oldest continuously inhabited European settlement in the United States
1585–1587	Sir Walter Raleigh leads an ultimately unsuccessful attempt to establish an English settlement in Roanoke, in present-day North Carolina
December 20, 1606	Virginia Company settlers leave London to establish the first permanent English settlement in North America
May 14, 1607	The first permanent English settlement in what is now the United States is established at Jamestown, Virginia; Colony of Virginia established permanently
November 11, 1620	*Mayflower Compact* is signed by English religious separatists seeking religious freedom on *Mayflower* and becomes first governing document of Plymouth Colony; days later, the Pilgrims land in present-day Plymouth, Massachusetts

June 1630	Puritan John Winthrop delivers "City on a Hill" sermon prior to landing at newly established Massachusetts Bay Colony
1642–1651	English Civil War between Royalists and Parliamentarians
January 30, 1649	King Charles I executed, English monarchy abolished, and Oliver Cromwell's parliamentarians go on to establish English Commonwealth
September 21, 1649	Maryland Toleration Act is the first act in the colonies regarding religious freedom
1660	English monarchy restored, Charles II becomes King
1663	King Charles II grants charter for Province of Carolina
November 1674	New Amsterdam ceded to Britain from Holland, will become New York City
Summer 1676	Bacon's Rebellion: Virginia planter leads failed rebellion against British governor and tries to drive all Native Americans from colony
March 4, 1681	William Penn establishes Province of Pennsylvania
1688	Glorious Revolution in England: King deposed, and English subjects granted Bill of Rights
1692–1693	Salem Witch Trials in Massachusetts
June 11, 1727	George II succeeds his father as King of Great Britain
1730s	First Great Awakening, a religious revitalization movement, sweeps the American colonies
April 21, 1733	Georgia Colony chartered by King George II, intended to act as buffer zone between British Carolinas and Spanish Florida

May 28, 1754	French and Indian War begins with Battle of Jumonville Glen; colonial forces under George Washington defeat French troops in present-day southwestern Pennsylvania
June–July 1754	The Albany conference; first meeting of representatives from all colonies
May–June 1755	British General Braddock's expedition to capture French Fort Duquesne (modern day Pittsburgh) fails, despite heroics from George Washington
1758–1760	Tide turns in French and Indian War; Britain and its colonies enjoy series of victories
May 16, 1760	French siege of Quebec fails
September 8, 1760	Montreal falls to the British, France surrenders
September 15, 1760	British flag is raised over Detroit, effectively ending the war
1761	The British make peace with the Cherokee Indians
February 10, 1763	The Treaty of Paris is signed ceding all French territory east of the Mississippi, except New Orleans, to the British. All French territory west of the Mississippi is given to the Spanish
April 5, 1764	The Sugar Act imposes taxes on specific goods specifically to raise revenue
March 22, 1765	The Stamp Act imposes a tax on many printed items in the colonies
March 24, 1765	The Quartering Act of 1765 requires the colonies to provide food and housing to British troops
March 18, 1766	The Stamp Act is repealed and replaced with the Declaratory Act, asserting Britain's full authority in the colonies

June 29, 1767	The Townshend Acts places duties on many items imported into America
March 5, 1770	The Boston Massacre occurs when British troops fire on a rock-throwing crowd
December 16, 1773	The "Boston Tea Party" takes place as residents disguised as Indians throw crates of tea into Boston Harbor
March—June, 1774	The Intolerable Acts, consisting of five punitive measures restricting the freedoms of the colonists, are passed
April 19, 1775	The Revolutionary War officially begins with the Battles of Lexington and Concord
May 10, 1775	American forces take the British fort at Ticonderoga, New York
June 14, 1775	The Continental Army is established by the Continental Congress
June 15, 1775	George Washington is appointed to commander-in-chief of the Continental Army
June 17, 1775	British troops defeat militia in the Battle of Bunker Hill in Charlestown, Mass.
July, 1775	Olive Branch Petition adopted by Continental Congress attempts to avoid full-blown war with Great Britain
August 22, 1775	King George III officially declares a state of open rebellion in the American colonies
November 28, 1775	The Continental Navy is established by the Continental Congress

July 4, 1776   The United States declares its independence from Britain by approving the Declaration of Independence

September 6, 1776   The first submarine, the Turtle, is used in Battle in New York Harbor

December 25, 1776   American forces cross the Delaware River and attack British forces at Trenton

September 19, 1777   American forces win the first Battle of Saratoga

November 15, 1777   Articles of Confederation adopted by the Second Continental Congress

December 17, 1777   American forces win the second Battle of Saratoga

February 6, 1778   The Continental Congress ratifies the Treaty of Alliance with France

July 9, 1778   The Continental Congress signs the Articles of Confederation

February 5, 1778   South Carolina is the first state to ratify the Articles of Confederation

July–November, 1778   North Carolina, Pennsylvania, Georgia, New Hampshire, and New Jersey ratify the Articles of Confederation

March 1, 1781   Articles of Confederation ratified

October 19, 1781   American and French forces win the Battle of Yorktown

December 31, 1781   Bank of North America chartered

August 7, 1782   General George Washington creates the Order of the Purple Heart (for soldiers wounded in battle)

September 3, 1783   The Treaty of Paris 1783, signed by Britain and the United States, officially ends the Revolutionary War and recognizes the United States as a sovereign nation

November 28, 1785	The Treaty of Hopewell, signed between U.S. representative Benjamin Hawkins and the Cherokee Indians, designates a boundary for white settlement in the West
1786–1787	Shays' Rebellion, an armed uprising by farmers in central Massachusetts who are burdened by debt and taxes, persuades some that the national government needs to be strengthened
August 8, 1786	The Continental Congress adopts the "Dollar" and decimal coinage
February 21, 1787	The Continental Congress adopts a resolution calling for a convention of state delegates to draw up a change to the Articles of Confederation
May 17, 1787	Delegates begin meeting in Philadelphia to draw up a change to the Articles of Confederation
May 25, 1787	George Washington is elected president of the Philadelphia convention
July 13, 1787	Northwest Ordinance of 1787 creates the first organized territory in the United States
September 17, 1787	Delegates at the Philadelphia convention approve the Constitution and send it to the Continental Congress
September 28, 1787	The Continental Congress sends the new Constitution to the states for ratification
October 27, 1787	The first of the Federalist Papers is published in a New York newspaper, calling for a Bill of Rights (written by Alexander Hamilton, James Madison, and John Jay)
June 21, 1788	The United States Constitution goes into effect after receiving the nine necessary state ratifications

July 4, 1789	First United States Congress passes the Hamilton tariff, enacting rates between 5 and 10 percent, as a source of government revenue
September 24, 1789	The First United States Congress passes the Judiciary Act of 1789, establishing the U.S. federal judiciary
September 25, 1789	The United States Congress adopts the Bill of Rights (containing the first 10 Amendments) and sends it to the states to be ratified
September 29, 1789	The United States Army is established
April 3, 1790	The United States Coast Guard is established
February 25, 1791	First Bank of the United States is chartered
December 15, 1791	The Bill of Rights (containing the first 10 Amendments) is ratified by three-fourths of the states and becomes a part of the U.S. Constitution
December 5, 1792	George Washington re-elected president of the United States; John Adams re-elected vice president
1793	Samuel Slater opens the first textile factory in Pawtucket, Rhode Island
February 1793	Congress passes Fugitive Slave Act, allowing slave owners to retrieve run-away slaves
February 18, 1793	The U.S. Supreme Court rules that a citizen of one state may sue a citizen of another state in federal court
March 14, 1794	Eli Whitney receives patent for cotton gin
March 27, 1794	The United States Navy is established
May 8, 1794	The United States Post Office is established

July 1794	Whiskey Rebellion: a tax resistance movement spurred by western dissatisfaction with national policies formulated in the east
1795	The Jay Treaty, between the United States and Great Britain, increases trade between the nations and avoids war
November 3, 1796	John Adams elected second president of the United States
June 10, 1797	The Treaty of Tripoli, between the United States and Tripoli, seeks to avoid privateering in the Mediterranean Sea
1797–1800	XYZ affair: ensues from poor diplomatic relations between France and the United States that leads to the Quasi War
January 8, 1798	The 11th Amendment is added to the Constitution
June/July 1798	Alien and Sedition Acts are passed
July 11, 1798	The United States Marine Corps is established
Autumn 1800	Election of 1800: Thomas Jefferson and John Adams tie in Electoral College
December 12, 1800	Washington, D.C. becomes the official capital of the United States
February 17, 1801	After 36 ballots, House of Representatives elects Thomas Jefferson president
February 24, 1803	*Marbury v. Madison* decided: Forms basis of principle of judicial review, the right for the courts to deem legislation unconstitutional
April 30, 1803	The United States purchases the Louisiana Territory for $15 million, containing what is now Arkansas, part of Colorado, Iowa, Louisiana, part of Minnesota, Missouri, part of Montana, part of North Dakota, part of Oklahoma, South Dakota, and part of Wyoming

March 10, 1804	Louisiana Purchase completed with France
May 1804	Lewis and Clark expedition sets off to explore Louisiana Purchase
June 15, 1804	The 12th Amendment revised presidential election procedures
July 11, 1804	Vice President Aaron Burr kills Alexander Hamilton in duel
Autumn 1804	Thomas Jefferson reelected president by 45.6 percent margin
November 18, 1805	Lewis and Clark reach the Pacific Ocean
September 23, 1806	Lewis and Clark return from exploring the Louisiana Territory
August 17, 1807	Robert Fulton invents steamboat; North River Steamboat sets off from New York City
December 22, 1807	Congress passes Embargo Act of 1807, curtailing trade with European states
1808	American slave trade with Africa ends
Autumn 1808	Secretary of State James Madison defeats Charles Pinckney to become fourth American president
June 18, 1812	War of 1812: United States declares war on Britain due to trading conflicts and British treatment of American vessels
Autumn 1812	Incumbent James Madison prevails over Federalist DeWitt Clinton in wartime presidential election
August 24, 1814	British troops burn Washington, D.C., but are forced back to Baltimore
December 24, 1814	Treaty of Ghent ends War of 1812
January 8, 1815	United States wins Battle of New Orleans, as news of the Treaty of Ghent has not yet reached America

Autumn 1816	Democrat-Republican James Monroe defeats Federalist Rufus King with nearly 70 percent of the popular vote to become fifth president
April 28–29, 1817	Rush-Bagot Treaty with Britain demilitarizes Great Lakes
February 19, 1819	United States and Spain sign Adams-Onis Treaty, which cedes Florida to the United States and settles western border with Spain
March 3, 1820	Missouri Compromise reached in Congress: Slavery prohibited in northern portion of Louisiana Purchase
Autumn 1820	James Monroe is elected to a second term as president with no opposition
December 2, 1823	Monroe Doctrine announced: U.S. will intervene if any European state interferes in affairs in Western Hemisphere
Oct.–Dec. 1824	Election of 1824 among John Quincy Adams, Andrew Jackson, and two other candidates is inconclusive, as no candidate receives majority of electoral votes
February 9, 1825	John Quincy Adams elected president by vote in House of Representatives
October 26, 1825	Erie Canal opens: First navigable passage between East Coast and Great Lakes
July 4, 1826	Thomas Jefferson and John Adams die within hours of one another on Independence Day
October 30, 1828	Tennessee's Andrew Jackson becomes the first Democrat elected president
August 21, 1831	Nat Turner leads slave rebellion in Southampton County, Virginia

1832	Jackson vetoes the charter renewal of the Second Bank of the United States, bringing to a head the Bank War and ultimately leading to the Panic of 1837
November 2, 1832	President Jackson easily secures second term in White House
November 24, 1832	South Carolina passes "Ordinance of Nullification," declaring that certain federal tariffs are invalid in South Carolina
1835–1840	Alexis de Tocqueville's *Democracy in America* published
October 2, 1835	Texas War of Independence begins
March 6, 1836	Battle of the Alamo: Texans resist larger Mexican army in San Antonio for days before Santa Anna's army storms the fort
April 21, 1836	Texans win Battle of San Jacinto and secure independence
November 3, 1836	Martin Van Buren becomes last sitting vice president to be elected president until George H.W. Bush in 1988
May 10, 1837	Panic of 1837 begins as speculative currency bubble bursts, five-year recession begins
1838	"Trail of Tears": Forced removal of the Cherokee Nation from the southeastern U.S. leads to more than 4,000 deaths
March 9, 1841	U.S. Supreme Court rules in favor of rebelling slaves in Amistad case; John Quincy Adams argues the case for the Africans

April 4, 1841	President William Henry Harrison dies after only a month in office, Vice President John Tyler assumes presidency
August 9, 1842	Webster-Ashburton Treaty establishes clear boundaries between U.S. and British Canadian territories
June 1842–Jan. 1843	Attempt to impeach President Tyler over his use of the veto fails
November 1, 1844	Democrat James K. Polk wins presidency with promises to annex Texas
March 3, 1845	Florida becomes 25th U.S. state
October 10, 1845	United States Naval Academy opens
December 29, 1845	Republic of Texas annexed, and immediately becomes 26th U.S. state
April 26, 1846	Mexican-American War begins, stemming from territorial disputes and American annexation of Texas
August 8, 1846	Wilmot Proviso, which would have banned slavery in lands acquired in Mexican-American war, introduced. It will never pass
August 10, 1846	Smithsonian Institution established
January 24, 1848	California Gold Rush begins: Gold discovered at Sutter's Mill
February 2, 1848	Treaty of Guadalupe Hidalgo ends Mexican-American War. The United States gains what is now California, Nevada, Utah, and parts of Arizona, Colorado, New Mexico, and Wyoming as a result of the treaty
November 7, 1848	Zachary Taylor, a Whig and a moderate on the issue of slavery, is elected president
December 6, 1849	Harriet Tubman escapes from slavery on the "Underground Railroad"

July 9, 1850	Zachary Taylor dies of gastroenteritis; Millard Fillmore becomes the thirteenth president of the United States
August, 1850	Congress adopts the Compromise of 1850, which admits California to the Union as a free state, but does not forbid slavery in other territories acquired from Mexico
September 18, 1850	Fugitive Slave Bill passes, requiring the return of runaway slaves to their masters.
October 23–24, 1850	The first national women's rights convention, held in Worcester, Mass., attracts delegates from nine states
March 20, 1852	The complete version of *Uncle Tom's Cabin* is published
September, 1852	Robert E. Lee appointed head of West Point Military Academy
November 2, 1852	Democrat Franklin Pierce elected fourteenth president of the United States
December 30, 1853	"Gadsden Purchase": Mexico sells the United States 29,640 square miles of territory in what is now southern Arizona and New Mexico for $10 million
February 28, 1854	"Kansas-Nebraska Act": Introduced by Stephen Douglas, opened Kansas and Nebraska territories to white settlement and repealed the Missouri Compromise line restricting slavery in northern part of the Louisiana Purchase
1856–1858	"Bleeding Kansas": John Brown and six companions murder five pro-slavery men at Pottawatomie Creek in Kansas. A war of reprisals ensues leaving more than 200 dead
November 4, 1856	James Buchanan elected fifteenth United States president

March 6, 1857	*"Dred Scott* Case": the Supreme Court rules that the U.S. Constitution and the Bill of Rights were not intended to apply to African Americans and that the Missouri Compromise was unconstitutional
August 24, 1857	"Panic of 1857": Nearly 5,000 businesses fail in the economic recession
October 16, 1859	John Brown leads raid on the federal arsenal at Harpers Ferry, Virginia (now West Virginia)
November 6, 1860	Abraham Lincoln wins a four-candidate field to become the sixteenth president of the United States
December 20, 1860	South Carolina secedes from the Union
February 4, 1861	Representatives from six seceding states adopt a Confederate constitution in Montgomery, Alabama
February 9, 1861	Jefferson Davis is elected president of the Confederate States of America
April 12, 1861	Civil War begins with attack on Fort Sumter: Confederates fire on the South Carolina installation. After over a day of bombardment, federal troops surrender
July 18, 1861	"First Battle of Bull Run": The confederacy wins the first major land battle of the Civil War
March 10, 1862	The United States issues its first paper currency, "greenbacks"
May 20, 1862	"Homestead Act": Gives settlers title to 160 acres if they work the land for five years
September 17, 1862	"Battle of Antietam": Union troops halt the Confederate invasion of the North
September 22, 1862	"Emancipation Proclamation": President Lincoln declares that on Jan. 1, 1863, slaves in areas still in rebellion will be declared free

March 3, 1863	Congress initiates a draft for all men aged 20 to 45
July 3–4, 1863	"Battle of Gettysburg": The largest battle of the Civil War is won by General Meade and the Union army
November 19, 1863	President Lincoln delivers Gettysburg Address at dedication of war cemetery
April 12, 1864	"Fort Pillow": Confederate cavalry massacres African American soldiers after they had surrendered
July 30, 1864	"Battle of the Crater": Union troops dig a 586-foot tunnel underneath Confederate lines and fill it with 8,000 lbs. of gunpowder
November 8, 1864	President Lincoln decisively defeats his former top general, Democrat George McClellan, in 1864 presidential election
April 9, 1865	Robert E. Lee surrenders to Ulysses S. Grant at Appomattox Courthouse, Civil War ends in Union victory
April 14, 1865	John Wilkes Booth assassinates President Lincoln at Ford's Theatre. Andrew Johnson becomes the seventeenth president of the United States
December 18, 1865	The 13th Amendment to the Constitution abolishes slavery
April 9, 1866	"Civil Rights Act": Citizenship and civil rights are granted to all persons born in the United States
March 2, 1867	"Reconstruction Act": Imposes martial law on the southern states and splits them into five military districts
March 30, 1867	"Seward's Folly": The United States buys Alaska from Russia for 7.2 million dollars
February 24, 1868	The U.S. Senate acquits President Andrew Johnson of all 11 Articles of Impeachment

July 28, 1868	The 14th Amendment to the Constitution grants citizenship to anyone born in the United States and guarantees due process and equal protection before the law
December 25, 1868	President Johnson issues an unconditional pardon to all those who participated in the southern rebellion
November 3, 1868	Civil War General Ulysses S. Grant is elected the second Republican president of the United States
May 10, 1869	The Transcontinental Railroad is completed
March 30, 1870	The 15th Amendment to the Constitution guarantees the right to vote to all citizens
March 1, 1875	"Civil Rights Act of 1875": Guarantees the equal use of public accommodations and forbids the exclusion of African Americans from jury duty
February 27, 1877	Rutherford B. Hayes is declared the nineteenth president of the United States following a contested election with Samuel Tilden
July–September, 1881	President James Garfield is shot by Charles Guiteau. Chester Arthur becomes the twenty-first president of the United States following Garfield's death on September 19
May 6, 1882	"Chinese Exclusion Act": Bars Chinese immigration for a period of 10 years
January 16, 1883	"Pendleton Act": Establishes a Civil Service Commission and the filling of government positions by merit
October 28, 1886	The Statue of Liberty is dedicated
February 4, 1887	"Interstate Commerce Act": Requires railroads to charge reasonable rates
July 2, 1890	"Sherman Anti-Trust Act": Establishes federal limitations on corporate monopolies

December 29, 1890	"Wounded Knee Massacre": More than 150 Lakota Sioux Indians are killed by federal troops
January 1, 1892	Ellis Island is opened up for screening European immigrants entering the United States
May 10, 1894	"Pullman Strike": Workers strike after wages are cut leading to an American Railway Union boycott
May 18, 1896	*"Plessy v. Ferguson"*: Supreme Court rules that segregation of blacks and whites is permitted under the Constitution so long as both races receive equal facilities
February 15, 1898	The battleship *Maine* blows up while anchored in Havana's harbor. Many suspect Spain behind the attack, and the Spanish-American war begins in April
August 12, 1898	The Spanish-American War ends in American victory, with the U.S. acquiring the Philippines, Puerto Rico, and Guam
July 7, 1898	President McKinley approves the annexation of Hawaii
March 14, 1900	Gold Standard Act: Establishes gold as the only standard for redeeming paper money
1900–1901	U.S. helps European states and Japan put down Boxer Rebellion in China
September 14, 1901	William McKinley assassinated by anarchist in Buffalo, New York, Vice President Theodore Roosevelt becomes president
1901–1909	Key Progressive Era legislation, including stricter regulations on worker safety, monopolies, railroads, and environmental protection, enacted under President Roosevelt
June 16, 1903	Ford Motor Company founded

December 17, 1903	The Wright brothers make their first powered flight in the Wright Flyer
May 4, 1904	United States begins work on Panama Canal, which will take ten years to complete
November 4, 1904	Roosevelt defeats Democratic challenger Alton B. Parker in a landslide, is elected to a full term as president
December 1904	Theodore Roosevelt announces the "Roosevelt Corollary" to the Monroe Doctrine, allowing the United States to intervene to "stabilize" Latin American economies
September 5, 1905	Roosevelt negotiates Treaty of Portsmouth to end Russo-Japanese War, receives Nobel Peace Prize in 1906
April 18, 1906	7.9 magnitude San Francisco earthquake and subsequent fire destroys much of city
July 26, 1908	Federal Bureau of Investigation established
August 12, 1908	First Model T automobile produced
February 8, 1910	Boy Scouts of America chartered
1912	New Mexico and Arizona become states
April 15, 1912	RMS *Titanic* sinks
October 14, 1912	Theodore Roosevelt shot, but not killed, while campaigning for the Bull Moose Party in Milwaukee
November 5, 1912	New Jersey Governor Woodrow Wilson wins three-way race for president with 42 percent of popular vote
February 3, 1913	Congress ratifies 16th Amendment, which allows the creation of a federal income tax

April 8, 1913	17th Amendment, allowing for popular election of senators, becomes law

April 8, 1913 — 17th Amendment, allowing for popular election of senators, becomes law

December 23, 1913 — Federal Reserve Act, establishing central banking system, signed by President Wilson

July 28, 1914 — World War I begins as the Ottoman Empire declares war on Bosnia; Allies and Central Powers begin fighting later in summer 1914, United States remains neutral

August 15, 1914 — First ship passes through Panama Canal, completing 10-year construction project

September 12, 1914 — Allied forces win the first Battle of the Marne

May 7, 1915 — RMS *Lusitania*, a British passenger ship, sunk by German U-Boat off the coast of Ireland; 128 American civilians killed

November 7, 1916 — Woodrow Wilson elected to second term; Jeannette Rankin, a Republican from Montana, becomes first woman elected to Congress

November 13, 1916 — Allied forces win the Battle of the Somme

April 2, 1917 — Wilson declares war on Central Powers, U.S. enters World War I

Autumn 1917 — First U.S. troops fight against German forces on Western Front in France

January 8, 1918 — President Wilson announces his "Fourteen Points"

September 26, 1918 — The Meuse-Argonne Offensive, the final Allied offensive on the Western Front, begins

November 11, 1918 — The Allied and Central Powers sign an armistice, ending combat in World War I

January 29, 1919 — 18th Amendment becomes law, Prohibition begins

June 28, 1919	The Treaty of Versailles is signed, though it and the League of Nations are ultimately rejected by the United States Congress
August 16, 1920	19th Amendment added to Constitution, gives women right to vote
November 2, 1920	First presidential election in which women can vote; Republican Warren C. Harding wins in landslide
November 1921	Washington Naval Conference: Powers agree to curtail warship construction
1921–1923	Teapot Dome Scandal: President Harding accused of taking bribes
August 2, 1923	Harding dies of massive heart attack; Calvin Coolidge succeeds him
July 21, 1925	"Scopes Monkey Trial" about teaching evolution in schools decided
May 20, 1927	Charles Lindbergh makes first trans-Atlantic flight
October 6, 1927	*The Jazz Singer*, the first "talkie" (motion picture with sound) is released
August 28, 1928	Kellogg-Briand Pact to make war "illegal" among U.S., European powers, and Japan
November 6, 1928	Herbert Hoover elected U.S. president in landslide
October 29, 1929	"Black Tuesday" stock market crash; Great Depression begins
1930–1936	"Dust Bowl": Dust storms cause severe economic and ecological damage in Great Plains
May 1, 1931	Empire State Building opens in Manhattan
September 19, 1931	Japanese invasion of Manchuria; Japan begins to build empire in East Asia

Nov. 8, 1932	Democrat Franklin D. Roosevelt wins all but 6 states in 1932 presidential election
January 23, 1933	20th Amendment fixes the dates of term commencement for Congress and the president
Jan–April 1933	Roosevelt's "First 100 Days" begin New Deal: Massive government efforts to ease Great Depression launched
December 5, 1933	21st Amendment ends Prohibition
August 14, 1935	President Roosevelt signs Social Security Act, creating an old-age insurance program
May 6, 1937	Hindenburg disaster; 36 killed
May 27, 1937	Golden Gate Bridge completed
1937–1938	"Second Great Depression": After several years of modest recovery, economy falls back into recession
September 1, 1939	Nazi Germany invades Poland, World War II begins in Europe
September 4, 1939	France and Great Britain declare war on Germany
September 21, 1939	"Cash-Carry" signed by President Roosevelt, allowing U.S. to sell supplies to World War II participants
September 28, 1939	Germany and the Soviet Union sign the Molotov-Ribbentrop Pact, temporarily keeping the USSR out of World War II
June 4, 1940	The British evacuate more than 300,000 soldiers from Dunkirk, France back across the English Channel following a failed invasion
June 22, 1940	France surrenders to Germany
October 16, 1940	Benjamin Davis becomes the first black general in the United States Army

November 5, 1940	Franklin D. Roosevelt elected to unprecedented third term as president
March 1941	"Lend-Lease" begins: U.S. stays neutral in World War II but begins supplying material to Allies
June 22, 1941	Germany invades the Soviet Union
August 14, 1941	U.S. and U.K. sign Atlantic Charter; becomes foundation of wartime and postwar cooperation
December 7, 1941	Japanese forces attack the United States naval base at Pearl Harbor, Hawaii
December 8, 1941	The United States declares war on Japan
December 11, 1941	Germany and Italy declare war on the United States
August 7, 1942	United States Marines land at Guadalcanal
February 2, 1943	200,000 German soldiers surrender at Stalingrad
November 28, 1943	Churchill, Roosevelt, and Stalin meet in Tehran to discuss possible second front in Europe
June 6, 1944	D-Day: Allied forces invade Normandy; second front established in Europe
June 22, 1944	G.I. Bill signed: Will fund education for millions of returning soldiers
July 1944	Bretton Woods Conference designs postwar financial system
August 25, 1944	Allied troops liberate Nazi-occupied Paris
December 16, 1944	A German surprise attack begins the Battle of the Bulge
December 24, 1944	Allied forces push the German troops past the German border
January 12, 1945	American forces liberate the Philippines

February 4, 1945	Roosevelt, Churchill, and Stalin meet at Yalta to discuss organization of postwar Europe
April 12, 1945	Franklin Delano Roosevelt dies; Harry S. Truman becomes president
May 8, 1945	VE Day: Nazis surrender and World War II ends in Europe
June 26, 1945	The United Nations is established
July 12, 1945	American forces take Okinawa
July 17, 1945	Truman, Atlee, and Stalin meet at Potsdam Conference to discuss fate of defeated Axis powers
August 6, 1945	The United States drops the first atomic bomb, on Hiroshima, Japan
August 9, 1945	The United States drops the second atomic bomb, on Nagasaki, Japan
September 2, 1945	VJ Day: Japan unconditionally surrenders to the United States, ending World War II
July 4, 1946	The Philippines, a United States protectorate, gains its independence
October 1, 1946	Nazi war criminals receive sentencing at the Nuremberg trials
October 17, 1946	Winston Churchill proclaims "an iron curtain has swept across the continent (Europe)," beginning the Cold War
March 12, 1947	Truman Doctrine declares: "The policy of the United States to support free peoples who are resisting attempted subjugation by armed minorities or by outside pressures"
April 15, 1947	Jackie Robinson breaks color barrier in baseball

April 1947	General Agreement on Tariffs and Trade (GATT) signed by 23 countries
June 5, 1947	Marshall Plan established
June 23, 1947	Taft-Hartley Act curtails union power
June 1948–May 1949	Berlin Blockade: West supplies lifeline to besieged city
July 26, 1948	Truman desegregates armed forces
August 1948	Alger Hiss accused of spying for Soviets in House Un-American Activities Committee
November 2, 1948	"Dewey Defeats Truman": President Truman defeats Republican Thomas Dewey in stunning upset
April 4, 1949	North Atlantic Treaty Organization (NATO) formed
August 29, 1949	Soviet Union tests its first atomic bomb
October 1, 1949	Communists defeat Nationalists in China, People's Republic declared
1949	Germany is divided into East and West
February 9, 1950	Senator Joseph McCarthy's Wheeling, WV speech alleges communists in U.S. government, era of "McCarthyism" begins
April 14, 1950	National Security Council Memo 68 (NSC-68) published, becomes blueprint for American Cold War strategy
June 25, 1950	Korean War begins; WWII hero General Douglas MacArthur in command of UN forces
September 15, 1950	UN forces take Inchon
October 7, 1950	UN forces recapture Seoul

January 4, 1951	North Korean/Chinese forces recapture Seoul
February 27, 1951	22nd Amendment sets presidential term limits to two terms or ten years
April 11, 1951	General Douglas MacArthur fired by Truman for comments that contradict official U.S. policies on Korean War
November 4, 1952	Dwight D. Eisenhower becomes first Republican elected president since 1928
June 19, 1953	Rosenbergs executed for sharing nuclear secrets with Soviets
July 27, 1953	Korean War ends in armistice
August 19, 1953	Shah of Iran returns to power in CIA-orchestrated coup known as Operation Ajax
March–June 1954	Army-McCarthy hearings discredit McCarthyism
May 7, 1954	Fall of Dien Bien Phu; end of French rule in Indochina
April–May 1954	Geneva Conference: Vietnam partitioned
May 17, 1954	U.S. Supreme Court decides *Brown v. Board* of Education
1954–1955	First Taiwan Strait Crisis: Communist China lays siege on Quemoy and Matsu Islands; Eisenhower sends in U.S. Navy
April 12, 1955	Jonas Salk develops polio vaccine
May 17, 1955	Warsaw Pact signed between Soviet Union and satellite states
December 1, 1955	Rosa Parks incident leads to Montgomery Bus Boycott
June 29, 1956	Interstate Highway Act passes

November 6, 1956	President Eisenhower handily reelected to second term
January 5, 1957	Eisenhower Doctrine announced: U.S. will aid any state threatened by communist aggression
September 1957	Little Rock, Arkansas school desegregation
September 9, 1957	President Eisenhower signs Civil Rights Act of 1957
October 4, 1957	Soviets launch Sputnik; "space race" begins
July 1958	Lebanon Crisis: U.S. troops land in Lebanon to prevent communist takeover
July 29, 1958	NASA formed
September 2, 1958	National Defense Education Act signed
January 1, 1959	Cuban Revolution: Fidel Castro overthrows pro-U.S. regime
January 1959	Alaska and Hawaii become states
May 1, 1960	U-2 incident: American spy plane shot down over Soviet territory
September 26, 1961	First Nixon-Kennedy debate
November 8, 1960	Senator John F. Kennedy narrowly defeats Vice President Richard Nixon in presidential election
January 3, 1961	U.S. ends diplomatic relations with Cuba
March 29, 1961	The 23rd Amendment gives representaion to Washington, D.C. in the electoral college
April 17, 1961	Bay of Pigs Invasion fails to topple Castro government in Cuba
May 5, 1961	Alan Shepard becomes first American in space on Freedom 7
June–November 1961	Berlin Crisis: Standoff between West and USSR over status of German capital

1961	U.S. sends first major delegation of advisers and troops to South Vietnam, officially beginning U.S. involvement in Vietnam War
February 20, 1962	John Glenn is first American to orbit Earth
October 1962	Cuban Missile Crisis
August 28, 1963	March on Washington; Martin Luther King, Jr. "I have a dream" speech
November 22, 1963	John F. Kennedy assassinated; Vice President Lyndon Johnson becomes president
January 23, 1964	24th Amendment prohibits revocation of voting rights due to non-payment of taxes
August 2, 1964	Gulf of Tonkin Resolution authorizes president to use conventional military force in Southeast Asia; U.S. military involvement in Vietnam escalates
May 22, 1964	President Johnson proposes "Great Society," the elimination of poverty and discrimination through large government programs
July 2, 1964	Civil Rights Act of 1964 enacted
October 27, 1964	Ronald Reagan delivers "A Time For Choosing" on behalf of GOP presidential candidate Barry Goldwater
November 3, 1964	Incumbent Lyndon Johnson defeats Goldwater, winning 61 percent of the popular vote
July 30, 1965	Social Security Act of 1965 creates Medicaid and Medicare
August 1965	Watts riot in Los Angeles
June 13, 1966	*Miranda v. Arizona* establishes "Miranda rights"
February 10, 1967	25th Amendment codifies the process of presidential succession

Summer 1967	Race riots across various American cities
April 4, 1968	Martin Luther King, Jr. assassinated
June 5, 1968	Presidential candidate Robert F. Kennedy assassinated
January 1968	Viet Cong launches Tet Offensive
April 11, 1968	Civil Rights Act of 1968 makes discrimination in housing illegal
July 1, 1968	U.S. signs Nuclear Non-Proliferation Treaty
November 5, 1968	Republican Richard Nixon defeats Democratic Vice President Hubert Humphrey by less than a percentage point in presidential election
January 1969	Richard Nixon implements "Vietnamization," which will gradually hand combat responsibilities from U.S. to South Vietnamese troops, as U.S. policy
July 20, 1969	Neil Armstrong walks on the moon, Earth's only natural satellite
May 4, 1970	Kent State shootings in Ohio
July 1, 1971	26th Amendment establishes eighteen as the minimum voting age
February 1972	Richard Nixon goes to China, beginning a process that will restore diplomatic relations between the U.S. and China
May 26, 1972	U.S. signs Anti-Ballistic Missile Treaty with USSR
November 7, 1972	President Richard Nixon defeats anti-war candidate George McGovern in a 49-state landslide
January 22, 1973	*Roe v. Wade* Supreme Court ruling overturns state laws against abortion
January 27, 1973	Paris Peace Accords end American troop involvement in Vietnam

October 1973	OPEC oil embargo begins, leading to spikes in U.S. oil and gas prices
July 1974	The House Judiciary Committee votes to impeach President Nixon over his involvement in the Watergate scandal
August 9, 1974	Richard Nixon resigns presidency over Watergate, and Vice President Gerald R. Ford becomes president
September 8, 1974	Ford pardons Nixon
April 30, 1975	Fall of Saigon
September 17, 1978	President Jimmy Carter brokers Camp David Accords between Israel and Egypt
March 28, 1979	Partial meltdown at Three Mile Island nuclear power plant
November 4, 1979	Iran hostage crisis begins as 66 Americans are taken hostage in Tehran
May 1980	Mount St. Helens eruption in Washington kills 57
July 1980	U.S. boycotts Summer Olympics in Moscow to protest 1979 Soviet invasion of Afghanistan
November 4, 1980	Former actor and California Governor Ronald Reagan defeats incumbent Jimmy Carter in 1980 presidential election
January 20, 1981	American hostages in Tehran are freed as Ronald Reagan is sworn in as fortieth president of the United States
March 30, 1981	Attempted assassination of Ronald Reagan by John Hinckley
August 13, 1981	Ronald Reagan signs Kemp-Roth Tax Cut

September 25, 1981	Sandra Day O'Connor becomes first woman on the U.S. Supreme Court
March 23, 1983	President Reagan announces the Strategic Defense Initiative
October 23, 1983	241 U.S. Marines killed by suicide bomb in Lebanon
November 6, 1984	Ronald Reagan wins a second term in a decisive landslide, securing 49 of 50 states
November 1985	Ronald Reagan and Soviet premier Mikhail Gorbachev meet in Geneva, marking the beginning of a warming of relations between the U.S. and the Soviet Union
January 28, 1986	Space Shuttle Challenger explodes shortly after take-off from Cape Canaveral, Florida
November 1986	Iran-Contra Scandal Breaks
June 12, 1987	In a speech in Berlin, President Reagan challenges Soviet leader Mikhail Gorbachev to "tear down this wall" and open Eastern Europe to political and economic reform
October 19, 1987	Dow Jones Industrial Average falls 22.6 percent in single session on "Black Monday"
December 8, 1987	Reagan and Gorbachev sign INF treaty, the first arms-control agreement to reduce the superpowers' nuclear weapons
November 8, 1988	Vice President George Bush defeats Massachusetts Governor Michael Dukakis in 1988 presidential election
November 9, 1989	Berlin Wall falls in Germany, the most visible sign of the end of communism in Eastern Europe
August 2, 1990	Iraqi forces invade Kuwait

January 16, 1991	United Nations authorities forces to launch air war against Saddam Hussein's Iraq, beginning Operation Desert Storm
February 23, 1991	UN ground forces liberate Kuwait.
February 28, 1991	A cease fire is signed between the United Nations and Iraq
December 25, 1991	The Soviet Union officially dissolves, Cold War ends
May 7, 1992	27th Amendment disallows laws regarding congressional salary to go into effect until the beginning of the subsequent session
November 3, 1992	Arkansas Governor Bill Clinton elected president, winning 43 percent of the popular vote in a 3-way race with incumbent George H.W. Bush and independent Ross Perot
January 1, 1994	North American Free Trade Agreement (NAFTA) goes into effect
November 8, 1994	In mid-term elections, Republicans win majorities in House and Senate for first time since 1955
April 19, 1995	Timothy McVeigh bombs Oklahoma City federal building, 168 killed
June 25, 1996	19 U.S. servicemen and one Saudi killed in al Qaeda attack on Khobar Towers in Saudi Arabia
November 5, 1996	Bill Clinton decisively elected to second term
August 7, 1998	2 American embassies (Dar Es Salaam, Tanzania and Nairobi, Kenya) in eastern Africa are destroyed by terrorist bombs
August 20, 1998	American forces launch air strikes at 2 targets in retaliation for the American embassy bombings: a terrorist training facility in Afghanistan, and a chemical plant in Sudan

December 16–18, 1998	American forces launch air strikes at targets in Iraq
December 19, 1998	The U.S. House of Representatives approves 2 of 4 Proposed Articles of Impeachment against President Bill Clinton
March 23, 1999	NATO begins launching air strikes against Yugoslavia
December 31, 1999	Panama gains control of the Panama Canal from the United States
October 12, 2000	Al Qaeda attacks USS *Cole*, 17 servicemen killed
December 12, 2000	George W. Bush declared winner of presidential election: U.S. Supreme Court rules in favor of George W. Bush in *Bush v. Gore*, ending 5-week ballot recount drama and delivering Bush Florida's 25 electoral votes and, consequently, the presidency
September 11, 2001	September 11 terrorist attacks; 19 terrorists hijack four planes and crash them into the World Trade Center, the Pentagon, and a field in Shanksville, Pennsylvania, killing nearly 3,000 people
October 7, 2001	"Operation Enduring Freedom": Coalition forces invade Afghanistan
November 25, 2002	Department of Homeland Security created
February 1, 2003	Space Shuttle Columbia disintegrates over Texas
March 20, 2003	Coalition forces invade Iraq
November 2, 2004	Incumbent George W. Bush defeats Senator John Kerry in presidential election
August 23–30, 2005	Hurricane Katrina devastates the Louisiana, Mississippi, and Alabama coastlines, killing at least 1,836 people and causing $81 billion in damage, making it the costliest natural disaster in U.S. history

December 2007	"Great Recession" of late 2000s officially begins
September 2008	Stock market crashes, financial crisis of 2008 begins
November 4, 2008	Democrat Barack Obama elected first African-American president of United States
February 19, 2009	President Obama signs $787 billion stimulus package, intended to jumpstart weak U.S. economy
March 23, 2010	President Obama signs Patient Protection and Affordable Care Act—also referred to as "Obamacare"—after highly contentious national debate
April 20, 2010	Explosion on oil rig *Deepwater Horizon* causes oil to gush into the Gulf of Mexico for three months in the largest oil spill in the history of the industry

ACKNOWLEDGMENTS

THIS BOOK, LIKE ALL BOOKS, IS MUCH MORE A TEAM PROJECT THAN AN individual accomplishment. There are quite a few people I would like to thank for their support and assistance in making this dream a reality.

My husband Jimmy, who provided support and assistance throughout this project with grace and patience, thank you. Without your help, and encouragement, this book would not have happened. Our children, Maggie and Robert Cushman, heard "not right now—Mommy has to finish her book" more times that I would like to admit. Thank you both for your patience and love.

To my mom, Jackie Gingrich, thank you for your encouragement and thank you for helping with Maggie and Robert so I could focus on writing.

A special thanks to my father, Newt Gingrich, and his wife Callista. Dad spent his precious free time reviewing this book and crafting an introduction; Callista provided great support for this project.

Kathy Lubbers, my sister, provided advice, support, and resources. With her help, this is a much better book than it would have been otherwise.

Kim Mallen, my super assistant, who can do just about anything, thank you for keeping me organized and tying up loose ends.

Research and editing provided by Brady Cassis, Michelle Selesky, Caitlin Laverdiere, Adam Minchew, and Ellery Kauvar were a gift from God right when I needed it. Thank you for your research, time, editing, and thoughtful advice. This book is much, much better due to your involvement.

Craig Wiley, my agent, for assisting me through the contract phase and working with us to make this book a success.

Sonya Harrison, for making sure there is time on Dad's schedule to make everything happen. Thank you for working miracles.

Joe DeSantis, for your support and encouragement, and your assistance in marketing and promoting.

Cynthia Counts of Counts and Associates and her team, Nima Adabi and Amanda Hyland, thank you for your great legal work and fast turn-around time.

James Fitts' picture makes me look better than I do in real life. Thank you.

For ongoing encouragement, Mary Beth Hicks, friend, columnist, and author—it's been great to have your weekly advice and thoughts.

Bill Smith, Wright Mitchell, and Thornton Kennedy, thank you for reviewing the list and providing suggestions.

This project has been fun from the start. It has been a pleasure working with the publishing professionals at Regnery Publishing. Marji Ross, president and publisher, thank you for your wonderful ideas, insight, and inspiration. Anneke Green, thank you for your persistence and cheerfulness while editing my work. Both were extremely helpful! Mary Beth Baker and Farahn Morgan in editorial, Sekayi Brunson in art, Jeanne Crotty in marketing, and Laura Bentz, and Kara Verducci in publicity, thank you all for your hard work to make this book a success for all involved. I so appreciate the opportunity to work with this incredible team.

To our American service men and women, thank you for your service and sacrifice. Without you, we would not have the freedoms that we enjoy.

SOURCES

"A TIME FOR CHOOSING (The Speech—October 27, 1964)" The Public Papers of President Ronald W. Reagan. Ronald Reagan Presidential Library.

Abraham Lincoln First Inaugural Address, Final Version, March 1861. Transcribed and annotated by the Lincoln Studies Center, Knox College, Galesburg, Illinois. Available at Abraham Lincoln Papers at the Library of Congress, Manuscript Division (Washington, D.C.: American Memory Project, [2000-02]).

Associated Press text of United Nations Representative Jeane J. Kirkpatrick's speech as delivered Aug. 20 to the Republican National Convention, in Dallas, TX.

Berlinski, Claire, *There is No Alternative: Why Margaret Thatcher Matters* (New York: Basic Books, 2008).

Bernstein, R.B., *Thomas Jefferson* (New York, Oxford University Press, 2003).

Butterfield, L.H., editor. *Adams Family Correspondence*, vol.1: pp. 369-371. Cambridge, Massachusetts: Belknap Press of Harvard University Press, 1963-1993.

Cox, Mike, "Baker Talk," April 11, 2006, *Texas Escapes Online Magazine*.

Dalton, Kathleen, *Theodore Roosevelt: The Strenuous Life* (New York, Vintage, 2007).

Davis, Kenneth C., *A Nation Rising: Untold Tales of Flawed Founders, Fallen Heroes, and Forgotten Fighters from America's Hidden History* (New York: Smithsonian Books, 2010).

Dolan, Anthony R. "Four Little Words," *Wall Street Journal*, November 8, 2009.

Ellis, Joseph J., *Founding Brothers: The Revolutionary Generation* (New York: First Vintage Books, 2000).

Evans, Thomas W., *The Education of Ronald Reagan* (New York: Columbia University Press, 2006).

Facsimile of the Bliss copy of the Gettysburg Address reproduced on an envelope. Library of Congress, Rare Book and Special Collections Division, Alfred Whital Stern Collection of Lincolniana.

Ferling, John, *Adams Vs. Jefferson: The Tumultuous Election of 1800* (New York: Oxford University Press, 2004).

Flexner, James Thomas, *Washington the Indispensable Man* (Boston, New York, Toronto, London: Little, Brown and Company, 1969).

Galoway, Terry, *Together We Cannot Fail: FDR and the American Presidency in Years of Crisis* (Naperville, Illinois: Sourcebooks, 2009).

Holzer, Harold, *Lincoln at Cooper Union: The Speech that Made Abraham Lincoln President* (New York: Simon & Schuster, 2004).

Holton, Woody, *Abigail Adams* (New York: Free Press, 2010).

"Inaugural Address of President John F. Kennedy Washington, D.C. January 20, 1961." The Public Papers of President John F. Kennedy. John F. Kennedy Presidential Library and Museum.

"Joint Address to Congress Leading to a Declaration of War Against Japan December 8, 1941." Our Documents: Declaration of War, Franklin D. Roosevelt Library and Museum Website; version date 2009.

Lodge, Henry Cabot, *Daniel Webster*, 9th ed. (Boston: Houghton, Mifflin and Company, 1887).

Meacham, Jon, *Franklin and Winston: An Intimate Portrait of an Epic Friendship* (New York: Random House, 2003) .

McCullough, David, *John Adams* (New York: Simon & Schuster, 2001).

Morris, Edmund, *Theodore Rex* (New York: Random House 2001.)

National Notary Association, *Why Coolidge Matters: How Civility in Politics Can Bring a Nation Together* (California: National Notary Association, 2010).

Pohl, James W., *The Battle of San Jacinto* (Texas State Historical Association, 2010

"Remarks on East-West Relations at the Brandenburg Gate in West Berlin June 12, 1987." The Public Papers of President Ronald W. Reagan. Ronald Reagan Presidential Library.

Theodore Roosevelt, *The Strenuous Life: Essays and Addresses*, (New York: The Century Co.).

Tyler Moses Coit, *Patrick Henry* (Washington, D.C., Heritage E Books, 2010).

The Papers of Thomas Jefferson, Volume 33: 17 February to 30 April 1801. (Princeton University Press, 2006), 148–52.

White, Ronald C., Jr. *A. Lincoln* (New York: Random House, 2009).

William Writ, *Sketches of the Life and Character of Patrick Henry*, Revised ed. (Ithaca, NY: Mack, Andrus, 1845), 89.

Introducing Regnery's
Essential American Library
Starter DVD
Over 1,200 Documents & Works of American History

Simply insert the disk from the back of the book into your computer, install the software as prompted, and then enjoy your Essential American Library Starter DVD, which includes:

- First-Hand Accounts
- Classic Histories
- Key Political Works
- Founding Documents
- Biographies
- Presidential Addresses
- Supreme Court Cases
  and much more

Easily find the information you need using the award-winning
Folio Views™ text retrieval system

INCREDIBLE BONUS OFFER: Unlock the
US Constitution Coach Kit